Get Going With QuickBooks® 2018 for Windows

Technical Learning Resources

This guide is intended for use with QuickBooks Desktop 2018. The practice files will not work properly if QuickBooks Desktop 2018 is not installed on your computer or laptop. Refer to the Before You Get Started lesson in this guide for instructions on downloading and activating the trial software.

t l r
technical learning resources

Copyright Notice

Get Going With QuickBooks® 2018 for Windows
ISBN # 978-1-942020-04-2
Item # GG2018
© TLR, 2018. Published in January 2018.

Disclaimer

Trademark Acknowledgments

All product names and services mentioned in this publication are trademarks or registered trademarks of their respective companies. They are used throughout this publication for the benefit of those companies, and are not intended to convey endorsement or other affiliation with the publication.

Other Acknowledgments

Executive Editors: Edward F. Thaney and Scott T. Gerken

Project and Production Managers: Lori Laney and Brandy Halstead

Developer: Carene Kulis

Technical Learning Resources is affiliated with Thaney & Associates, CPA's

Special Notice

Publisher: Technical Learning Resources
Voice: (877) 223-5740
Web: www.tlr-inc.com

Contents

Before You Get Started

Introduction

This training guide is dedicated to providing you with a flexible, high-performance learning system. This dedication has resulted in a unique and progressive training method. Unlike other training methods that focus on theory or high-tech training products that overwhelm you, this training method provides a simple approach to learning computer software. Each guide is written to assume the user has no prior computer skills. If you are using the software for the first time, you will be introduced to its primary features. If you are familiar with the software, you will quickly learn the new features and functionality of this version. Regardless of your skill level, you will learn with the greatest of ease.

Our Training Philosophy

Three core principles are the foundation of every training guide:

- You learn best by doing.

- The most important evaluation of your progress comes from you.

- Training should be flexible and allow you to focus on only the skills you need to learn.

Training Guide Features

This training guide provides instructions for downloading the accompanying practice files from the www.tlr-inc.com web site. The practice files encourage quick and easy learning and reinforce the development of new skills. This training guide is based on the above principles and uses the following features to ensure that you learn the most skills in the least amount of time.

Step-by-Step Instruction

Lessons are written in a simple and concise language, and use step-by-step instructions to perform software tasks. This hands-on approach is the essence of skills application and ensures successful learning. You can complete each lesson in 45 minutes or less, which will dramatically improve your ability to retain new skills.

Confidence Building

Learning objectives are defined at the beginning of each lesson. The practice section at the end of each lesson allows you to determine whether you have met the objectives. To help you monitor the accuracy and success of your work within each lesson, this guide includes computer responses, narration and screen captures. The combination of continuous feedback and post-lesson practice helps you develop confidence that strengthens ongoing learning.

Self-contained Lessons

Each lesson within a training guide is self-contained. For example, there's no need to complete lessons 1-4 if you prefer to learn lesson 5. Because lesson modules are self-contained, you can pinpoint needed skills, master them, and move on. This flexibility allows for self-paced learning so you can learn what you want, when you want, and apply new skills immediately.

How to Use This Guide

General Conventions

In this lesson, you will learn:

Lesson objectives are stated at the beginning of each lesson. A quick glance at the objectives will give you a brief description of what you will learn in the lesson.

Concept

This paragraph explains why the objectives are important, and how the objectives might be used in an actual situation.

Scenario

The scenario paragraph sets the stage for each lesson. The scenario is explained, and a general overview presents the tasks you will perform in the lesson.

In this lesson, you have learned:

This section provides a summary of the topics covered in the lesson. Check the items listed in this section to see if you have learned them thoroughly.

Practice

The practice section enables you to reinforce new skills with additional tasks similar to those performed in the lesson. If you have trouble completing the practice section, refer back to the lesson for help before proceeding.

Instructional Conventions

Procedural Steps

Step-by-step instructions are in the form of numbered steps.

Example:

1. Click to close the Control Panel

Steps are divided into columns. Following the step number, the first column contains the action. The second column contains the item on which the action is being performed. The third column contains the intent of the step, or additional information that is needed.

Many steps include keystrokes.

Example:

2. Press to move to the next field

Multiple keys may appear in a step. If the keys listed are the same, press the keys one after the other; if the keys listed are different, the first key is held while pressing the second key.

Steps may direct you to select a command from a menu.

Example:

3. Select   File : Exit   from the menu bar

Steps directing you to type a specific amount, date, word, or phrase are in boldface.

Example:

4. Type   **30**   in the Amount field

Steps directing you to type variable information, such as the date, are in boldface and are enclosed by square brackets.

Example:

5. Type   **[today's date]**   in the Date field

For example, if today's date is November 1, 2018, you would type 11/01/2018.

Some steps do not fit the three-column structure.

Example:

6. Use the scroll bars to move around the report

A diamond bullet indicates a one-step procedure.

Example:

◆ Use the scroll bars to move around the report

Icons

Lessons frequently contain tips, shortcuts, or warnings for the tasks being performed. Such instances are indicated by the following icons:

 The **Quick Tip** icon provides useful shortcuts for common tasks. Quick Tips also explain events or conditions that may occur.

 The **Quick Fix** icon provides solutions to small problems and inconsistencies that may arise. Quick Fix icons also mark information that instructs you to change the application's settings or preferences to better fit the lesson.

 The **Caution** icon indicates that it may be easy to perform a step incorrectly. Pay close attention to the step-by-step instructions when you see the Caution icon.

Prerequisites

You can successfully complete this training guide without any prior software knowledge or computer experience. A basic understanding of the computer operating system you are using is recommended.

System Requirements

This training guide does not include the Intuit QuickBooks software; however, it does include access codes to the free trial version of the software, so that you may use this guide along with the practice files. Before using this guide, verify that the software is installed on your computer. This training guide works with the following application:

• QuickBooks® Pro or QuickBooks Premier 2018 for Microsoft® Windows

Note: The QuickBooks Simple Start software is not recommended for use with the QuickBooks guides.

Customized Settings for This Guide

Displaying File Extensions

It is recommended that you display file extensions while using this guide. By default, file extensions are hidden, so you must perform the following procedure to display them.

Note: You may want to remember to hide extensions between lessons or upon completion of using this guide.

1. Click (Windows Start button)

The Windows Start menu displays.

Note: Depending on your operating system, these steps and the icons on your computer may be slightly different.

2. Select

The Control Panel opens:

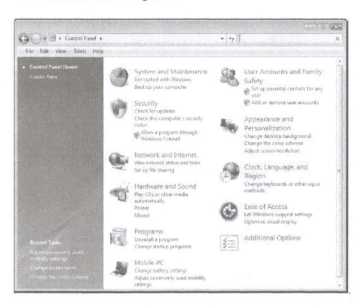

Note: Your computer's control panel may look different.

3. Select   Tools : Folder Options   from the Control Panel menu bar

The Folder Options window opens:

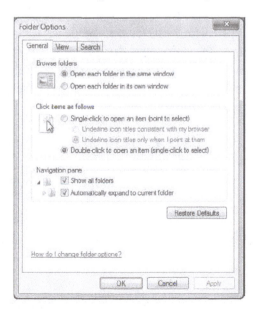

Note: Your computer's Folder Options may look different.

4. Select   the View tab

The View page displays:

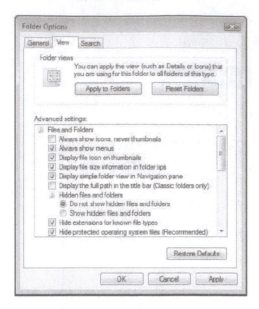

5. Click   the Hide extensions   to deselect it
                           for known file types
                           check box

6. Click   to close the Folder Options window

You return to the Control Panel.

7. Click   to close the Control Panel

Dates

The current day, month, and year on your computer are always displayed when using the QuickBooks application. Therefore, the dates that display in this training guide will be different from the dates that display on your screen. We strongly recommend that you temporarily change your computer's date setting to November 1, 2018 while taking this course, so that the dates you see on your screen match the dates in this guide.

Note: The following steps work with a Windows Vista™, Windows 7, and Windows 8 operating system. Depending on your operating system, these steps may be slightly different.

To change your computer's date,

1. Click   the time   displayed in the lower-right corner of
                                               your screen

Note: If your computer does not display the time, right-click in the lower-right corner of the screen and select the Adjust date/time option from the menu that displays.

A calendar opens:

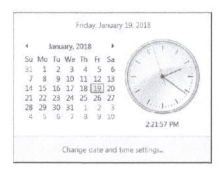

2. Click   the Change date and time settings link

The Date and Time window opens:

3. Click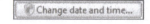

Note: If a User Account Control dialog box displays asking for permission to continue, click the Continue button.

The Date and Time Settings window opens:

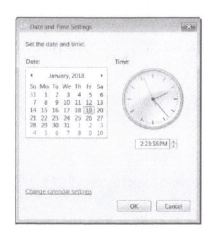

4. Click   ▸ at the top of the calendar to scroll to November, 2018

5. Click   1   in the calendar (if necessary)

6. Click   [OK]   to return to the Date and Time
                                    window

7. Click   [OK]   to close the Date and Time window

Your computer's date should now be set to November 1, 2018.

Training Objectives

After completing this training guide, you should be able to:

- Set up a company

- Work with lists

- Set up inventory

- Sell your product

- Invoice for services

- Process payments

- Work with bank accounts

- Enter and pay bills

- Use the EasyStep Interview

Downloading the Practice Files

The practice files you use to complete the lessons in this guide can be downloaded from the tlr-inc.com web site. This section provides instructions for unzipping the practice files to a folder you create on the C: drive of your computer.

Note: The steps in this section may be different, depending on the web browser and browser version you are using. The following steps work with Internet Explorer.

1. Open   the www.tlr-inc.com   in Internet Explorer
               web site

The TLR web site opens.

2. Click   the Practice Files tab   at the top of the page

The QuickBooks practice files display.

3. Click   Get Smart with QuickBooks 2018

A dialog box opens asking if you want to open or save the StudentsBooks2018.zip file:

Do you want to open or save **StudentBooks2018.zip** (169 MB) from **tlr-inc.com**?   Open   Save ▾   Cancel   ×

Note: Your dialog box may appear different.

4. Click   Open

The StudentBooks2018.zip file downloads. When the file has completed downloading, the WinZip - StudentBooks2018.zip dialog box displays:

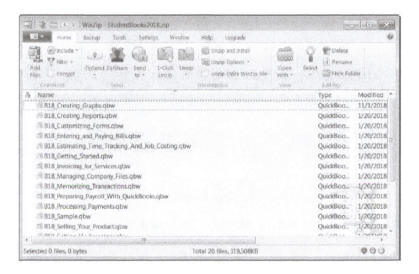

5. Click   Unzip

A drop-down menu displays:

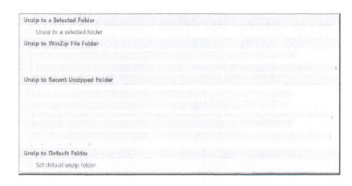

Note: Your window will be different.

6. Select   Unzip to a selected folder

The Unzip dialog box displays:

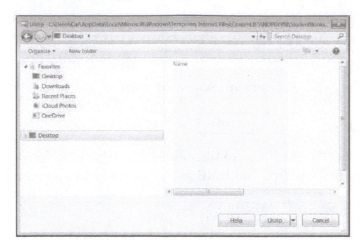

Note: The folder and file locations that display in your window will be different.

7. Navigate   to the C drive

Note: If you prefer to install the practice files to another drive, navigate to that drive.

8. Click

A blank new folder displays in the Unzip window.

9. Type   **Books2018**   to name the new folder

10. Press

11. Click

A Winzip dialog box displays while the practice files are unzipped to the Books2018 folder on the C drive:

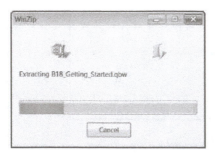

The dialog box closes when all files are unzipped.

Quick Tip. You can use the practice files as many times as you want. To guarantee you perform every lesson with "fresh" files, we recommend that you delete the current Books2018 folder and then follow these steps every time you use this guide.

Opening Practice Files

Most lessons in this guide have a corresponding practice file, which is indicated at the beginning of each lesson. Before starting a lesson, be sure to open the correct practice file using the method below.

To open a practice file,

1. Start   QuickBooks 2018

2. Select   File : Open or   from the menu bar
    Restore Company

The Open or Restore Company window opens:

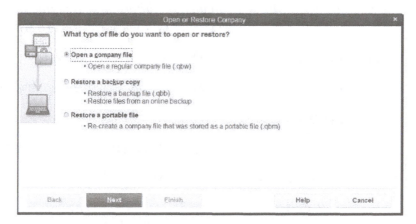

3. Verify that Open a company file is selected

4. Click   [Next]

The Open a Company window displays:

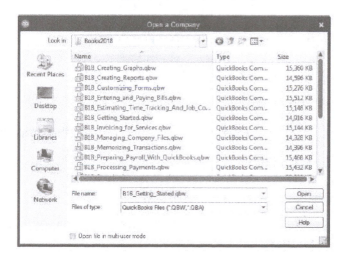

5. Navigate   to the Books2018 folder (if necessary)

6. Select   the file you want to open

7. Click   [Open]

This guide demonstrates the process of opening a file in further detail in the first lesson that requires you to open a practice file. The following abbreviated method will be shown after that lesson:

    ◆   Open   the file   using the method described in Before You Get Started

Downloading the Trial Software

This guide is intended for use with QuickBooks Desktop 2018. The practice files will not work properly if QuickBooks Desktop 2018 is not installed on your computer or laptop.

Note: The steps in this section may be different, depending on the web browser and browser version you are using. The following steps work with Internet Explorer.

To download the QuickBooks Desktop Pro trial software:

1.   Open   the www.tlr-inc.com web site   in Internet Explorer

The TLR web site opens.

2.   Click   the Trial Download tab   at the top of the page

The Intuit QuickBooks web site opens.

Note: If the QuickBooks Desktop Pro 2018 software information does not display, click the Change link next to QuickBooks Desktop Pro. When the Select dialog box opens, click QuickBooks Desktop Pro in the left pane. The right pane of the dialog box is populated with the QuickBooks Desktop Pro versions. Click 2018 to return to the Downloads and Updates page.

3.   Click   Download

A dialog box opens asking if you want to open or save the Setup_QuickBooksPro2018.exe file.

4.   Click   the down arrow   next to the Save button

A drop-down menu displays.

5.   Select   Save as   from the drop-down menu

The Save As dialog box displays.

6.   Navigate   to the C drive

Note: If you prefer to download the QuickBooks executable file to another drive, navigate to that drive.

7.   Double-click   the Books2018 folder

8.   Click   Save   to download the executable file to the Books2018 folder

When the download is complete, a dialog box displays.

9. Click   Run

Note: If a User Account Control dialog box displays asking if you would like to allow the program to make changes to your computer, click Yes.

The Intuit Download Manager dialog box displays while the file is downloaded. When the download is complete, the QuickBooks Financial Software PRO Series - InstallShield Wizard opens. The InstallShield Wizard will guide you through the QuickBooks installation process.

10. Click   Next   to extract the installation files

The Intuit QuickBooks Desktop Installer window displays the Welcome to QuickBooks Desktop window.

11. Click   Next

The License Agreement window displays.

12. Select   the I accept the terms   check box
                    of the license
                    agreement

13. Click   Next

The License and Product Numbers window displays. The license and product numbers entered in this window are located on the inside cover of your QuickBooks guide.

14. Type   **[the License Number]**   in the License Number fields

15. Type   **[the Product Number]**   in the Product Number fields

16. Click   Next

The Choose your installation type window displays.

17. Verify   Express (recommended)   is selected

18. Click   Next

The QuickBooks Desktop Installer window displays while the software is installed. When the software installation is complete, a Congratulations window displays.

19. Click   Open QuickBooks   to open the QuickBooks application

Note: If you cannot click the Open QuickBooks button, you may need to click the Close button and then restart your computer for QuickBooks to finish the installation.

Evaluation Criteria

The back of this guide contains important materials. Please take a moment to review the materials before using this guide.

Before Training Skill Evaluation

This training guide is designed to meet the course objectives stated at the beginning of each lesson. Prior to using the guide, rate your skill level for each objective.

After Training Skill Evaluation

After completing the guide, rate your skill level again. This evaluation helps to determine whether you met the objectives of each lesson.

Training Guide Evaluation

Rate your satisfaction level with guide objectives. This evaluation allows for comments and suggestions, and is invaluable in helping us to provide you with the best educational materials possible. Please complete the evaluation and return it to the address provided on the evaluation form.

Ordering Training Guides

If you are interested in ordering more copies of this guide, or are interested in other training guides, you may use the order form available at the back of this guide or log on to tlr-inc.com.

Getting Started

In this lesson, you will learn how to:

- ❏ Start QuickBooks
- ❏ Set QuickBooks preferences
- ❏ Identify components of the QuickBooks operating environment
- ❏ Use QuickBooks Help
- ❏ Identify common business terms
- ❏ Exit QuickBooks

Concept

Although most business owners are predominantly concerned with revenue, running a business involves many other tasks. Depending on the type of business you have, you may need to invoice customers, record customer payments, pay bills to vendors, manage inventory, and—in your spare time—analyze your company's financial data to determine where to focus your next efforts. QuickBooks is a tool you can use to automate the tasks that you already perform as a business owner.

This course is an introduction on how to use QuickBooks to best meet the needs of your business. The main objective is to introduce you to QuickBooks's basic features and give you an opportunity for hands-on practice. You will learn about the types of information you need to track in your business, and how to enter that information and track it in QuickBooks. By the time you complete the course, you will have a good idea of how an accounting software package can save time and help organize business finances. When you are ready to use QuickBooks, you will be familiar with the most common tasks and will know where to find information about more advanced features.

Scenario

To get the most out of QuickBooks, it is important to be proficient and comfortable with QuickBooks's features. In this lesson, you will learn how to start QuickBooks, how to set QuickBooks preferences, and how to identify the various components of the QuickBooks operating environment, including the Title Bar, Menu Bar, Icon Bar, and QuickBooks desktop. You will also learn about the QuickBooks Insights page, which provides a quick read of your business performance, the Home page, which enables you to move through the windows necessary to accomplish your business tasks, and the Company Snapshot, an area where you can quickly view how well your business is doing. This lesson also demonstrates how to use the QuickBooks help and introduces you to common business terms so you will be ready to set up your company. As a final step, you will learn how to exit from QuickBooks.

Practice Files: B18_Getting_Started.qbw

Starting QuickBooks

When QuickBooks is installed, the installation program places a QuickBooks application icon on the desktop and creates a QuickBooks submenu under the All Programs or Programs menu of the Start button.

Note: For this lesson, set your computer's date to 11/1/2018 before opening the QuickBooks file, as recommended in the Before You Get Started lesson. This will ensure that the dates you see on your screen match the dates in this lesson.

To start QuickBooks,

1. Double-click   the QuickBooks Pro icon   on the desktop

Quick Tip. You can also select All Programs : QuickBooks : QuickBooks Pro 2018 from the Windows Start menu. If a Let's get your business set up quickly window opens, close it to display the No Company Open window.

QuickBooks opens and displays the No Company Open window:

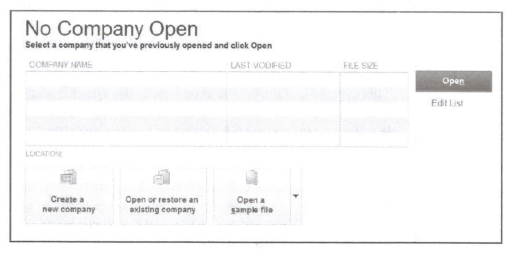

Note: If you have already opened a company file in QuickBooks 2018, the company file will display in the No Company Open window. If this is the first time you are using QuickBooks 2018, an additional window may open displaying information about how QuickBooks uses your internet connection.

This window allows you to create a new company file, open or restore an existing company file, or open a sample file. For this exercise, you will open an existing company file.

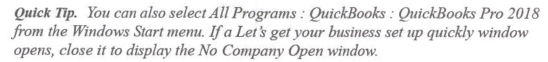

2. Click

The Open or Restore Company window opens:

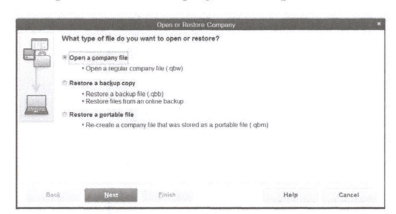

Note: Depending on the version of QuickBooks you are using, your window may display additional options. For example, the QuickBooks Accountant version will display an option for Converting an Accountant's Copy Transfer File.

This window allows you to open or restore a QuickBooks file.

3. Verify   Open a company file   is selected

4. Click   [Next]

The Open a Company window displays:

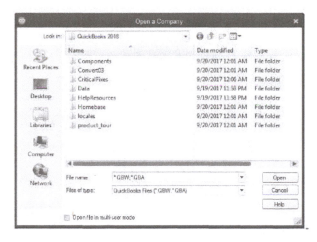

Note: The files and folders displayed in your window may be different.

By default, this window opens to the folder where you last saved or opened a QuickBooks file.

5. Click   the drop-down arrow   in the Look in field

A drop-down menu displays.

6. Click the letter that corresponds to the hard drive (the drive where you unzipped the QuickBooks files in the Before You Get Started lesson)

All folders in the hard drive display in the area below the Look in field.

7. Double-click   the Books2018 folder

All QuickBooks files in the Books2018 folder display:

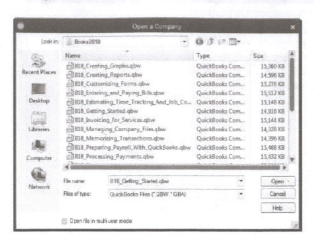

Note: If your system is not set up to display file extensions, you will not see the .qbw extension. Refer to the Displaying File Extensions section in the Before you Get Started lesson for instructions on displaying file extensions.

8. Select   B18_Getting Started.qbw   from the list of files

9. Click   [Open]

The QuickBooks Login dialog box displays:

This dialog box informs you that you must login as a QuickBooks Administrator in order to open the company file. When you create a company file, you can password-protect the file in order to prevent unwanted users from accessing your company's information.

10. Type   **Canalside2**   in the Password field

Note: Passwords are case-sensitive.

11. Click   OK

Note: A Set Up an External Accountant User dialog box and a QuickBooks Usage Study dialog box may also display. Click the X in the upper-right corner of these dialog boxes to close them.

QuickBooks opens the file and displays the Home page with a Reminders window:

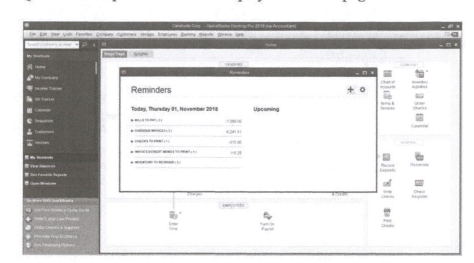

Note: Your QuickBooks window may open to the Home page with a Welcome message and yellow What's New message boxes describing some of QuickBooks new features. You can click anywhere in the application window to hide the What's New message boxes. Then, select Company : Reminders from the menu bar to display the Reminders window. In addition, depending on your screen resolution, your QuickBooks window may open with the Icon Bar located at the top of the window below the menu bar, and the Account balances and Do More with QuickBooks areas may display on the right side of the window.

Note: If you did not change your computer's date as recommended in the Before You Get Started lesson, your Reminders window will display different reminders.

The Reminders window displays all reminders and notifications in one single location. It lists all of the QuickBooks tasks you need to complete, such as bills to pay, checks to print, and inventory to order, and displays items that are due, or overdue, such as invoices. You can choose which tasks to be reminded of, and how and when you'll see the reminder. For example, ten days before a bill is actually due, you can have QuickBooks remind you to pay it. This window even displays system notifications, and notes from accountants Clicking a bolded heading in the Reminders window displays further information about that task.

12. Click Bills to Pay in the Reminders window

The Bills to Pay heading expands to display all bills that need to be paid:

Note: If you did not change your computer's date as recommended in the Before You Get Started lesson, the bills to pay will be different.

From this window, you can double-click a bill to open the Enter Bills window and pay the bill.

13. Click   ✖   to close the Reminders window

Note: If you are using an Accountant's edition of QuickBooks, an Accountant Center will display. Deselect the Show Accountant Center when opening a company file check box and then close the Accountant Center.

Setting QuickBooks Preferences

You can customize various aspects of QuickBooks to suit both your personal needs and the needs of your business. For example, you can set general preferences, such as configuring how a keyboard key works in QuickBooks, or you can set more specific preferences, such as identifying which reminders display in the Reminders list.

In this exercise, you will turn off pop-up messages for services and products so they do not display when working in this QuickBooks company file.

1. Select   Edit : Preferences   from the menu bar

The Preferences window opens with the My Preferences tab of the General category displayed:

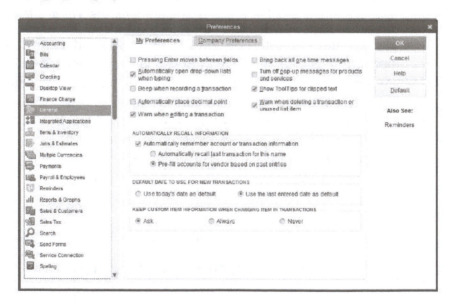

Note: If the Preferences window opens with another category selected, click the General category.

QuickBooks general preferences allow you to customize how certain functions and keys work in QuickBooks. The My Preferences tab allows you to modify how QuickBooks works for you when working in this company file, but not for other QuickBooks users. The Company Preferences tab allows you to modify how QuickBooks works for all users working in the company file.

Note: Only an administrator can change settings on the Company Preferences tab.

On the My Preferences tab,

2. Select   the Turn off pop-up messages   check box
                   for products and services

3. Click   [OK]

The Preferences window closes. QuickBooks will no longer display pop-up messages for any product or service.

Identifying Components of the QuickBooks Operating Environment

QuickBooks provides multiple tools to quickly and easily access various tasks and features.

The QuickBooks operating environment includes the following main elements:

- Title Bar

- Menu Bar

- Icon Bar

- QuickBooks Desktop

Title Bar

Menu Bar

Icon Bar

QuickBooks
Desktop

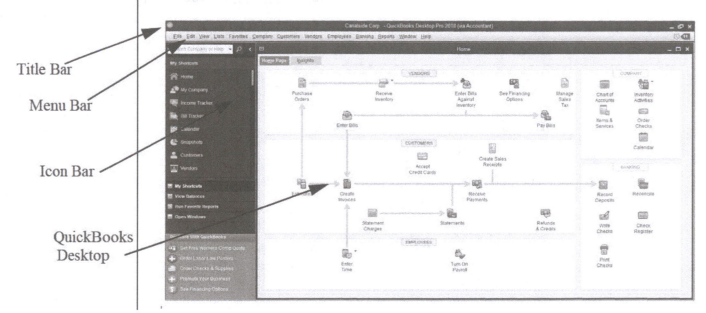

Note: Your QuickBooks window may display the Icon Bar at the top of the window. To display the Icon Bar on the left side of the window, so that your window matches the screens in this guide, select View : Left Icon Bar from the menu bar.

Title Bar

| ⊕ | Canalside Corp - QuickBooks Desktop Pro 2018 | _ □ ✕ |

The title bar, located at the top of the screen, displays the name of the QuickBooks company file that is currently open (Canalside Corp.) and the name of the software program (QuickBooks Desktop Pro 2018). If you maximize the window displayed in the QuickBooks desktop, the name of the window currently displayed in the desktop will be in brackets in the title bar. For example, when the Home page window is displayed and maximized, Home appears in brackets; when the Enter Bills window is displayed and maximized, Enter Bills appears in brackets.

By double-clicking the title bar when the QuickBooks window is maximized, you minimize the window. By double-clicking the title bar when the QuickBooks window is minimized, you can maximize the window or restore it to its previous size and location. By clicking and dragging the title bar, you can move the QuickBooks window (when it is not maximized). The title bar also provides the following buttons:

▬ Minimize	Reduces the QuickBooks window to the taskbar on the bottom of the screen
⌐₧ Restore	Restores the QuickBooks window to its previous size and location
☐ Maximize	Enlarges the QuickBooks window to fill the screen
✕ Close	Closes the QuickBooks application

Quick Tip. *A title bar also displays for each QuickBooks window that you open and can be used in the same manner.*

Menu Bar

| File   Edit   View   Lists   Favorites   Company   Customers   Vendors   Employees   Banking   Reports   Window   Help |

All of QuickBooks's various commands can be found in the drop-down menus of the menu bar. The menu bar provides quick and easy access to all of QuickBooks tasks and features.

Note: Depending on the QuickBooks edition you are using, your menu bar may display additional menus.

Quick Tip. *Software programs designed for Windows make extensive use of the right mouse button to produce shortcut menus. When using the software, you can click the right mouse button to see if there is a shortcut menu for the procedure with which you are working.*

Icon Bar

Search

Shortcuts

Control Pane

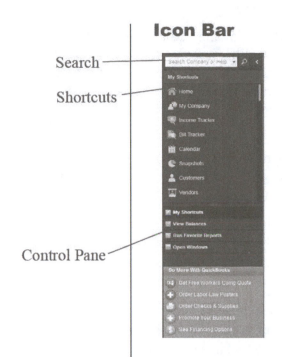

The Icon Bar includes a search field allowing you to search within your company file or within the QuickBooks help. It also includes shortcuts that give you one-click access to the QuickBooks tasks and features you use most. Instead of selecting a command from a menu, you simply click the shortcut in the Icon Bar.

Note: You can minimize the Icon Bar by clicking ◄ *(the Collapse Pane arrow) next to the search field.*

The Control Pane allows you to switch from displaying shortcuts to displaying other sections, such as viewing balances, running favorite reports, and opening windows.

Note: Depending on the QuickBooks edition you are using, your Icon Bar may display additional icons.

The following are some of the shortcut icons included on the Icon Bar:

 Opens the Home page, allowing you to start common business tasks. Click this icon at any time to return to the Home page.

 Opens the My Company window, displaying important information about your company file at a glance.

 Opens the Income Tracker, making it easy to find and work with unbilled sales (estimates and sales orders), unpaid sales (open and overdue invoices), and paid sales (payments and sales receipts).

 Opens the Bill Tracker, making it easy to manage vendor-related payables, such as bills and purchase orders

 Opens a calendar allowing you to quickly view all transactions and tasks entered into QuickBooks. For each day, QuickBooks displays a summary of transactions entered, transactions due, and tasks to be completed. The Calendar view allows you to quickly see important upcoming tasks or past due tasks.

 Opens the Company Snapshot, displaying real-time company, payment, and customer information.

 Opens the Customer Center, allowing you to view all of your customers and jobs and manage customer and job data and transactions. You can also view current customer balances, contact and billing information, and related transactions. You can also add customers and jobs and manage key customer tasks, such as creating invoices and receiving payments.

Vendors	Opens the Vendor Center, allowing you to view a list of vendor names, their contact and billing information, your current balance with a vendor, and your entire history with a vendor. From this window, you can easily add vendors and manage key vendor tasks, such as tracking and paying bills.
Employees	Opens the Employee Center, allowing you to view employee names, contact information, and payroll history. From this window, you can easily add new employees, edit current employee information, and enter hours worked for employees.
Bank Feeds	Opens the Online Banking Center, allowing you to view the most recent balances for your bank accounts, as well as download and create transactions. You must have accounts set up for online services to view the Online Banking Center.
Docs	Opens the Doc Center, allowing you to organize and store documents you use with QuickBooks, such as receipts and bills. From this window, you can add documents from your computer or scanner, attach documents to customers, vendors, employees, items, accounts, forms, and transactions, view and add document details, and search for documents. All of your documents are stored locally on your hard drive, at no cost.

Note: If you have an existing online subscription to QuickBooks Attached Documents, the Doc Center also displays documents you store online.

Reports	Opens the Report Center, allowing you to display detailed reports and graphs that answer questions about your business. The Report Center includes numerous preset reports and graphs that provide a comprehensive view of your company.
Invoice	Opens the Create Invoices window allowing you to create invoices.
Item	Opens the Item List window allowing you to record information about the products and services you buy and sell and for items that perform calculations, such as discounts and sales tax.
MemTx	Opens the Memorized Transaction list allowing you to manage the transactions you have memorized and the memorized transaction groups you have created.
Check	Opens the Write Checks - Checking window allowing you to write checks.

Note: Additional shortcut icons will display on your Icon Bar.

Quick Tip. *You can move the Icon Bar above the QuickBooks desktop by selecting View : Top Icon Bar from the menu bar. You can hide the Icon Bar by selecting View : Hide Icon Bar from the menu bar.*

Using QuickBooks Search

The Icon Bar includes a search field allowing you to enter a keyword and easily search the QuickBooks Help or within your company file. When searching within your company file, you can search across all areas to quickly find:

- Forms/transactions (invoices, estimates, and so on)

- People (customers, vendors, employees, and other names)

- List entries (items, tax items, and so on)

- Amounts and dates

- Menu commands

- Specific text within notes, descriptions, memos, and transactions

In this exercise, you will use the search field in the Icon Bar to search for all instances of the word "Plumbing" in your company file.

1. Type **Plumbing** in the search field located on the Icon Bar

2. Click

QuickBooks displays the search results in a Search window:

Note: If your search results do not display, click the Update search information link below the Last Update text in the Search window to display the search results. You may also need to click the Search icon in the Search window again.

The search results identify how many records were found and from which areas of QuickBooks. In this example, "Plumbing" was found in ten records, including Transactions, Vendors, and Item records.

3. Position   the mouse cursor   over the first search result for the vendor PJ's Plumbing for $450.00

The PJ's Plumbing vendor record becomes shaded in light blue:

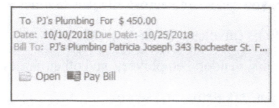

QuickBooks now displays the actions that can be performed on this record, including opening the bill in the Enter Bills window or opening the Pay Bills window to pay the bill.

4. Click   to close the Search window

Customizing the Icon Bar

The Icon Bar is customizable. You can select which icons display on the Icon Bar, as well as control their appearance, order, and the way in which they are grouped.

To customize the Icon Bar,

1. Select   View :   from the menu bar
                   Customize Icon Bar

The Customize Icon Bar window opens:

From this window, you can add icons to the Icon Bar for tasks you perform on a daily basis, such as printing invoices or purchase orders. You can also delete icons for tasks that you do not perform often. In addition to deciding which features to include or exclude on the Icon Bar, you can reorder icons, group icons, and select different graphics and descriptions for icons.

To add an icon,

2. Click

The Add Icon Bar Item window opens:

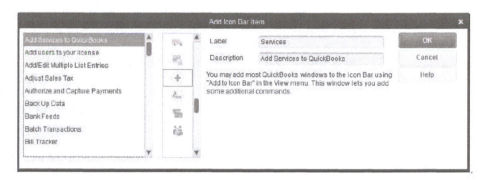

Note: Depending on the version of QuickBooks you are using, your window may display additional items and may open with a different item selected.

This window allows you to add an item to the Icon Bar and specify the icon's graphic, label, and description. For example, if you frequently use a calculator in your business, you may want to add the Calculator icon to the Icon Bar.

3. Select   Calculator   from the list of available icons (scroll down if necessary)

For this example, you will leave the default graphic, label, and description.

4. Click

Calc displays at the bottom of the list in the Customize Icon Bar window:

Quick Tip. *You can quickly add most open windows to the Icon Bar by selecting View : Add [name of window] to Icon Bar from the menu bar. For example, if the Create Estimates window is open, select View : Add "Create Estimates" to Icon Bar from the menu bar. This adds the Create Estimates icon to the Icon Bar.*

To reorder the icons on the Icon Bar,

5. Position   the mouse pointer   over the small diamond to the left of Calc

The mouse pointer becomes a four-directional arrow ⊕, indicating that you can drag the item up or down.

6. Click and hold   the left mouse button

7. Drag   the mouse pointer   up to the top of the list until the dotted line displays below Calendar in the Icon Bar Content List

8. Release   the left mouse button   to drop the icon into the new position

The Customize Icon Bar window should resemble the figure below:

To delete an icon from the Icon Bar,

9. Select   Docs   from the Icon Bar Content list (scroll down)

10. Click   Delete

Docs is removed from the Icon Bar Content list:

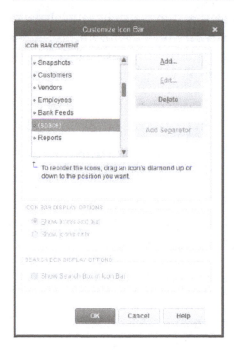

11. Click [OK] to close the Customize Icon Bar window

The Calculator (Calc) icon now displays below the Calendar icon and the Docs icon has been removed:

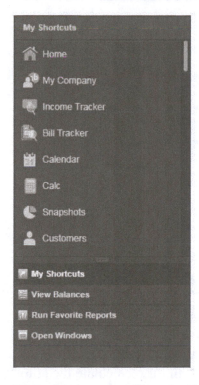

Note: You may need to scroll down to see that the Docs icon no longer displays.

The QuickBooks Desktop

The space below the menu bar and to the right of the Icon Bar is known as the QuickBooks desktop and is where the QuickBooks Home page, Company Snapshot, QuickBooks Centers, and other task windows display. Basically, this is the area where all windows display and where you will perform all of your business tasks.

Forms, Registers, and Lists

When working in QuickBooks, you will spend most of your time using the software's basic elements: forms, registers, and lists.

Forms

You will record most of your daily business transactions on a QuickBooks form, which looks just like a paper form.

To view an example of the form you will use when you want to enter a bill from one of your vendors,

- ◆ Click in the Vendors area of the Home page

The Enter Bills window opens:

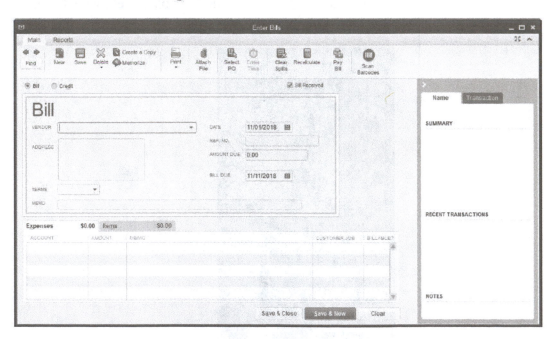

QuickBooks forms have a simplified layout allowing you to easily complete tasks. For example, on the Enter Bills form, all of the tasks related to paying a bill are located at the top of the window. You can attach a file to a bill, select an open purchase order to create a bill from, or recalculate the amount of a bill.

After you provide information on the Enter Bills form, QuickBooks automatically does the accounting for you. For example, when you pay a bill for a business expense, QuickBooks automatically puts a transaction in your accounts payable register to show the payment you made. (Accounts payable is the money owed by your business to vendors.) QuickBooks also records the check in your checking account, keeps your records up-to-date, and provides a running balance of what you owe at any time.

Registers

The register is another basic QuickBooks feature. Just as you can use a paper checkbook register to enter transactions from your checking account—checks written, other withdrawals from your account, and deposits—a QuickBooks register shows all the activity in one account. Almost every QuickBooks account has its own register.

To view an example of an Accounts Receivable register,

1. Click 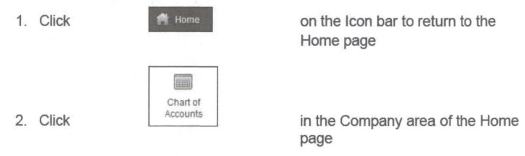 on the Icon bar to return to the Home page

2. Click in the Company area of the Home page

The Chart of Accounts opens:

Quick Tip. You can display the Chart of Accounts by clicking the Chart of Accounts icon in the Company area of the Home page, by selecting it from the Lists menu, or by clicking the Chart of Accounts (Accnt) icon on the Icon Bar.

3. Double-click   Accounts Receivable   in the Name column

The Accounts Receivable register opens:

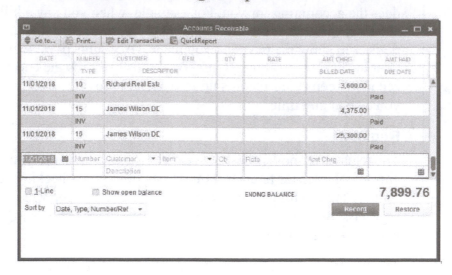

The register shows information about invoices billed to customers: the date of the invoice, the name of the customer, the amount of the invoice, and the date the invoice is due. It also shows payments you have received against your invoices. The right column of the register gives you a running balance of your accounts receivable, so you always know how much you are owed.

Lists

In addition to forms and registers, you will also work with QuickBooks lists. There are lists displayed when you open QuickBooks Centers, such as the list of vendors that displays in the Vendor Center. There are also lists that open in separate windows, such as the Chart of Accounts or the Item List.

You fill out most QuickBooks forms by selecting entries from a list. Lists help you enter information consistently and correctly, thus saving time. For example, when you are completing an invoice and you select an item from the Item List, QuickBooks not only fills in the name of the item, but also the description, rate, and total amount charged for the item.

To view an example of an Item List,

- Select   Lists : Item List   from the menu bar

The Item List opens:

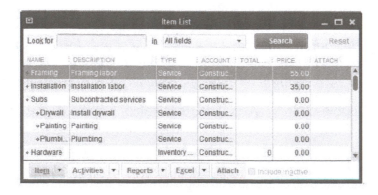

QuickBooks allows you to perform a variety of activities from lists using menu buttons located at the bottom of each list. For example, if you want to add an item to the Item List, you can select New from the Item button.

Open Windows

When you have multiple windows open, you may find it useful to display a list of the windows that are open in one convenient location. The Icon Bar allows you to easily view all windows that are open and also allows for one-click access to these open windows.

To view a list of all open windows,

1. Click  in the Control Pane of the Icon Bar

Note: Your Open Windows button may only display an icon and not the text "Open Windows".

A list of all open windows displays in the Icon Bar:

The window currently displayed is listed at the top of the Open Windows list. All other windows can be accessed by clicking the name of the window in the list.

2. Click My Shortcuts in the Control Pane of the Icon Bar

The list of shortcuts displays in the Icon Bar.

3. Click Home in the Icon Bar

The Home page displays.

 Quick Tip. You can also select Window on the menu bar to view a list of all open windows. To bring a window to the front, simply select the name of the window from the Windows menu.

The QuickBooks Home Page

When you open a company file, a Home page tab and an Insights tab display. The Home page displays clickable icons and is designed to allow for direct access to major QuickBooks features and common business tasks.

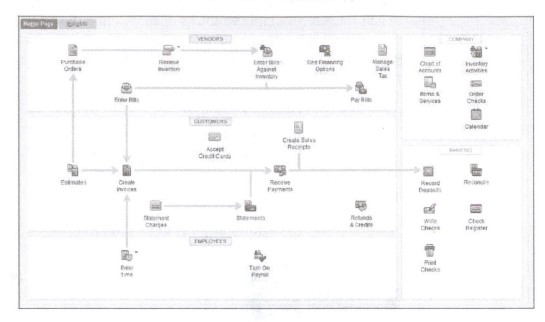

Workflow arrows are also displayed to help you understand how tasks are related to one another and to help you decide what task to perform next. These workflows are displayed in an easy-to-follow format that helps you work more efficiently.

Note: The workflow arrows suggest a logical progression of business tasks; however, you may perform tasks in any order you prefer.

The Home page groups different types of business activities and pictorially shows the flow of activities within each grouping. Related business tasks are grouped into the following categories:

- Vendors

- Customers

- Employees

- Company

- Banking

Each category contains clickable icons enabling you to perform tasks relevant to that category. These icons allow for fast, single mouse-click navigation to registers, lists, and forms that are most commonly used in typical business transactions. To start a task, you simply click the icon for that task.

Positioning the cursor over an icon displays a description of the icon's function:

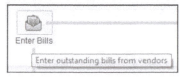

The description disappears after you point away from the icon.

Customizing the Home Page

The Home page that displays when you start QuickBooks is based on your company file preferences, or how you answered the questions about your business in the EasyStep Interview. If you need to change which icons are displayed on the Home page, you can customize it.

Note: You must be in single-user mode to customize the Home page.

To customize the Home page,

1. Select   Edit : Preferences   from the menu bar

The Preferences window opens with the My Preferences tab of the General category displayed.

2. Select   Desktop View   from the list of preferences

The My Preferences tab of the Desktop View category displays:

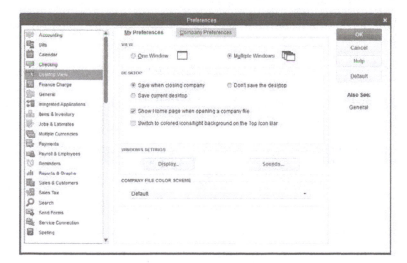

These preferences allow you to customize your QuickBooks desktop, such as determining the windows that display when you open a company file.

Quick Tip. QuickBooks now allows you to display windows on multiple monitors. To use multiple monitors, select the Desktop View option in the Preferences window and then click Display in the Window Settings area to change your monitor settings.

3. Click   the Company Preferences tab

The Company Preferences tab displays:

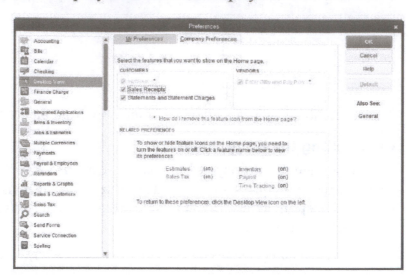

This tab allows you to show or hide icons for specific features on the Home page. To hide the Statements and Statement Charges icons in the Customers area of the Home page,

4.	Deselect	the Statements and Statement Charges check box	in the Customers area

You can show or hide other icons on the Home page, by enabling or disabling that feature in QuickBooks. For example, your company may no longer track time for its employees and therefore, you no longer need to display the Enter Time icon on the Home page.

5.	Click	the Time Tracking link	in the Related Preferences area

Because you have made changes to the Desktop View preferences, a Save Changes dialog box displays:

6.	Click	Yes

A Warning dialog box displays informing you that QuickBooks must close all open windows to change this preference:

7. Click

The Company Preferences tab of the Time & Expenses category displays:

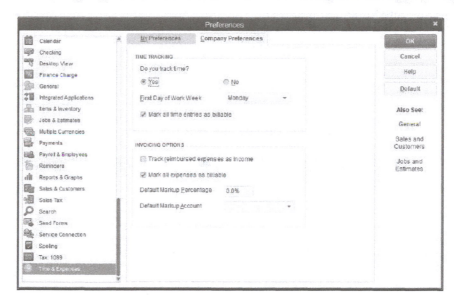

8. Select   **No**   in the Time Tracking area

9. Click   OK

10. Click   Home   in the Icon Bar

The Home page opens:

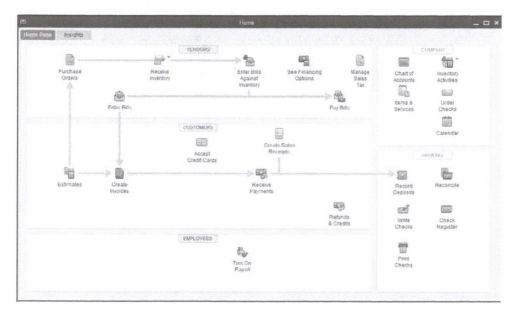

The Statements and Statement Charges icons in the Customers area of the Home page no longer display. Also, the Enter Time icon no longer displays in the Employees area of the Home page.

The Insights Page

The Insights page allows you to quickly get a read of your business performance by allowing you to view your profit and loss, income and expenses, and top customers at a glance.

To access the Insights page,

1. Click next to the Home Page tab below the menu bar

The Insights page opens:

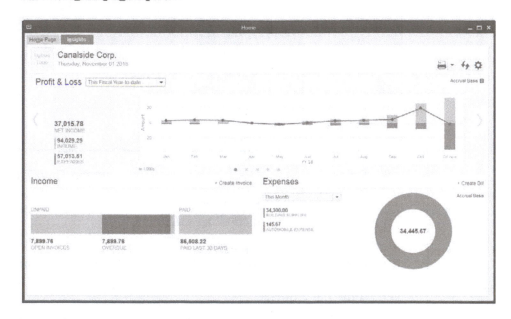

Note: If you did not change your computer's date as recommended in the Before You Get Started lesson, your Insights window will look slightly different.

The Insights page is divided into three panes: a center pane, an Income pane, and an Expenses pane.

* The center pane includes left and right arrows that allow you to move between different data views, such as the Profit & Loss view, the Prev Year Income Comparison view, the Top Sales by Customers view, the Business Growth view, and the Net Profit Margin.

* The Income pane displays open and overdue invoices, and any paid invoice over the last 30 days.

* The Expenses pane displays all major expenses over the selected time period.

Quick Tip. You can also add a company logo to this page, print the page, and even save the page as a PDF.

Note: Only the QuickBooks administrator has access to the Insights page when a company file is initially set up. To provide another user access to this page, the administrator must edit that user's role.

The Company Snapshot

The Company Snapshot allows you to easily view real-time company, payment, and customer information and perform tasks from a single area.

To access the Company Snapshot,

1. Click  on the Icon Bar

The Company Snapshot window opens.

2. Click  in the upper-right corner of the Company Snapshot window

The Company Snapshot window is maximized:

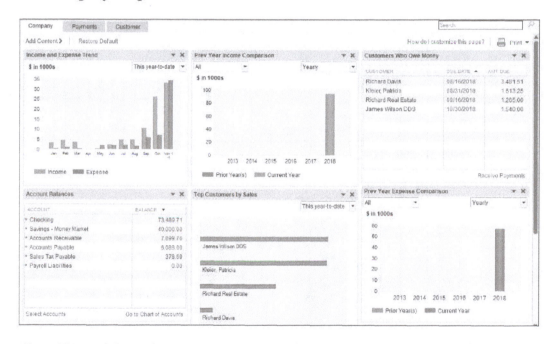

Note: If you did not change your computer's date as recommended in the Before You Get Started lesson, your window may look different.

The Company Snapshot includes three tabs: a Company tab, a Payment tab, and a Customer tab.

The Company tab consists of the following sections:

Income and Expense Trend	Displays the money going in and out of your business over time. It provides a graphical snapshot of how your business is doing and lets you compare monthly income and expenses.
Prev Year Income Comparison	Displays how much money you're making this year compared to previous years for any or all accounts. You can view monthly, quarterly, weekly, or yearly comparisons.

Customers Who Owe Money	Displays balances owed by customers.
Account Balances	Displays all bank, accounts receivable, accounts payable, credit card, asset, liability, and equity accounts. You can add accounts to this list by clicking the Select Accounts link.
Top Customers By Sales	Displays who your top five customers are based on sales for a given period of time.
Prev Year Expense Comparison	Displays how much money you're spending this year compared to previous years for any or all accounts. You can view monthly, quarterly, weekly, or yearly comparisons.
Expense Breakdown	Displays your company's biggest expenses.

3. **Click** the Payments tab

The Payments tab of the Company Snapshot opens:

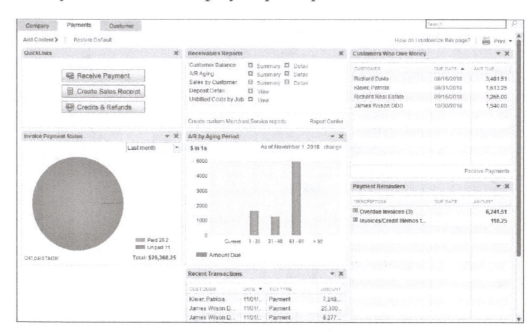

The Payments tab consists of the following sections:

QuickLinks	Allows you to add short-cut buttons for the tasks you use most often, such as receiving payments, creating sales receipts, and issuing credits and refunds.
Receivables Reports	Displays summary and detailed views of the following standard QuickBooks reports: Customer Balance, A/R Aging, Sales by Customer, Deposit Detail, and Unbilled Costs by Job.

Customers Who Owe Money	Displays a list of customers with outstanding invoices. The due date is displayed in red when an invoice is overdue.
Invoice Payment Status	Displays a graphical representation of paid and unpaid invoices by billing date range.
A/R by Aging Period	Displays how much each customer owes you and any balance overdue by the number of days.
Payment Reminders	Displays which customers have overdue invoices (and the total dollar amount), money waiting to be deposited, and memorized invoices.
Recent Transactions	Displays recent transactions your company has had with customers. You can view all or individual transactions, and sort by most recent transactions.

4. Click   the Customer tab

The Customer tab of the Company Snapshot opens:

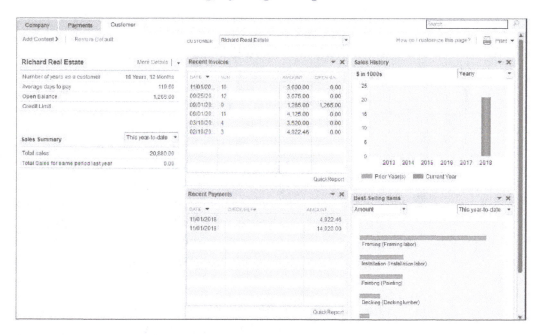

Note: Select Richard Real Estate from the Customer drop-down menu at the top of the window if it is not already selected.

The Customer tab offers a consolidated view of a customer's purchase history, average days to pay, and outstanding balance, and allows you to identify top customers by revenue and payment consistency.

The Customer tab consists of the following sections:

Customer Summary	Displays summary information about the selected customer, including how long they have been a customer, their open balance, and their credit limit.
Sales Summary	Displays the total sales for the selected customer.
Recent Invoices	Displays the date, invoice number, amount, and open balance due for the last ten invoices for the customer.
Recent Payments	Displays the last ten payments received from the customer.
Sales History	Displays a sales history for a particular period of time and compares it to the same time in prior periods.
Best-Selling Items	Displays the items the customer bought most for a specific period.

Using QuickBooks Help

There are a variety of ways to get help while using QuickBooks.

Help menu	The Help menu is the last menu on the menu bar and contains commands that access different elements of the Help system. Selections from this menu include opening QuickBooks Desktop Help, showing or hiding new features in this release of QuickBooks, accessing support resources, finding a local QuickBooks expert, sending feedback online, setting up an Internet connection, opening the Year-End Guide, adding QuickBooks services, accessing the App Center, updating QuickBooks Desktop, managing user licenses, resetting Intuit ID settings, viewing the QuickBooks Desktop privacy statement, learning about automatic updates, viewing QuickBooks usage and analytics studies, and viewing QuickBooks Desktop software license information.
QuickBooks Help windows	When you press the F1 key, select Help : QuickBooks Desktop Help from the menu bar, enter a keyword in the search field of the Icon Bar, or click any other Help buttons or Help links displayed in a window, the Have a Question? window displays. This window lists topics relevant to the currently displayed window, area, or button where the mouse pointer is located. From this window, you can click any of the links displayed for further information, or search for help on a specific topic to display a Help Article window.

Identifying Common Business Terms

Chart of Accounts

When you keep books for a business, you want to track where your income comes from, where it goes, what your expenses are for, and what you use to pay them. You track this flow of money through a list of accounts called the Chart of Accounts. The Chart of Accounts displays balance sheet accounts first, followed by income accounts, and then expense accounts.

Assets, Liabilities, and Equity

Assets

Assets include both what you have and what other people owe you. The money people owe you is called accounts receivable, or A/R for short. QuickBooks uses an Accounts Receivable account to track the money owed to you.

The rest of your company's assets may include checking accounts, savings accounts, petty cash, fixed assets (such as equipment or trucks), inventory, and undeposited funds (money you have received from customers, but have not yet deposited in the bank).

Liabilities

Liabilities are what your company owes to other people. The money you owe for unpaid bills is your accounts payable, or A/P for short. QuickBooks uses an Accounts Payable account to track all the money you owe different people for bills.

A liability can be a formal loan, an unpaid bill, or sales and payroll taxes you owe to the government.

Equity

Equity is the difference between what you have (your assets) and what you owe (your liabilities):

- Equity = Assets - Liabilities

If you sold all your assets today and you paid off your liabilities using the money received from the sale of your assets, the money you would have left would be your equity.

Your equity reflects the health of your business, because it is the amount of money left after you satisfy all your debts. Equity comes from three sources:

- Money invested in the company by its owners or stockholders

- Net profit from operating the business during the current accounting period

- Retained earnings or net profits from early periods that have not been distributed to the owners or stockholders

Quick Tip. If you have a sole proprietorship (where the existence of the business depends solely on your efforts), you can check the value of your owner's equity by creating a QuickBooks balance sheet report.

Cash versus accrual bookkeeping

When you begin your business, you should decide which bookkeeping method to use. The bookkeeping method determines how you report income and expenses on your tax forms. QuickBooks allows you to switch between the cash and accrual reports at any time—you are not required to select only one method.

Check with your tax adviser or the IRS before choosing a bookkeeping method for tax purposes.

Cash basis

Many small businesses record income when they receive the money, and expenses when they pay the bills. This method is known as bookkeeping on a cash basis. If you have been recording deposits of your customers' payments, but have not been including the money customers owe you as a part of your income, you have been using the cash basis method. Similarly, if you have been tracking expenses at the time you pay them, rather than at the time you first receive the bills, you have been using the cash basis method.

Accrual basis

In accrual-basis bookkeeping, you record income at the time of the sale, not at the time you receive the payment. You enter expenses when you receive the bill, not when you pay it.

Most accountants feel that the accrual method gives you a truer picture of your company's finances.

How your bookkeeping method affects QuickBooks

You enter transactions the same way in QuickBooks, whether you use the cash or the accrual method.

QuickBooks is set up to prepare your reports on an accrual basis. For example, it shows income on a profit and loss statement for invoices as soon as you record them, even if you have not yet received payment.

Quick Tip. If you would like to prepare reports on a cash basis, you can change this setting by selecting Edit : Preferences from the menu bar. When the Preferences window opens, select the Reports & Graphs preference, click the Company Preferences tab, and select the Cash option in the Summary Reports Basis area.

Measuring Business Profitability

Two of the most important reports for measuring the profitability of your business are the balance sheet and the profit and loss statement (also called an income statement). These are the reports most often requested by certified public accountants (CPAs) and financial officers. For example, banks request both documents when you apply for a loan.

The balance sheet

A balance sheet is a financial snapshot of your company on a particular day. It shows:

- What you have (assets)

- What people owe you (accounts receivable)

- What your business owes to other people (liabilities and accounts payable)

- The net worth of your business (equity)

The profit and loss statement

A profit and loss (P&L) statement, also called an income statement, shows your income, expenses, and net income (= income - expenses). QuickBooks's profit and loss statements allow you to summarize the income and expenses of your business by category.

Exiting QuickBooks

Unlike most other Windows programs, QuickBooks does not require you to save your data before exiting, because it performs an automatic save while you are working and every time you exit the program.

To close the company file and exit QuickBooks,

1. Select   File : Close Company   from the menu bar

The company file closes.

Note: If you want QuickBooks to open to this company file the next time the application is started, you do not need to close the company. However, it is recommended that you close the company file if you are using QuickBooks on a network.

2. Select   File : Exit   from the menu bar

Quick Tip. You can also click ☒ *in the title bar of the QuickBooks window.*

The QuickBooks application closes.

Review

In this lesson, you have learned how to:

- ☑ Start QuickBooks
- ☑ Set QuickBooks preferences
- ☑ Identify components of the QuickBooks operating environment
- ☑ Use QuickBooks Help
- ☑ Identify common business terms
- ☑ Exit QuickBooks

Practice: None

Setting Up a Company

In this lesson, you will learn how to:

❑ Create a QuickBooks company

❑ Use the Chart of Accounts

Concept

QuickBooks allows you to enter and store a wide variety of information about your company and the way it does business. When you set up your company and enter the company address, business type, and taxing policy, QuickBooks will then add this data automatically to invoices, checks, purchase orders, and reports. This data can be edited as your company changes and grows.

Scenario

In this lesson, you are the owner of Canalside Corp., which does new building construction and remodeling. You will use the QuickBooks express set up feature to set up your company and its Chart of Accounts. You will then work with the Chart of Accounts by adding account numbers to accounts. You will also search for an account, edit an account, add an account, delete an account, move an account, and add subaccounts. As a final step, you will enter account opening balances to accounts in the Chart of Accounts.

Practice Files: Created in this lesson

Creating a QuickBooks Company

A QuickBooks company contains all of the financial records for a single business. Before you can use QuickBooks, you need to tell QuickBooks about your company so that it can set up your company file.

Choosing a Start Date

Before you start entering your company data, you need to choose a QuickBooks start date. The start date is the date on which you give QuickBooks a financial snapshot of your company's assets and liabilities.

After you decide on a start date, you will enter all your company's transactions from that date on. You should choose a start date that is not too far in the past. Many business owners like to use the last day of a financial period as their start date, such as the end of the last fiscal year, last quarter, or last month. You need to enter all historical transactions from the day after your start date through today. For example, if you decide on a start date of March 31, you would enter your historical transactions from April 1 through the current date.

How Many Company Files Should You Set Up?

If you operate a business enterprise, the IRS expects you to show all sources of income and to document all business expenses that you claim as deductions. Therefore, for tax purposes it is best to set up a separate QuickBooks company for each business enterprise you report on your tax forms.

Entering a Company Name and Address

When you create a new QuickBooks company, QuickBooks will ask you about the type of business you own. It uses your answers to create the appropriate accounts and lists.

You are going to create a new QuickBooks company for a business named Canalside Corp., a company that does both new construction and remodeling. As the owner, you can then use QuickBooks to set up and run your company, and to produce reports and graphs to help you analyze your business.

Note: For this lesson, it is recommended that you do not change your computer's date as recommended in the Before You Get Started lesson. Changing your computer's date will prevent certain steps in this lesson from working properly.

To create your company,

1. Start QuickBooks

QuickBooks opens displaying the QuickBooks application window with a No Company Open window:

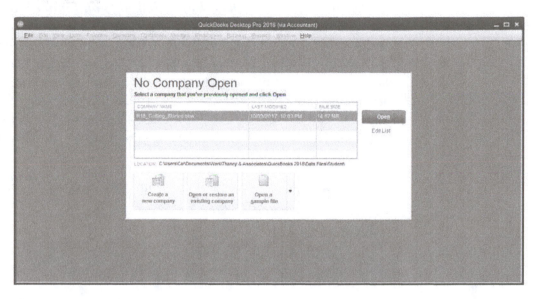

 Caution. *If an Administrator was set up in the last company file you accessed and you did not log out when previously exiting QuickBooks, you will be prompted to log in. If the QuickBooks Login dialog box displays, click the Cancel button.*

2. Click

QuickBooks opens, displaying the QuickBooks Setup window:

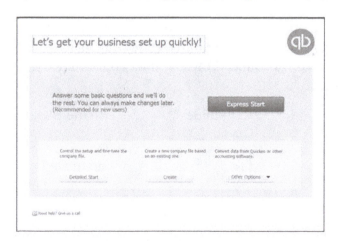

The QuickBooks Setup window allows you to create a new company file using an express or advanced setup process. For this lesson, you will use the express method, the quicker of the two processes.

Note: The Detailed Start button takes you through the EasyStep Interview, which is covered in Appendix A.

3. Click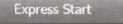

Note: If an Enter your email address window opens, enter the email address associated with your company and click the Validate button to allow QuickBooks to determine if your email address is linked to an Intuit account. If you have an Intuit account, you should enter the same email address used with your Intuit account in order to link your company file to the Intuit account. Linking your email address to your Intuit account allows you to easily access additional apps and services directly from QuickBooks. If you do not have an Intuit account, you should enter the email address for your business and QuickBooks will create an Intuit account during the set up process. After validating your email address, additional fields may display allowing you to enter or create an Intuit account password.

The Glad you're here screen of the setup process opens:

This screen allows you to tell QuickBooks how your business is organized so that the appropriate accounts can be created for the business and tax form lines can be assigned to those accounts. You also enter contact information for your business on this screen.

4.	Type	**Canalside Corp.**	in the Business Name field
5.	Press	Tab	to move to the Industry field

Note: Your Industry field may display a different industry or may be blank.

This field allows you to select your company's type of industry in order to customize QuickBooks to work best for your business. When you create a new QuickBooks company, you should select an industry type that most closely matches your type of business. QuickBooks will then automatically create a preset Chart of Accounts for your company. If your business does not fall into a specific industry listed, select the one that is closest to get a head start on creating your own Chart of Accounts. After you have created your new company file, you can modify the Chart of Accounts to suit your needs.

6. Type   **Con** (for construction)   in the Industry field

A drop-down menu displays:

> Construction General Contractor
> Construction Trades (Plumber, Electrician, HVAC, etc.)
> Professional Consulting

7. Select   Construction General   from the drop-down menu
                  Contractor

Quick Tip. *Clicking the Help me choose link displays a window allowing you to select various industries and view the accounts QuickBooks recommends for that industry.*

8. Click   in the Business Type field

A drop-down menu displays:

> Sole Proprietorship
> Partnership or LLP
> Single-Member LLC (Form-1040)
> Multi-Member LLC (Form-1065)
> Corporation
> S Corporation
> Non-Profit
> Other / None

9. Select   S Corporation   from the drop-down menu

10. Type   **11-2345678**   in the Employer Identification
                                         Number (EIN) field

11. Type   **401 Lewis Ave.**   in the Address field

12. Press   `Tab`   twice to move to the City field

13. Type   **Fairgrave**   in the City field

14. Select   NY   from the State drop-down menu
                                         (scroll down)

15. Type   **11111**   in the Zip field

16. Verify that U.S. is selected in the Country field

17. Type   **555-555-5555**   in the Phone field

Based on your selections on this screen, QuickBooks automatically sets up your company file with certain features and creates a Chart of Accounts.

To review the features and accounts QuickBooks has automatically selected for your company,

18. Click   Preview Your Settings

The Features Selected tab of the Preview Your Company Settings window opens:

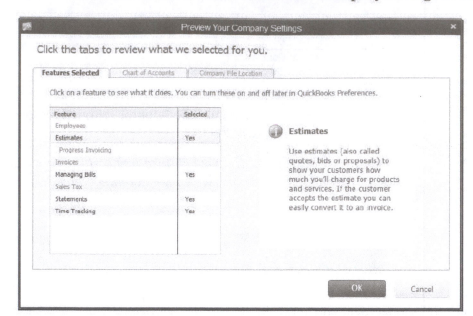

This tab allows you to view the features QuickBooks has automatically selected for your company based on your industry. The word "Yes" will display in the Selected column for any feature QuickBooks selected. You can select a feature to learn more about it.

19. Select   the Managing Bills feature

QuickBooks displays information about managing bills:

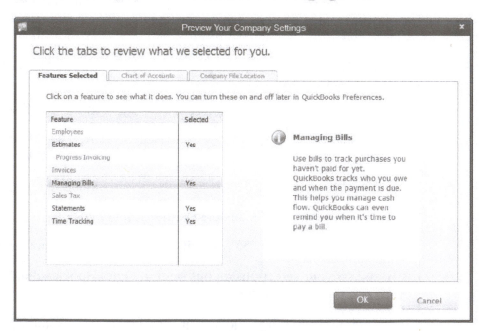

Quick Tip. After you have created your company file, you can turn any feature on or off in the Preferences window.

20. Click   the Chart of Accounts tab

The Chart of Accounts tab displays:

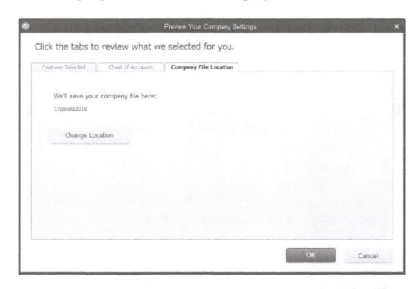

This tab displays the predefined Construction General Contractor accounts that QuickBooks will create for your business. You can select a check box in the Account Name column to include that account or deselect a check box to exclude the account.

21.	Select	the Janitorial Expense account check box	to add the account to the Chart of Accounts (scroll down)
22.	Click	the Company File Location tab	

The Company File Location tab displays:

This tab displays the location on your computer where QuickBooks will save your company file. By default, QuickBooks names the new file using the company name and places it in the directory where you last saved or opened a file.

Note: If the Books2018 folder does not display, click the Change Location button and navigate to the folder.

23. Click OK   to return to the QuickBooks Setup window

24. Click   Create Company

A Working dialog box displays while the new company file is created. After QuickBooks finishes creating the company file, the next screen in the setup process displays:

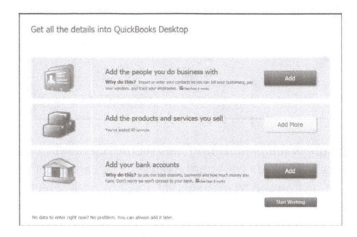

This screen allows you to easily add critical business information to your company file, including customers, vendors, and employees, products and services, and bank accounts. These processes are covered in detail in other lessons within this guide; therefore. you will not add this information for this lesson.

25. Click   Start Working

The New Feature Tour opens in the QuickBooks window:

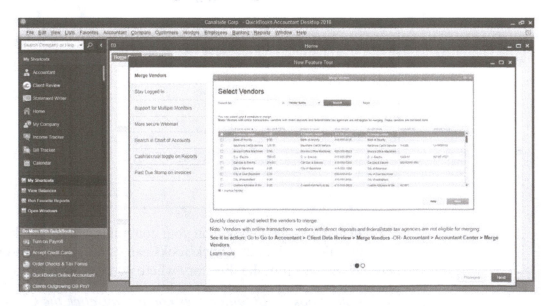

Note: Your QuickBooks window may display the Icon Bar at the top of the window and account balances on the right side of the window.

The New Feature Tour allows you to view the new features in QuickBooks.

26. Click to close the New Feature Tour

The QuickBooks Home page displays.

Quick Tip. *You can open the New Feature Tour at any time by selecting Help : New*
Features > New Feature Tour from the menu bar.

Using the Chart of Accounts

The Chart of Accounts is a list of all of your company's accounts and account
balances. You can use it to track the amount of money your company has, the
money your company owes, and the amount of money coming in and out of your
company. For example, if you want to track all of the money you spend on office
supplies, you would set up an Office Supplies account in the Chart of Accounts.

When you created your QuickBooks company file, QuickBooks automatically set
up a chart of accounts for the company. Your first task is to customize the Chart of
Accounts and enter account beginning balances. First, you need to display the
Chart of Accounts for Canalside Corp.

1. Click in the Company area of the Home
    page

The predefined Chart of Accounts opens:

Note: The size of your Chart of Accounts may be different. You may resize the
window, as necessary.

Notice the buttons at the bottom of the window. You can use these buttons to add,
edit, or perform other activities on the entries in the Chart of Accounts. When you
click a button, a drop-down menu displays. The available options are determined
by the entry that is currently selected in the Chart of Accounts.

Every Chart of Accounts has two basic types of accounts:

• Balance sheet accounts

• Income and expense accounts

Balance Sheet Accounts

Accounts that display on a balance sheet are balance sheet accounts. Balance sheet accounts include assets, liabilities, and equity. QuickBooks provides various types of balance sheet accounts you can create as you customize your company's Chart of Accounts. These include:

• Bank Accounts - used to track checking, savings, and money market accounts.

• Accounts Receivable (A/R) Accounts - used to track transactions related to the customers that owe you money, including invoices, payments, refunds, and statements.

• Other Current Asset Accounts - used to track assets that are likely to be converted to cash or used up in one year, such as petty cash and security deposits.

• Fixed Asset Accounts - used to track depreciable assets your company owns that are not likely to be converted to cash within one year, such as equipment or furniture.

• Other Asset Accounts - used to track any asset that is neither a current asset nor fixed asset, such as long-term notes receivable.

• Accounts Payable (A/P) Accounts - used to track transactions related to money you owe, including bills and any credit you have with vendors.

• Credit Card Accounts - used to track credit card purchases, bills, and payments.

• Other Current Liability Accounts - used to track liabilities that are scheduled to be paid within one year, such as sales tax, payroll taxes, and short-term loans.

• Loan Accounts - used to track the principal your business owes for a loan or line of credit.

• Long-Term Liability Accounts - used to track liabilities to be paid over periods longer than one year, such as loans or mortgages.

• Cost of Goods Sold - used to track the direct costs to produce the items your business sells, such as cost of materials, cost of labor, shipping, freight, and delivery, and subcontractors.

• Equity Accounts - used to track owner's equity, including capital investment, owner's draw, and retained earnings.

Income and Expense Accounts

Income and expense accounts track the sources of your company's income and the purpose of each expense. When you record transactions in one of your balance sheet accounts, you usually assign the amount of the transaction to one or more income or expense accounts. For example, not only do you record that you took money out of your checking account, but you also keep track of what you spent the money on — utilities, office supplies, postage, and so on.

If you scroll down in the Chart of Accounts, you will notice that QuickBooks does not display a balance for income and expense accounts in the Chart of Accounts. To see income and expense account balances, you can select the income or expense account in the Chart of Accounts and click the Reports button at the bottom of the window to display a drop-down menu, then select QuickReport.

Using Account Numbers

By default, account numbers are not displayed in the Chart of Accounts. Although you are not required to use account numbers, your accountant may recommend that you do so. If you would like to display account numbers, you can specify this in the Preferences window.

To use account numbers:

1. Select   Edit : Preferences   from the menu bar

The Preferences window opens with the My Preferences tab of the General category displayed:

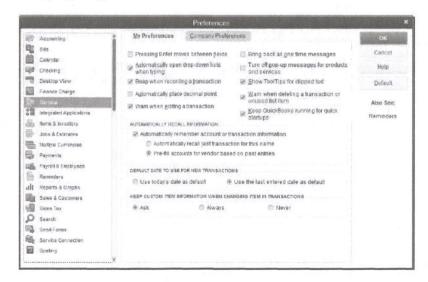

Note: Your Preferences window may open with a different category selected.

2. Select   the Accounting   from the list on the left
                   category

The My Preferences tab of the Accounting category displays.

3. Click   the Company Preferences tab

The Company Preferences tab of the Accounting category displays:

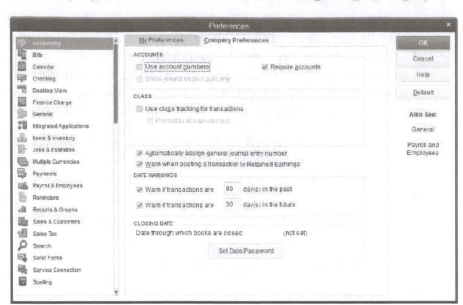

4. Click   the Use account   to select it
                   numbers check box

QuickBooks will now include account numbers in the chart of accounts, in all account fields, and on reports and graphs. A Number field will also display in the New Account and Edit Account windows.

5. Click   OK

The Preferences window closes and the Chart of Accounts displays:

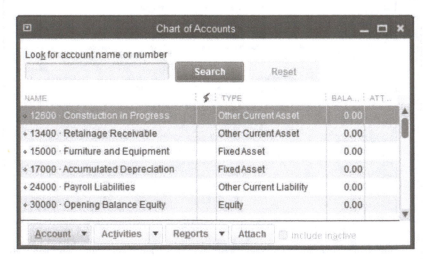

QuickBooks has inserted account numbers before account names in the Chart of Accounts.

Note: Now that you have added account numbers, you may want to resize the Chart of Accounts so that you can view the account names completely.

Quick Tip. After turning the account number preference on, you can run the Account Listing Report to view and print your company's accounts and account numbers.

Searching for an Account

The search feature in the Chart of Accounts allows you to quickly find an account by its name or number.

1. Type   Janitor   in the Look for account name or number field

2. Click

The search results display in the Chart of Accounts:

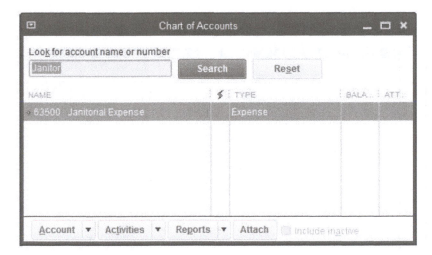

Editing an Account

The Chart of Accounts is your most important list because it shows how much your business has, how much it owes, how much money you have coming in, and how much you are spending. Because you chose a preset Chart of Accounts when you created the new company, you need to make a few changes to the list.

Any of the preset accounts that do not suit your needs can be edited. For example, QuickBooks automatically adds a Repairs and Maintenance expense account, but you may prefer to give it a different name. In this exercise, you will change the name of the Janitorial Expense account to Dumpster Rental, as well as change the description of the account.

Quick Tip. Before modifying the preset chart of accounts, you should have your accountant review the Chart of Accounts that QuickBooks has set up for you. You may need to add accounts and subaccounts, delete accounts, or move accounts. It is important to decide on an account structure prior to entering transactions.

With 63500 - Janitorial Expense already selected in the Name column,

1. Click   at the bottom of the window

A drop-down menu displays:

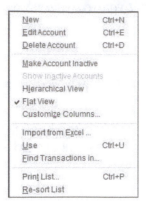

2. Select **Edit Account** from the drop-down menu

The Edit Account window opens:

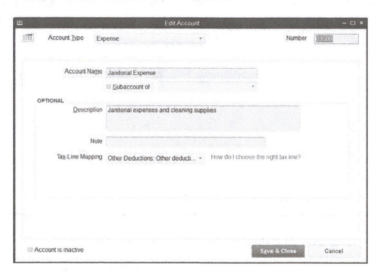

Notice that the account number is automatically selected in the Number field.

3. Type **68700** to replace 63500 in the Number field

4. Press **Tab** to move to the Account Name field

Janitorial Expense becomes highlighted in the Account Name field.

5. Type **Dumpster Rental** to replace Janitorial Expense

6. Press **Tab** twice to move to the Description field

The text becomes highlighted in the Description field.

7. Type **Bulk trash and construction debris removal**

8. Click **Save & Close** to return to the Chart of Accounts

9. Click in the Chart of Accounts

The search results are cleared.

10. Scroll to the bottom of the Chart of Accounts

The Janitorial Expense account is renamed Dumpster Rental and listed in numerical order:

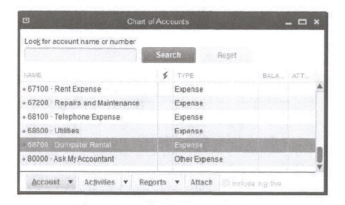

Adding an Account

You will most likely need to add accounts to the Chart of Accounts. For example, your business will need a checking account.

To add a checking account to the Chart of Accounts,

1. Click at the bottom of the window

A drop-down menu displays.

2. Select New from the drop-down menu

The Add New Account: Choose Account Type window opens:

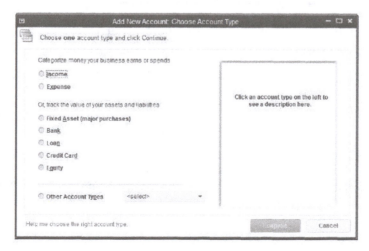

This window allows you to select the type of account you would like to add.

3. Select Bank

Examples of bank accounts display in the right area of the window:

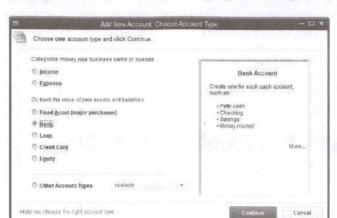

4. Click Continue

The Add New Account window opens:

Bank is automatically selected in the Account Type field and the cursor displays in the Number field.

5. Type **10000** in the Number field

6. Press **Tab** to move to the Account Name field

7. Type **Checking** in the Account Name field

8. Press **Tab** three times to move to the Bank Acct. No. field

9. Type **98765430** in the Bank Acct. No. field

The bank account number is the number that the bank has assigned to the account and is different from the QuickBooks account number.

10. Click Save & Close

A Set Up Bank Feed dialog box displays:

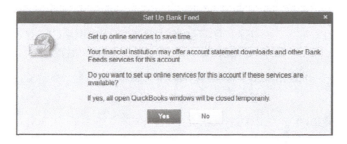

This dialog box informs you that your financial institution may offer account statement downloads and other online banking services for this account. For this lesson, you will not set up online banking services.

11. Click No

The new Checking account is added to the Chart of Accounts:

12. Repeat steps 1 through 11 to add a Savings account with a QuickBooks account number of 11000 and a bank account number of 12223330.

The new Savings account is added to the Chart of Accounts:

Deleting an Account

The preset Chart of Accounts may have accounts that are not appropriate for your type of business. For example, you may not have any rent fees in your type of business and therefore want to delete the Rent Expense account.

1. Select   67100 - Rent   in the Chart of Accounts (scroll
                    Expense   down)

2. Click

A drop-down menu displays.

3. Select   Delete Account   from the drop-down menu

A Delete Account dialog box displays asking if you are sure you want to delete this account:

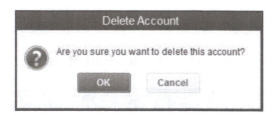

4. Click   OK

QuickBooks deletes the Rent Expense account from the Chart of Accounts.

Note: You cannot delete a "used" account (one that already has been used for expenses); you can only delete "unused" accounts.

Moving an Account

The Chart of Accounts initially lists each account in alphabetical order within each account type (income, expense, etc.). When you add account numbers, the accounts are listed in numerical order. Within an account type, you can change an account's position in the list.

In this exercise, you will position the Office Supplies expense account after the Bank Service Charges expense account.

Note: You should resize the Chart of Accounts for this exercise to make it larger.

To move the Office Supplies expense account,

1. Select   the diamond to the   in the Chart of Accounts
                    left of the 64900 -
                    Office Supplies
                    account

The cursor changes to a four-directional arrow.

2. Click and hold   the left mouse button

3. Drag   the cursor   until the dotted line displays below the 60400 - Bank Service Charges account

The cursor changes to a two-directional arrow as you drag the account, indicating that the account can be moved up or down.

4. Release   the mouse button   to drop the account into the new position

The Office Supplies expense account should now be listed after the Bank Service Charges expense account, similar to the figure below:

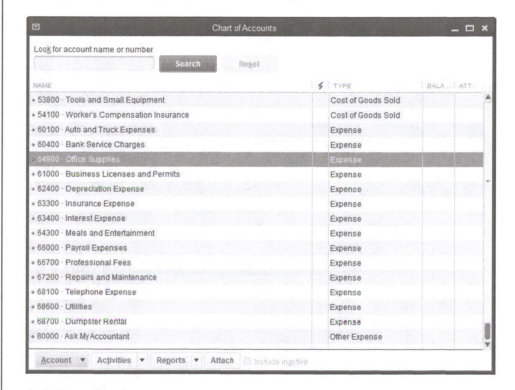

Adding Subaccounts

The Telephone Expense account has only one level with no subaccounts. Subaccounts are indented under their account type. If your business has two phone lines—one for a regular phone line and one for a cellular phone—and you want to track the amount you spend for each, you need to add two subaccounts to the Telephone Expense account.

1. Select   Telephone Expense   in the Chart of Accounts (scroll down, if necessary)

2. Click   Account ▼

3. Select   New   from the drop-down menu

The Add New Account: Choose Account Type window opens:

4. Select   Expense

A description of an expense account and examples of expenses display in the right area of the window.

5. Click   Continue

The Add New Account window opens:

Notice that Expense is already selected in the Account Type field and the cursor displays in the Number field.

6. Type   **68150**   in the Number field

7. Press   Tab   to move to the Account Name field

8.	Type	**Business Phone**	in the Account Name field
9.	Click	the Subaccount of check box	to select it
10.	Click	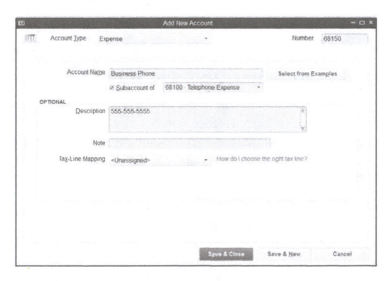	to the right of the Subaccount of field

A drop-down menu displays.

11.	Select	68100 - Telephone Expense	from the drop-down menu
12.	Press	Tab	to move to the Description field
13.	Type	**555-555-5555**	in the Description field

Your window should resemble the figure below:

14.	Click	Save & New	to add another subaccount

A blank Add New Account window opens with Expense displayed in the Account Type field.

15. Repeat steps 6 through 13 to add a Cell Phone with a QuickBooks account number of 68200 and a description of 555-555-3432 as another subaccount of Telephone Expense.

16.	Click	Save & Close	

The new Telephone Expense subaccounts display in the Chart of Accounts:

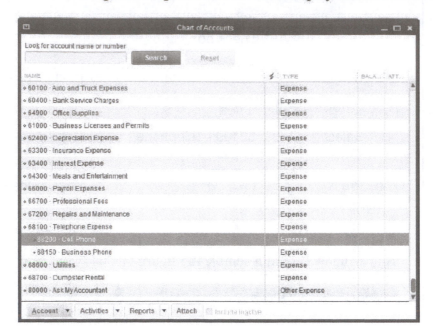

Entering Account Opening Balances

The Balance Sheet accounts in the QuickBooks Chart of Accounts start with an opening balance of zero. Before you begin working in QuickBooks, you should enter an opening balance for each Balance Sheet account as of your start date. The opening balance should reflect the amount of money in, or the value of, an account as of the start date of your records in QuickBooks.

The opening balance is important because QuickBooks cannot give you an accurate balance sheet (what your company owns and what it owes) without it. An accurate balance sheet gives you a true picture of your company's finances. Also, if you start with an accurate balance as of a specific date, you can reconcile your QuickBooks bank accounts with your bank statements, and your QuickBooks checking accounts will show the actual amount of money you have in the bank.

The easiest way to determine an account's opening balance is to work from an accurate balance sheet. If you have a balance sheet as of your start date, you can take the opening balance from there.

Let's assume the Canalside Corp. start date is today's date, and you, the owner, want to enter an opening balance for the checking account.

1. Select   10000 - Checking   in the Chart of Accounts (scroll to the top of the list)

2. Click   Account ▼

A drop-down menu displays.

3. Select   Edit Account   from the drop-down menu

The Edit Account window opens:

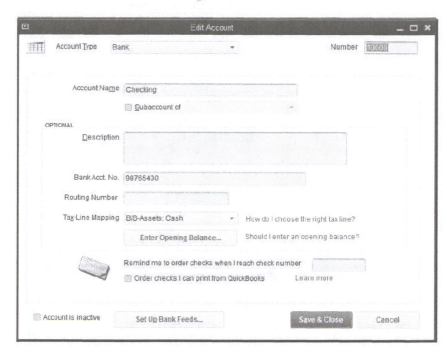

The opening balance for a QuickBooks bank account is the dollar amount you have in the bank on your start date. You can determine this amount by using the ending balance on the last bank statement before your start date, or you can use your bank account balance from a balance sheet prepared by your accountant.

4. Click   **Enter Opening Balance...**

The Enter Opening Balance: Bank Account window opens:

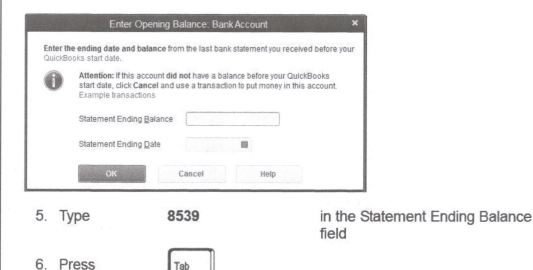

5. Type   **8539**   in the Statement Ending Balance field

6. Press   [Tab]

QuickBooks automatically inserts the appropriate comma, decimal point, and zeros for you when you move to another field.

7. Type **[yesterday's date in** in the Statement Ending Date field
mm/dd/yyyy format]

This date represents the ending date from the last bank statement you received before your QuickBooks start date.

Quick Tip. *You can also click* *and select the date on the calendar that displays.*

8. Click [OK]

You return to the Edit Account window.

9. Click [Save & Close]

Your Chart of Accounts should resemble the figure below:

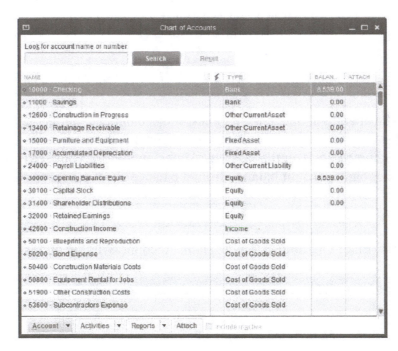

Notice that the Balance Total for the Checking account is now 8,539.00. The balance for the Opening Balance Equity account is also 8,539.00.

When you set up your company in QuickBooks as of a particular start date, you may already have company assets and liabilities as of that date. When you enter opening balances for your assets and liabilities, QuickBooks automatically enters the same amounts in an account called Opening Balance Equity. This account is created to ensure that you will have a correct balance sheet when you first set up your QuickBooks company.

Note: Your accountant may want to review the Opening Balance Equity account and make adjustments to reclassify entries to the proper account type.

Now, you will add an opening balance to the savings account to see how the Opening Balance Equity account is affected.

10. Select   Savings   in the Chart of Accounts

11. Repeat steps 2 through 9 to add an opening balance of $5,000.00 for the savings account as of yesterday's date.

Your Chart of Accounts should resemble the figure below:

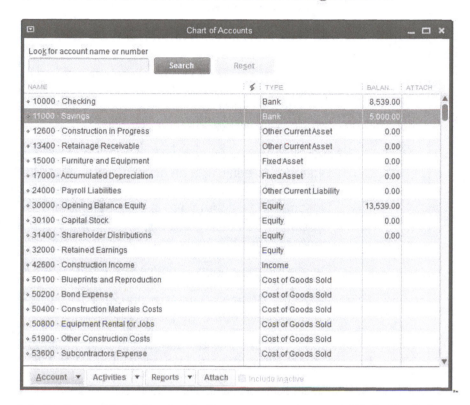

The Balance Total for the Savings account is now 5,000. The balance for the Opening Balance Equity account is now 13,539.00, an increase of 5,000.00.

Note: If you have entered an incorrect opening balance for an account, you can change it by clicking the Change Opening Balance button in the Edit Account window. You will then need to make any changes to the opening balance in the account's register.

12. Click   ☒   to close the Chart of Accounts

13. Select   File : Close Company   to close the company file

Review

In this lesson, you have learned how to:

☑ Create a QuickBooks company

☑ Use the Chart of Accounts

Practice:

1. Open the Canalside Corp. company file.

2. Open the Chart of Accounts and change the name of the Auto and Truck Expenses account to Fuel Expenses.

3. Add a Credit Card account to the Chart of Accounts with the name Business Credit Card, an account number of 11500, and an opening balance of $1,313.27 as of yesterday's date. Make a note in the Description field that there is a credit limit of $10,000.00. *Note: If a Set Up Bank Feed dialog box displays asking if you want to set up online services, click the No button.*

4. Delete the Insurance Expense account.

5. Move the Business Licenses and Permits expense account below the Professional Fees expense account.

6. Add a new income account called Remodeling as a subaccount of Construction Income. Use account number 42650.

7. Close the company file.

Working with Lists

In this lesson, you will learn how to:

- ❑ Create company lists
- ❑ Work with the Customers & Jobs list
- ❑ Work with the Employees list
- ❑ Work with the Vendors list
- ❑ Work with the Items list
- ❑ Work with other lists
- ❑ Manage lists

Concept

QuickBooks uses lists to maintain your company's information. There are lists displayed when you open QuickBooks Centers, such as the list of vendors that displays in the Vendor Center. There are also lists that open in separate windows, such as the Chart of Accounts or the Item List. QuickBooks uses the information contained in lists to fill in forms automatically.

Scenario

As you work with your company, you will need to change your QuickBooks lists from time to time. In this lesson, you will add a new customer, employee, vendor, and item to the lists that QuickBooks maintains. You will add custom fields to the lists, so that you can include information specific to your business. Because lists are in a constant state of fluctuation, you will learn how to sort a list, both alphabetically and in ascending or descending order, and merge two items on a list that were entered in two different ways, but are really the same. Next, you will rename an item in a list, delete an item, make an item inactive, and resize a column in a list. Finally, you will print a list so that you have your own hard copy.

Practice Files: B18_Working_With_Lists.qbw

Creating Company Lists

Lists, the framework of QuickBooks, are used to organize a wide variety of information, including data on customers, vendors, employees, items, and more. Lists help you enter information consistently and correctly, thus saving time.

The major benefit of storing information in a list is that after you enter the information, you never need to retype it. Think about how much information you use more than once in your business:

- Customers who purchase from you on a regular basis

- Vendors from whom you purchase your supplies

- Products or services you sell again and again

You fill out most QuickBooks forms by selecting entries from a list. For example, to pay a bill, you can select a vendor name from your vendor list on the Enter Bills form. QuickBooks will then enter the list information on the form for you. When you are dealing with repetitive information, it makes sense to use QuickBooks's lists. Type the information into a list once, and then use it over and over on checks, on invoice forms, or for any of your daily transactions.

You do not need to enter all the information for your company lists before you can begin working with QuickBooks. You can add information to lists as you go along, or you can set up your lists fully from the beginning.

1. Open   B18_Working   using the method described in
       With_Lists.qbw   Before You Get Started

A QuickBooks Login dialog box displays:

This dialog box informs you that you must login as a QuickBooks Administrator in order to open the company file.

2. Type   **Canalside2**   in the Password field

Note: Passwords are case-sensitive.

3. Click   OK

QuickBooks opens the file.

4. Click   to close the Reminders window

QuickBooks displays the Home page:

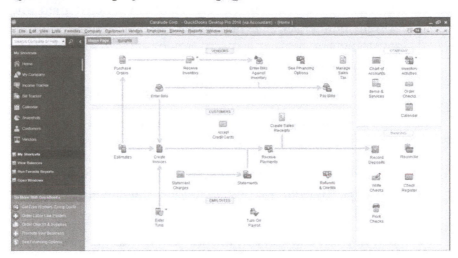

Note: Your QuickBooks window may be different and the Icon Bar may be located at the top of the window.

Working with the Customers & Jobs List

The Customers & Jobs list within the Customer Center stores information about the people and companies to whom you sell your products and services. QuickBooks uses the data in the Customers & Jobs list to automatically fill in estimates, invoices, statement charges, and various other forms as you sell your products and services.

Adding a New Customer

In this exercise, you will add a new customer to the Customers & Jobs list.

1. Click  on the Icon Bar

The Customer Center opens:

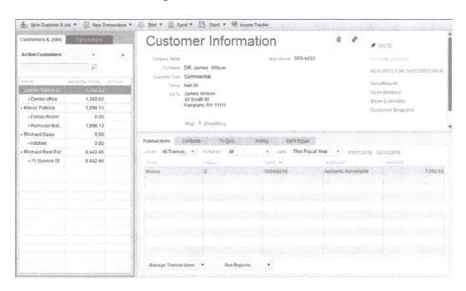

A customer refers to anyone who pays you for goods or services. The Customer Center displays information about all of your customers and their transactions in a single area. It contains names, addresses, and other information about your customers, as well as a description of the jobs or projects that you may want to track for each customer.

The Customer Center includes the following main components:

- A toolbar allowing you to perform tasks, such as adding new customers and jobs or creating estimates and invoices.

- A Customers & Jobs tab allowing you to view a list of your customers and jobs. You can use this tab to view and edit information for a single customer or job.

- A Transactions tab allowing you to view and manage transactions relevant to a customer, such as estimates, invoices, and sales receipts. You can use this tab to view specific transaction types for a customer. This tab includes drop-down menus allowing you to filter the information that displays by transaction type.

- A Customer Information or Job Information area (depending on the selection in the Customers & Jobs tab) displaying contact and billing information for the customer or job. This area includes an Attach button allowing you to attach documents to your customers and jobs and an Edit button allowing you to edit customer or job information.

- A Reports area allowing you to access and work with common customer and job reports.

- A Transactions tab allowing you to manage customer and job transactions, such as estimates and invoices, as well as view transaction reports. This tab includes drop-down menus allowing you to filter the transaction information that displays.

- A Contacts tab allowing you to add, edit, and delete customer and job contacts.

- A To Do's tab allowing you to add, edit, and delete customer and job to do items, as well as launch a to do report. This tab includes drop-down menus allowing you to filter the information that displays.

- A Notes tab allowing you to add, edit, and delete customer and job notes. This tab includes a Dates drop-down menu allowing you to filter the notes that display by date.

- A Sent Email tab allowing you to view and manage all emails sent to a customer or in regards to a customer.

The Customers & Jobs tab on the left side of the window displays a list of all customers. Each customer in the list can have multiple jobs (projects or accounts). Notice that the Balance Total column in the Customers & Jobs list contains open balances for many of the customers already.

To add a new customer,

2. Click  at the top of the window

A drop-down menu displays:

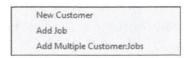

3. Select   New Customer   from the drop-down menu

The New Customer window opens with the Address Info tab displayed:

The New Customer window allows you to enter various types of information about a new customer, including addresses, contacts, credit limits, and payment terms. Information entered here will be used by QuickBooks to complete invoices and receipts automatically.

4. Type   **Smith Manufacturing**   in the Customer Name field

Quick Tip. When QuickBooks displays Smith Manufacturing in the Customers & Jobs list, it will be listed alphabetically by default. If you are entering individual names, you may want to enter the last name, then the first name, so that the Customers & Jobs list displays the name with the last name first. This is useful for alphabetical sorting of lists and reports.

5. Press

6. Type   **546.00**   in the Opening Balance field

Quick Tip. You may want to consider entering any outstanding invoices individually, rather than entering an amount in the Opening Balance field.

Leave the date that displays in the as of field.

7. Press 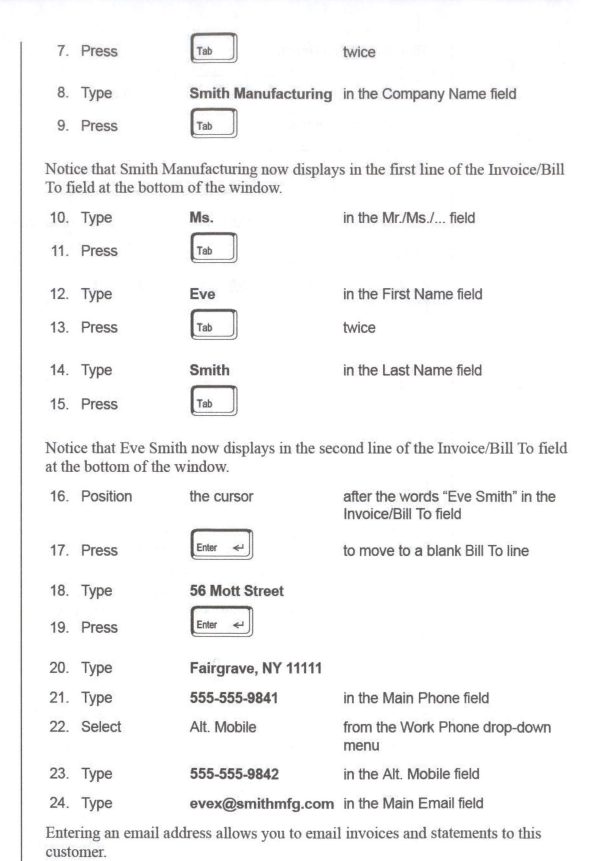 Tab   twice

8. Type   **Smith Manufacturing**   in the Company Name field

9. Press   Tab

Notice that Smith Manufacturing now displays in the first line of the Invoice/Bill To field at the bottom of the window.

10. Type   **Ms.**   in the Mr./Ms./... field

11. Press   Tab

12. Type   **Eve**   in the First Name field

13. Press   Tab   twice

14. Type   **Smith**   in the Last Name field

15. Press   Tab

Notice that Eve Smith now displays in the second line of the Invoice/Bill To field at the bottom of the window.

16. Position   the cursor   after the words "Eve Smith" in the Invoice/Bill To field

17. Press   Enter ⏎   to move to a blank Bill To line

18. Type   **56 Mott Street**

19. Press   Enter ⏎

20. Type   **Fairgrave, NY 11111**

21. Type   **555-555-9841**   in the Main Phone field

22. Select   Alt. Mobile   from the Work Phone drop-down menu

23. Type   **555-555-9842**   in the Alt. Mobile field

24. Type   **evex@smithmfg.com**   in the Main Email field

Entering an email address allows you to email invoices and statements to this customer.

 Quick Tip. *You can select different field titles from the drop-down lists next to each field. For example, you may prefer to change the Fax field to URL 1 or the Other 1 field to Facebook.*

To copy the billing information to the Ship To area,

25. Click Copy >>

The Add Shipping Address Information window opens:

This window allows you to edit and confirm the billing information that you are copying to the Ship To area.

26. Click OK

QuickBooks fills in the Ship To field with the information from the Bill To field.

 Quick Tip. *You can enter multiple shipping addresses for a customer by clicking the Add button next to the Ship To area.*

Your New Customer window should resemble the figure below:

You have now completed entering address information for this customer. QuickBooks allows you to enter additional customer and job information on the Payment Settings, Sales Tax Settings, Additional Info, and Job Info tabs.

27. Click   Payment Settings

The New Customer window displays the Payment Settings tab:

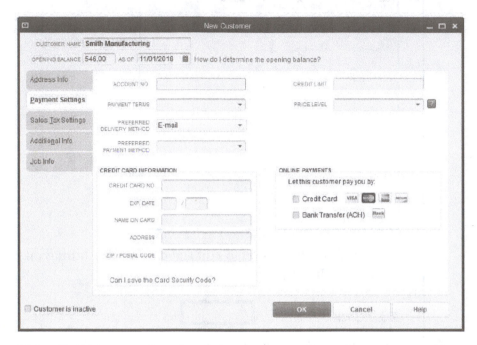

This tab allows you to enter customer account numbers, payment terms, preferred delivery, and preferred payment methods. For customer's who pay by credit card, you can enter credit card numbers and expiration dates. In addition, you can enter customer credit limits. QuickBooks will remember each customer's credit limit and warn you when a customer is about to exceed it.

28. Type   **12345**   in the Account No. field

29. Select   Net 30   from the Payment Terms drop-down menu

This selection specifies that the customer is required to pay the net amount (the total outstanding on the invoice) within 30 days of receiving this bill.

You will leave the default selection of E-mail in the Preferred Delivery Method field.

30. Select   Check   from the Preferred Payment Method drop-down menu

31. Type   **2500**   in the Credit Limit field

32. Click   the Sales Tax Settings tab

The New Customer window displays the Sales Tax Settings tab:

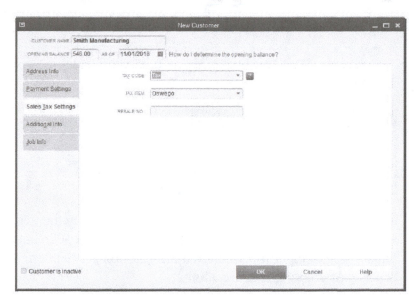

This tab allows you to specify a customer's sales tax information, including whether the customer has taxable or non-taxable sales. If the sales are taxable, you can then select the customer's default sales tax item. QuickBook will calculate the sales tax based on information provided for the sales tax item.

33. Click the Additional Info tab

The New Customer window displays the Additional Info tab:

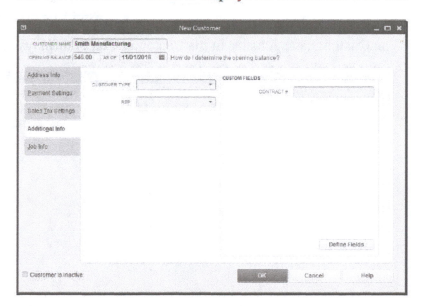

The Customer Type field enables you to track customers by different rules that you define. For example, you can categorize customers by how they learned about your business, such as by an advertisement, commercial, or referral.

In this exercise, you will use the Type field to categorize customers by the type of service Canalside Corp. provides them.

34. Type **Industrial** in the Customer Type field

35. Press Tab

A Customer Type Not Found dialog box displays telling you that Industrial is not in the Customer Type list:

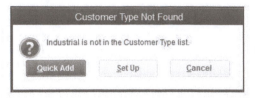

Clicking the Quick Add button allows you to set up the item with the minimum amount of data that QuickBooks needs to continue. Clicking the Set Up button allows you to enter more detailed information for the item, but interrupts the process of creating a new customer.

In this exercise, you will use the Quick Add feature.

36. Click Quick Add   to add Industrial to the Customer Type list

Quick Tip. *The Additional Info tab also allows you to add custom fields for a customer/job. You'll learn more about custom fields later in this lesson.*

37. Click OK   to add the customer and close the New Customer window

The Customers & Jobs list in the Customer Center displays Smith Manufacturing:

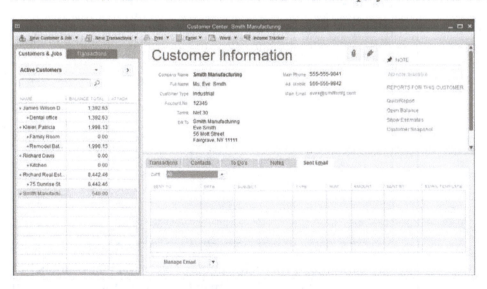

Customer data for Smith Manufacturing displays in the Customer Information area.

38. Close the Customer Center to return to the Home page

Quick Tip. *QuickBooks has several useful customer preset reports, including the Sales by Customer Summary and Detail reports, located within the Sales submenu of the Reports menu. These reports break down total sales by customer. The A/R Aging Summery and Detail reports, Customer Balance Summary and Detail reports, and Open Invoices reports located below the Customers & Receivables submenu of the Reports menu are also useful customer reports.*

Working with the Employees List

The Employees list within the Employee Center records information about your employees, including name, address, and Social Security Number. QuickBooks uses the information entered into the Employees list to track sales and fill in information on checks and other forms.

Adding a New Employee

To add a new employee to the Employees list,

1. Select   Employees :   from the menu bar
                      Employee Center

The Employee Center opens:

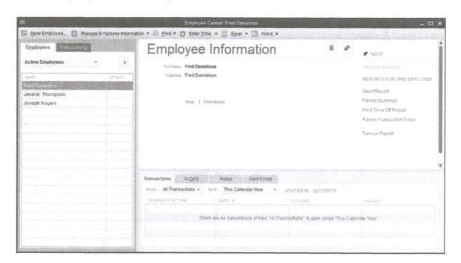

The Employee Center includes the following main components:

* A toolbar allowing you to perform such tasks as adding new employees or employee default settings.

* An Employees tab allowing you to view all employees, only active employees, or released employees (no longer active). You can use this tab to view and edit information for a single employee.

* A Transactions tab allowing you to view and manage transactions relevant to an employee, such as an employee's paychecks or year-to-date adjustments. You can use this tab to view specific transaction types for an employee. This tab includes a drop-down menu allowing you to filter the information that displays by date.

- An Employee Information area displaying contact information for the employee. This area includes an Attach button allowing you to attach documents to your employees and an Edit button allowing you to edit employee information.

- A Reports area allowing you to access and work with common employee reports.

- A Transactions tab allowing you to manage employee transactions. This tab includes drop-down menus allowing you to filter the transaction information that displays.

- A To Do's tab allowing you to add, edit, and delete employee to do items, as well as launch a to do report. This tab includes drop-down menus allowing you to filter the information that displays.

- A Notes tab allowing you to add, edit, and delete employee notes. This tab includes a Dates drop-down menu used to filter the notes that display by date.

- A Sent Email tab allowing you to view and manage all emails sent to an employee or in regards to an employee.

Note: If you subscribe to one of the QuickBooks payroll services or set up your company file to use manual payroll tax calculations, the Employee Center will also include payroll options. These payroll options allow you to easily manage your payroll and tax information.

The Employees tab on the left side of the window displays a list of employees. From the Employee Center, you can add a new employee to the list, edit an existing employee on the list, or delete an employee from the list if you have not used the employee name in any transactions.

2. Click 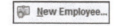 at the top of the window

The Personal tab of the New Employee window displays:

The New Employee window allows you to enter employee information.

3.	Type	**Mr.**	in the Mr./Ms./.. field for the Legal Name
4.	Type	**Cadan**	in the First field
5.	Type	**F**	in the M.I. field
6.	Type	**James**	in the Last field
7.	Press	Tab	twice to move to Social Security No.

Notice that Cadan James automatically displays in the Print on Checks as field.

8.	Type	**123-45-6789**	in the Social Security No. field
9.	Select	Male	from the Gender drop-down menu
10.	Type	**10/13/1975**	in the Date of Birth field
11.	Select	Single	from the Marital Status drop-down menu
12.	Select	Yes	from the US Citizen drop-down menu
13.	Select	No	from the Disabled drop-down menu in the Disability section
14.	Select	Yes	from the On File drop-down menu in the I-9 Form section
15.	Select	No	from the U.S. Veteran drop-down menu in the Military section
16.	Click	Address & Contact	

The Address & Contact tab displays:

You can enter an employee's address and contact information on this tab, including emergency contact information.

17. Enter the following information in the fields on this screen:

Address	**455 Park Avenue**
City	**Fairgrave**
State	**NY**
Zip	**11111**
Work Phone	**555-555-1819**
Contact Name (Primary Contact)	**Mark James**
Contact Phone	**555-555-7777**
Relation	**Father**
Contact Name (Secondary Contact)	**Carolyn James**
Contact Phone	**555-555-9999**
Relation	**Mother**

18. Click

The Additional Info tab displays:

You can enter the employee's account number, as well as any custom fields for the employee on this tab. You'll learn more about custom fields later in this lesson.

19. Click   OK

The New Employee: Payroll Info dialog box displays:

This dialog box asks if you want to set up this employee's payroll information now. Because you have not yet started to track payroll in QuickBooks,

20. Click   Leave As Is

QuickBooks displays the new employee on the Employees tab:

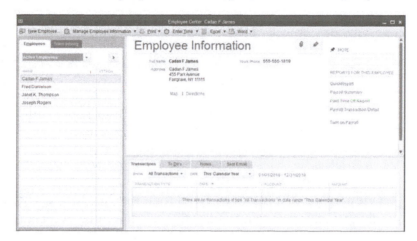

21. Close the Employee Center

Working with the Vendors List

The Vendors list within the Vendor Center is used to record information about the companies or people from whom you buy goods or services. QuickBooks uses the data in the Vendors list to automatically fill in purchase orders, receipts, bills, checks, and various other forms as you receive and pay for goods and services.

Adding a New Vendor

In this exercise, you will add a new vendor to the Vendors list.

1. Click   Vendors   on the Icon Bar

The Vendor Center opens:

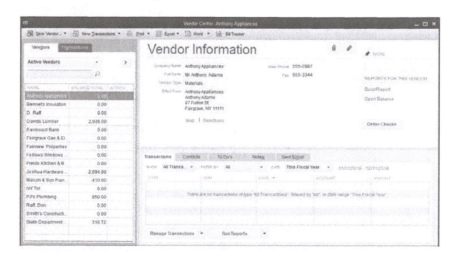

A vendor refers to any person or company you purchase products or services from. The Vendor Center displays information about all of your vendors and their transactions in a single area.

Note: If you have subcontractors or others who receive 1099s, you should add them as vendors. To properly set up these vendors, you will need their addresses and Tax ID numbers.

The Vendor Center contains the following main components:

- A toolbar allowing you to perform such tasks as adding new vendors, creating purchase orders, or paying bills.

- A Vendors tab allowing you to view a list of your vendors. You can use this tab to view and edit information for a single vendor.

- A Transactions tab allowing you to view and manage transactions relevant to a vendor, such as purchase orders, item receipts, and bills. You can use this tab to view specific transaction types for a vendor. This tab includes drop-down menus allowing you to filter the information that displays by transaction type.

- A Vendor Information area displaying contact and billing information for the vendor. This area includes an Attach button allowing you to attach documents to your vendors and an Edit button allowing you to edit vendor information.

- A Reports area that allows you to access and work with common vendor reports.

- A Transactions tab allowing you to manage vendor transactions, as well as view vendor transaction reports. This tab includes drop-down menus allowing you to filter the transaction information that displays.

- A Contacts tab allowing you to add, edit, and delete vendor contacts.

- A To Do's tab allowing you to add, edit, and delete vendor to do items, as well as launch a to do report. This tab includes drop-down menus allowing you to filter the information that displays.

- A Notes tab allowing you to add, edit, and delete vendor notes. This tab includes a Dates drop-down menu allowing you to filter the notes that display by date.

- A Sent Email tab allowing you to view and manage all emails sent to a vendor or in regards to a vendor.

The Vendors tab on the left side of the window displays a list of all vendors. From the Vendor Center, you can add a new vendor, edit an existing vendor record, use a vendor on a form, or run a report on a vendor.

2. Click 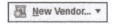 at the top of the window

A drop-down menu displays:

New Vendor
Add Multiple Vendors

3. Select   New Vendor   from the drop-down menu

The Address Info tab of the New Vendor window displays:

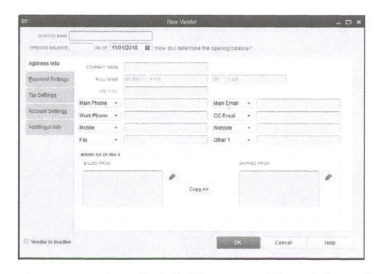

The New Vendor window allows you to enter information for a vendor, such as opening balance, address and contact information, payment, tax, and account settings, and any other additional information. Just like when you added a new customer, you begin by entering basic information on the Address Info tab.

To add Fields Electric as a new vendor,

4. Type   **Fields Electric**   in the Vendor Name field

This is the name under which the vendor information is alphabetically displayed in the Vendors list. If the vendor is an individual, you may want to enter the last name first, then the first name.

5. Type   **Fields Electric**   in the Company Name field

6. Type   **Mr.**   in the Mr./Ms./... field

Notice that Fields Electric now displays in the Billed From field.

7. Type   **Kevin**   in the First field

8. Type   **Fields**   in the Last field

9. Position   the cursor   after the words "Kevin Fields" in the Billed From field

10. Press   to move to a blank Bill To line

11. Type   **111 Oak Ridge Lane**

12. Press

13. Type **Fairgrave, NY 11111**

14. Click

The Tax Settings tab displays:

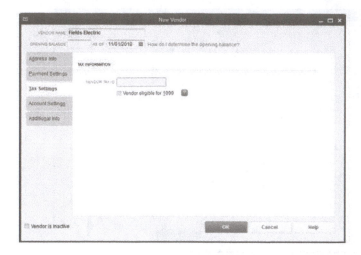

If you send 1099-MISC forms to this vendor, you will need to enter the vendor's Tax ID and select the Vendor eligible for 1099 check box. If the vendor is a sole proprietor, you should enter the vendor's social security number in the Tax ID field. If the vendor is not a sole proprietor, you should enter the vendor's nine-digit tax identification number in the Tax ID field.

15. Type **987-65-4321 (the vendor's social security number)** in the Vendor Tax ID field

16. Select the Vendor eligible for 1099 check box

This vendor is now set up as being eligible to receive a 1099.

Quick Tip. *You may want to review IRS rules regarding 1099s.*

The New Vendor window also includes a Payment Settings tab allowing you to specify vendor payment information, such as the vendor's account number, payment terms, and credit limit your company has with this vendor. QuickBooks will warn you when you are about to exceed the limit. The Account Settings tab enables QuickBooks to pre-fill expense accounts for payments to vendors, making it quicker and easier to accurately track expenses. For each vendor, you can choose up to three expense accounts that you typically use when you pay that vendor. The Additional Info tab allows you to specify the type of vendor this is, for example, if the vendor supplies contractors, equipment, or materials. From this tab, you can also add custom fields for vendors.

Note: For more information, refer to the QuickBooks Help by pressing the F1 key or selecting Help : QuickBooks Desktop Help from the menu bar while the New Vendor window is displayed.

17. Click OK

QuickBooks displays the new vendor in the Vendors list of the Vendor Center:

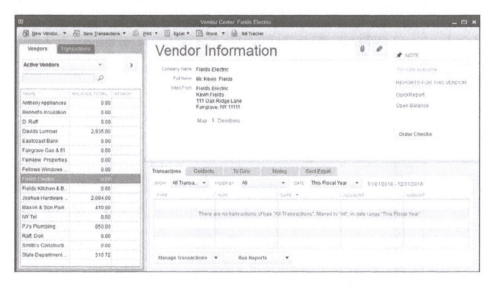

Notice that the new vendor's data displays in the Vendor Information area.

18. Close the Vendor Center

 Quick Tip. QuickBooks has several preset reports related to vendors. Some useful reports are the Purchases by Vendor Summary and Detail reports, located within the Purchases submenu of the Reports menu. These reports break down your purchases by vendor. There are additional preset reports related to vendors located within the Vendors & Payables submenu of the Reports menu, including the Vendor Balance Summary and Vendor Balance Detail reports.

Adding Custom Fields for Customers, Vendors, and Employees

QuickBooks allows you to add custom fields to the Customers & Jobs, Vendor, and Employees lists. Custom fields provide a way for you to track information specific to your business. When you add the custom fields on sales forms or purchase orders, the fields will be prefilled with the information you entered for that customer, employee, vendor, or item. You can use custom fields on invoices, credit memos, cash sales receipts, estimates (QuickBooks Pro), and purchase orders.

 Quick Tip. You don't always have to add custom fields to forms. You can also use custom fields as a way to record information just for your use, such as a credit rating for each customer. QuickBooks remembers the information you entered in the custom fields when you import and export data, and when you memorize transactions.

In this exercise, you will add a Job Title field for customers, a Certifications field for employees, and a Web Address field for vendors.

To add custom fields for customers, vendors, and employees,

1. Click  on the Icon Bar

The Customer Center opens:

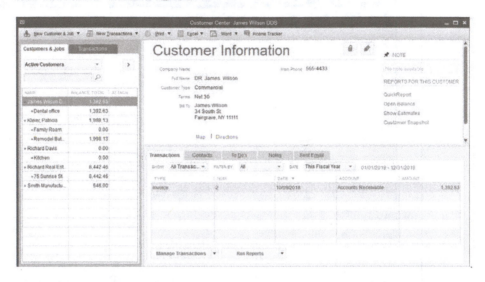

You can only add custom fields for customers, vendors, and employees through the New or Edit windows, for example, the New Customer or Edit Customer windows.

2. Select   Richard Davis   on the Customers & Jobs tab

3. Click in the Customer Information area

The Edit Customer window opens:

4. Click Additional Info

The Additional Info tab displays:

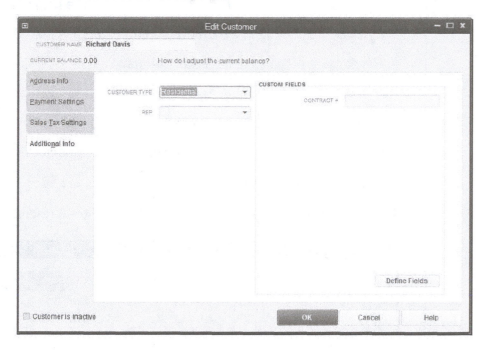

5. Click Define Fields

The Set up Custom Fields for Names window opens:

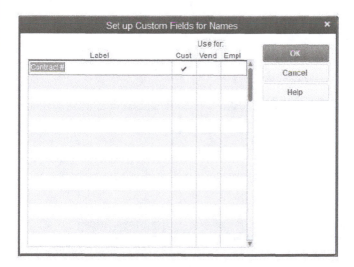

You can add multiple custom fields to the Customer, Vendor, and Employee lists. Notice that Canalside Corp. has already set up a custom field called Contract # for customers.

6. Click   in the first blank row   in the Label column

7. Type   **Job Title**   in the first blank Label row

8. Click   in the Cust column   across from Job Title

A check mark displays in the Cust column.

9. Click   in the next blank Label row

10. Type   **Certifications**   in the next blank Label row

11. Click   in the Empl column   across from Certifications

A check mark displays in the Empl column.

12. Click   in the next blank Label row

13. Type   **Web Address**   in the next blank Label row

14. Click   in the Vend column   across from Web Address

A check mark displays in the Vend column.

The Set up Custom Fields for Names window should resemble the figure below:

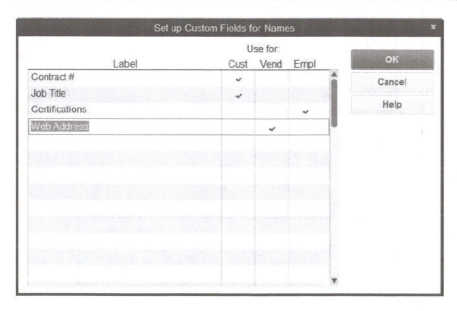

15. Click   [OK]

The following Information dialog box displays informing you that you have activated custom fields:

16. Click   the Do not display this message
                          in the future check box

17. Click   [OK]

QuickBooks adds the new custom field you set up for customers - the Job Title field - after the Contract # field in the Custom Fields area:

You can enter information in custom fields on the Additional Info tabs of the New Customer and Edit Customer windows, the New Vendor and Edit Vendor windows, and the New Employee and Edit Employee windows.

18. Click [OK] to close the Edit Customer window

The Customer Center displays.

19. Close the Customer Center

Working with the Item List

The Item List is used to record information about the products and services you buy and sell and for items that perform calculations, such as discounts and sales tax.

Items allow you to quickly enter data on forms, such as invoices and purchase orders. In addition to providing a quick method for entering data, items perform important accounting tasks in the background.

Quick Tip. Prior to setting up items, you should determine how much detail you want to include on your forms and set up your items with the same level of detail.

1. Click in the Company area of the Home page

The Item List opens:

Note: The size of your Item List may be different. You may resize and move the window as necessary.

2. Click   [Item ▼]   at the bottom of the window

A drop-down menu displays.

3. Select   New   from the drop-down menu

The New Item window opens:

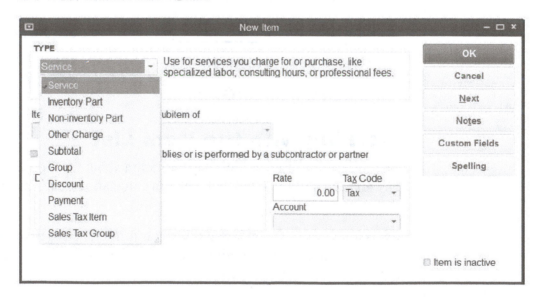

The New Item window allows you to select the type of item you want to enter. QuickBooks provides various item types to assist in filling out sales and purchase forms quickly.

Some item types, such as the service item or the non-inventory part item, record the services and products your business sells. Other item types, such as the sales tax item or discount item, are used to perform calculations in a sale.

The following table displays the item types available in QuickBooks:

Service	Used for services you charge for or purchase, such as professional fees or hours spent consulting.
Inventory Part	Used for items you purchase, track as inventory, and then resell.
Inventory Assembly	Used for assembled goods you build or purchase, track as inventory, and then resell. *Note: This option is only available in the Premier and Enterprise editions of QuickBooks.*
Non-inventory Part	Used for items you purchase, but don't track, such as office supplies, or materials you buy for a job that you charge to your customer.
Other Charge	Used for miscellaneous labor, material, or part charges such as delivery charges, setup fees, and service charges.
Subtotal	Used to total items on a form, which can be useful for applying discounts or surcharges to items.
Group	Used to link individual items that often display together on forms, so that they can all be added at once.
Discount	Used to subtract a percentage or fixed amount from a total or subtotal.
Payment	Used to record a partial payment already received at the time of the sale, which reduces the amount owed on an invoice.
Sales Tax Item	Used to calculate a single sales tax item at a rate that you pay to a single tax agency.
Sales Tax Group	Used to calculate and individually track two or more sales tax items that apply to the same sale, so the customer only sees the total sales tax.

Note: You will add a new item to the Item List in Lesson 4.

4. Click to close the New Item window

5. Click ☒ to close the Item List

 Quick Tip. *You can also close the Item List by pressing the Esc key.*

Working with Other Lists

There are many other lists in QuickBooks for you to use. The Lists menu on the menu bar allows you to view some of these other lists.

1. Select   Lists   from the menu bar

The Lists drop-down menu displays:

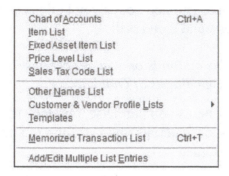

In addition to the Chart of Accounts and Item List, this menu includes a Fixed Asset Item List, a Price Level List, a Sales Tax Code List, an Other Names List, Customer & Vendor Profile Lists that include lists for items such as customer and vendor types, job types, terms, and vehicles, and a Memorized Transaction List.

Note: If you are using QuickBooks Premier, your menu will also include a Billing Rate Level List.

Other Names List

The Other Names list is used to store information about individuals or companies you do business with, other than customers, employees, and vendors. For example, this list could include a business partner or another company you partner with.

You can use a name from the Other Names list when you write checks or enter credit card charges; however, you cannot use a name from this list on other forms, such as the Create Invoices or Enter Bills forms. If you need to create an invoice for a name in the Other Names list, you would need to move the name to the Customers & Jobs list. If you need to create a bill for a name in the Other Names list, you would need to move the name to the Vendors list. The Other Names list is the only list where you can move a name to another list.

Note: If you try to use the same name in different lists, a Warning dialog box displays informing you that the name is already in use and that you cannot use a name in more than one list. QuickBooks suggests you append a letter or number to the name to differentiate it from the existing name.

Class List

QuickBooks allows you to identify different segments of your business, such as departments or locations, and set up a class for each segment. Then, as you create transactions, such as estimates, invoices, and bills, you can assign a class to each transaction. Because classes apply to transactions, they are not tied to any specific customer. This allows you to track account balances and create reports on income and expense by class, regardless of which customers are involved.

For example, as the owner of a construction company, you may have two different sites you are working at — a hotel building site and a parking garage site. You can set up a class for each site and every time you enter an invoice or bill, you assign the appropriate class to that bill. This allows you to track your account balances and produce income and expense reports by hotel site and parking garage site.

Quick Tip. In order to assign classes to transactions, you need to turn the class tracking feature on in QuickBooks by selecting Edit : Preferences from the menu bar. When the Preferences window opens, select Accounting in the left pane, click the Company Preferences tab, and select the Use class tracking check box.

Managing Lists

Lists are easy to manage in QuickBooks. You can sort lists, merge list items, rename list items, make list items inactive, resize list columns, and print lists.

Sorting Lists

You can sort many QuickBooks lists manually or alphabetically. To sort a list manually, you simply drag list items to new locations. Some of the lists that can be sorted this way include the Chart of Accounts, Item List, Fixed Asset Item List, Customer Type List, Vendor Type List, Job Type List, Memorized Transaction List, and the Customers & Jobs List.

If you have changed the order of a list by dragging items and then decide you would rather have an alphabetically sorted list, use the Re-sort List command. In the Chart of Accounts, the Re-sort List command sorts alphabetically within account type; in the Item List, the Re-sort List command sorts alphabetically within item type.

In this exercise, you will sort a list manually, then re-sort it back to alphabetical order.

1. Select　　　　　　Lists :　　　　　　　　　from the menu bar
    　　　　　　　　　Chart of Accounts

The Chart of Accounts opens:

Quick Tip. Resize the Chart of Accounts window to make it larger, so that it is easier to work with.

2. Click   the diamond   to the left of the Commissions Earned income account (scroll down the list)

The cursor changes to a four-directional arrow.

3. Hold   the left mouse button

4. Drag   the cursor   down until a dotted line displays below the Sales income account

The cursor changes to a two-directional arrow as you drag, indicating the item can be moved up and down the list.

5. Release   the mouse button   to drop the account into the new position

The Commissions Earned account now displays directly below the Sales account:

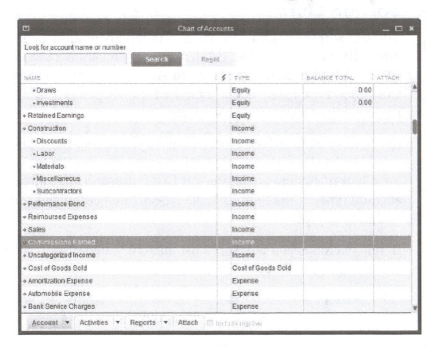

To re-sort the list alphabetically,

6. Click   at the bottom of the window

A drop-down menu displays.

7. Select   Re-sort List   from the drop-down menu

A Re-sort List? dialog box displays:

8. Click OK

The Chart of Accounts is re-sorted alphabetically within each account type:

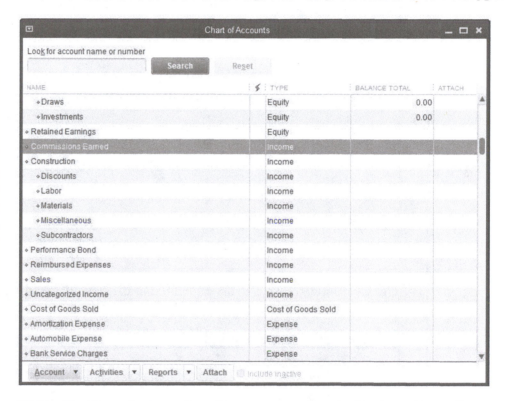

Notice the Commissions Earned account once again displays above the Construction account.

You can also sort the Customers & Jobs list within the Customer Center using the same method.

Note: You cannot sort the Vendors list or the Employees list using this method.

9. Close the Chart of Accounts

Sorting Lists in Ascending and Descending Order

Depending on your business, you may want to sort items in a list a specific way. For example, you may want to sort a list to show customers who owe you money (customers with the highest balances) at the top of the list.

To sort the Customers & Jobs list by customer balance,

1. Click  on the Icon Bar

The Customer Center opens:

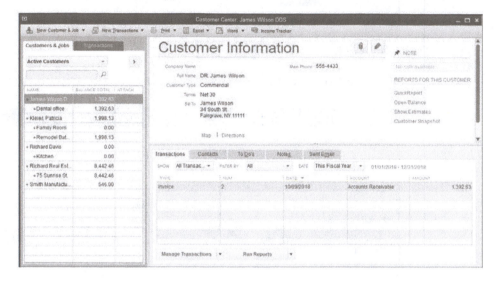

2. Click to the right of the Active Customers drop-down menu on the Customers & Jobs tab

The Customers & Jobs list is expanded to display details about each customer and job:

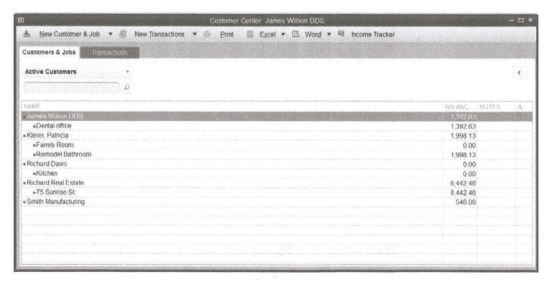

3. Click the Balance Total column heading

The Customers & Jobs list is sorted in ascending order by customer balance:

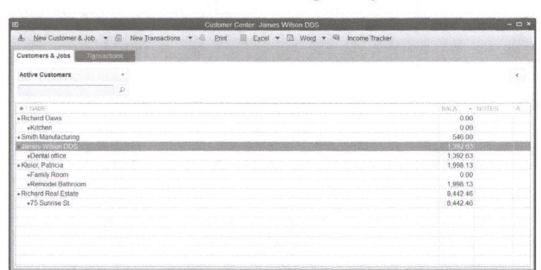

Notice there is now an arrow pointing up in the Balance Total column heading. This indicates the list is sorted in ascending order.

4. **Click** the Balance Total column heading again

The Customers & Jobs list is sorted in descending order by customer balance:

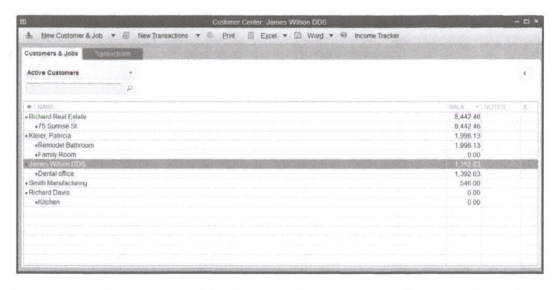

The arrow in the Balance Total column heading now points down to indicate the list is sorted in descending order. You can see the customers with the highest balances are displayed at the top of the list.

To return the list to its original order,

5. **Click** ◈ below the search field to the left of the Name column

The Customers & Jobs list is returned to its original order, alphabetically by customer name.

6. Click 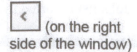 (on the right side of the window) to collapse the Customers & Jobs list

Note: If you don't click the collapse arrow, the next time you open the Customer Center, the Customers & Jobs list will display in expanded view.

7. Close the Customer Center

Merging List Items

In most lists, you can combine two list items into one. For example, you may find that you have been using two customers (because of different spellings) when you really need only one on your Customers & Jobs list. You can merge list items in the following QuickBooks lists: Chart of Accounts, Item, Customers & Jobs, Vendors, Employees, and Other Names.

Caution. *After list items have been merged, you cannot separate them.*

In the Vendors list, Don Raff was entered twice: once as D. Raff and once as Raff, Don. To merge them, you can edit the incorrect name to match the spelling of the correct name.

1. Click on the Icon Bar

The Vendor Center opens:

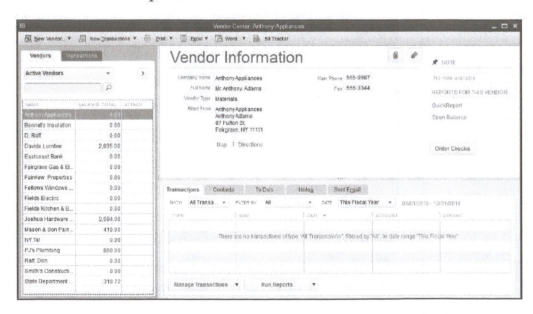

2. Select D. Raff from the list on the Vendors tab

D. Raff's vendor data displays in the Vendor Information area.

3. Click in the Vendor Information area

The Edit Vendor window opens:

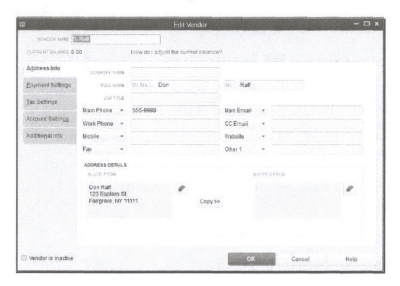

4. Type **Raff, Don** in the Vendor Name field to change it to the name you want to merge it with

5. Click OK

A Merge dialog box displays informing you that the name is already being used and asks if you would like to merge the names:

6. Click Yes

The Vendor List displays:

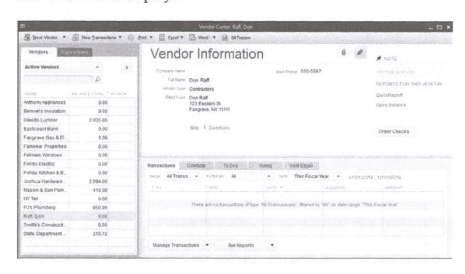

QuickBooks merges the two items and only Raff, Don is displayed in the Vendors list.

7. Close the Vendor Center

Renaming List Items

You can rename any list item. When you rename an item, QuickBooks modifies all existing transactions containing that item.

Caution. *If you do not want to change existing transactions, add a new name or item instead.*

In this exercise, you will rename an item in the Chart of Accounts.

1. Select   Lists : Chart of Accounts   from the menu bar

The Chart of Accounts opens:

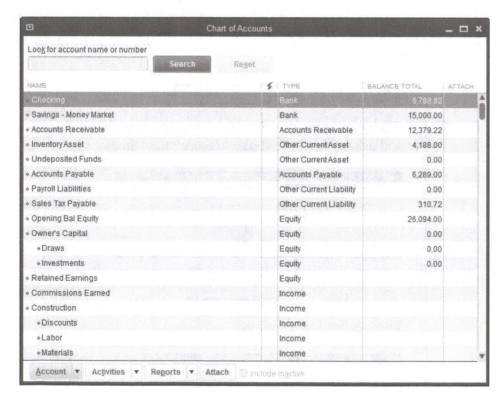

Note: The size of your Chart of Accounts may be different.

2. Select   Checking   in the Chart of Accounts, if necessary

3. Click   Account ▼   at the bottom of the window

A drop-down menu displays.

4. Select   Edit Account   from the drop-down menu

The Edit Account window opens:

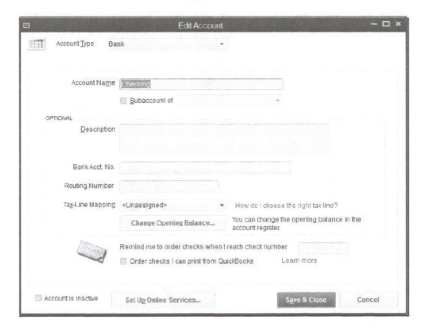

The word Checking is already selected in the Account Name field.

5. Type   **Business Checking**   to replace Checking in the Account
                  Account   Name field

6. Click   Save & Close

QuickBooks changes the name in the Chart of Accounts:

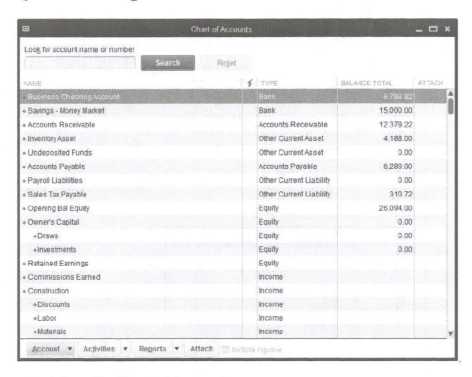

7. Close the Chart of Accounts

Deleting List Items

You can only delete list items that are not used in any transactions. If you attempt to delete a list item that is used in a transaction, QuickBooks will display a warning that the item cannot be deleted.

In this exercise, you will delete a list item.

1. Select   Lists : Item List   from the menu bar

The Item List opens:

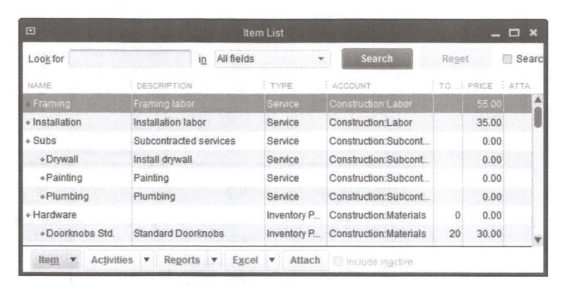

Note: The size of your Item List may be different. You may resize the window as necessary.

2. Select   Permits   in the Name column (scroll down the list)

3. Click   [Item ▼]   at the bottom of the window

A drop-down menu displays.

4. Select   Delete Item   from the drop-down menu

A Delete Item dialog box displays asking if you are sure you want to delete this item:

5. Click   [OK]   to delete the item

The Item List displays.

Notice the Permits item is no longer listed.

Making List Items Inactive

If you no longer want to use a list item that is used in transactions, you will not be able to delete it. Instead, you can make the item inactive.

In this exercise, you will make a list item inactive.

1. Select   Window   in the Name column (scroll up, if necessary)

2. Click   [Item ▼]   at the bottom of the window

A drop-down menu displays.

3. Select   Make Item Inactive   from the drop-down menu

The Window item no longer displays in the Item List:

Quick Tip. *To view inactive list items, select the Include inactive check box on the bottom of the Item List window. QuickBooks will display all items, active and inactive. If you need to make the item active again, select it from the list, click the Item button, and then select Make Item Active.*

Resizing List Columns

You can resize columns in a list to make them wider or narrower. You may want to resize a list column when the column is too narrow and you can't read all of the data in the column. In this exercise, you will resize a column in the Item List.

With the Item List displayed,

1. Position	the cursor	on the dividing line between the Description and Type column headers

The cursor changes to a bar with two-directional arrows.

2. Click and hold	the left mouse button	on the dividing line
3. Drag	the cursor	to the right to make the Description column wider until you can read all of the finance charge text in the Description column
4. Release	the mouse button	

Your Item List should resemble the figure below:

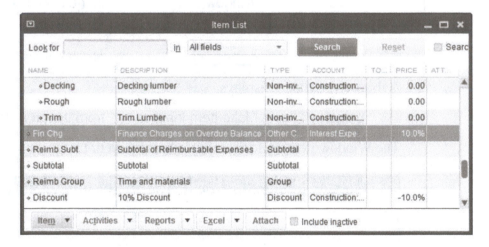

The Description column is now wider.

Note: Your window may be different depending on the size of your Item List. Although the size may vary, the concept of resizing list columns is still the same.

5. Close the Item List

Printing a List

You can print a QuickBooks list for reference, or you can print a list to a file to use in your word processor or spreadsheet. QuickBooks prints lists just as they are displayed on screen. For example, if the Customers & Jobs list is expanded and sorted by balance total, QuickBooks prints the expanded list sorted by balance total.

Note: You must have a printer driver and printer installed on your computer or network in order to print a list.

In this exercise, you will print the Customers & Jobs list.

1. Click  on the Icon Bar

The Customer Center opens displaying the Customers & Jobs list.

2. Click at the top of the window

A drop-down menu displays:

Customer & Job List
Customer & Job Information
Customer & Job Transaction List

This drop-down menu allows you to select the type of list you want to print.

3. Select   Customer & Job List   from the drop-down menu

Note: If a List Reports dialog box displays informing you about using the list report feature to print lists, click the OK button.

The Print Reports window opens:

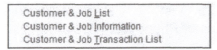

Note: Your Print Reports window may be different depending on your operating system and the name of your printer.

Note: If your computer is not set up to print, click the Cancel button to close the Print Reports window.

Quick Tip. *If you would like to preview the list on screen, click the Preview button.*

4. Click

QuickBooks displays a message as it sends the print job to your printer, then displays the Customer Center. When the Customers & Jobs list is printed, the customer names, jobs, and balance totals will print.

5. Close the Customer Center

Printing a List Report

QuickBooks has preset reports that allow you to report on the information in your QuickBooks lists. For example, you can create a phone list or a contact list for your customers, employers, and vendors. Or, you can create a price list for the items in your QuickBooks Item List.

To create a list report:

1. Select   Reports : List   from the menu bar
                      Customer Phone List

The Customer Phone List window opens:

2. Click   [Print]   in the Customer Phone List window

A drop-down menu displays:

Report
Save As PDF

3. Select   Report   from the Print drop-down menu

The Print Reports window opens.

4. Click

Note: If your computer is not set up to print, click the Cancel button to close the Print Reports window.

The Customer Phone List prints exactly as it is displayed on screen.

5. Close the Customer Phone List window

Review

In this lesson, you have learned how to:

- ☑ Create company lists
- ☑ Work with the Customers & Jobs list
- ☑ Work with the Employees list
- ☑ Work with the Vendors list
- ☑ Work with the Items List
- ☑ Work with other lists
- ☑ Manage lists

Practice:

1. Add a new customer to the Customer Center using the following data:

Customer Name:	Rhodes Advertising
Opening Balance:	$234.00
Full Name:	Ms. Sheila H. Rhodes
Invoice/Bill To:	300 Lewis St., Suite #3
	Fairgrave, NY 11111
Main Phone:	555-555-6767
Fax:	555-555-6777
Ship To:	Same as Invoice/Bill To
Payment Terms:	Net 15
Tax Code:	Non
Customer Type:	Commercial

2. Add a new employee to the Employee Center using the following data:

Legal Name:	Mr. Brian Johnson
Social Security No.	123-45-6788
Address:	701 Bailey Road
	Fairgrave, NY 11111
Work Phone:	555-555-9834

3. Add a new vendor to the Vendor Center using the following data:

Vendor Name:	Jerry's Painting Co.
Full Name:	Mr. Jerry Mathews
Main Phone:	555-555-5432
Account No.:	082-4343
Payment Terms:	Net 30
Credit Limit:	1000
Vendor Tax ID:	111-22-3333
Vendor eligible for 1099:	Yes

4. Add a custom field named Referred By to the Customers and Vendors lists.

5. In the Item List, delete the Drywall item.

6. In the Item List, make the Appliances item inactive.

7. In the Item List, resize the Type column to make it wider.

8. Close the company file.

Setting Up Inventory

In this lesson, you will learn how to:

- ❑ Enter inventory
- ❑ Order inventory
- ❑ Receive inventory
- ❑ Pay for inventory
- ❑ Manually adjust inventory

Concept

Many businesses that stock inventory do not know the accurate number of units they have on hand or on order at any particular time, and they have no way of getting that information quickly. If you use QuickBooks to manage your inventory, you will be able to track the number of items you have in stock and the value of your inventory after every purchase and sale. As you order inventory items, receive the items, and later sell items from inventory, QuickBooks automatically tracks each inventory-related transaction for you. You will always know the status of your inventory and, as a result, will have a more accurate picture of your business's assets.

Scenario

QuickBooks tracks your inventory; therefore, when you receive or sell items, you need to add them to your QuickBooks file. In this lesson, you will add a new part to your Item List, which tracks your inventory. You will create a purchase order for stock that you need to add to your inventory, then you will receive and pay for the inventory. Finally, you will manually adjust the inventory to account for damaged goods.

Practice Files: B18_Setting_Up_Inventory.qbw

Entering Inventory

For you to track inventory, you must enter each inventory item into the Item List as an inventory part. After you enter an item, QuickBooks will automatically keep track of it as you sell or reorder it.

To enter an item into inventory,

1. Open   B18_Setting_Up   using the method described in
                  Inventory.qbw   Before You Get Started

A QuickBooks Login dialog box displays:

This dialog box informs you that you must login as a QuickBooks Administrator in order to open the company file.

2. Type   **Canalside2**   in the Password field

Note: Passwords are case-sensitive.

3. Click

QuickBooks opens the file.

4. Click   to close the Reminders window

QuickBooks displays the Home page:

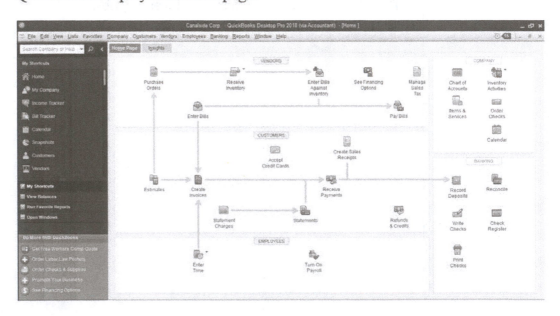

Before you can track inventory, you need to verify the inventory tracking feature is turned on in QuickBooks.

5. Select   Edit : Preferences   from the menu bar

The Preferences window opens:

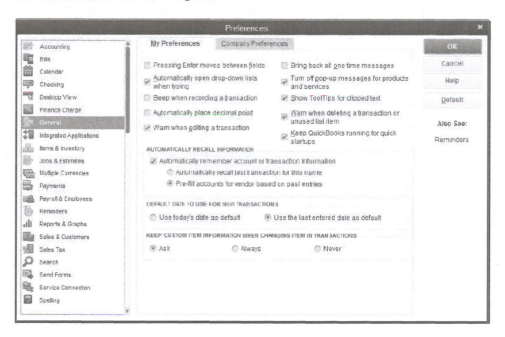

Note: Your Preferences window may display a different selection.

6. Select   the Items & Inventory   from the list on the left
                   category

7. Click   the Company Preferences tab

The company preferences for items and inventory are displayed:

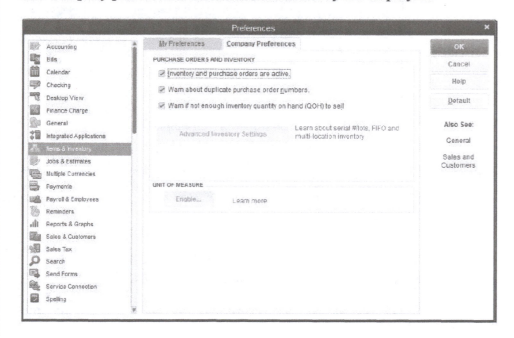

Note: If you are using the QuickBooks Premier version, your Company Preferences tab may be slightly different.

This tab allows you to enable or disable the ability to track inventory and use purchase orders in your company file.

8. Verify the Inventory and purchase orders are active check box is selected

Quick Tip. QuickBooks uses the average cost method to determine the value of inventory, rather than the last in, first out (LIFO) or first in, first out (FIFO) method. However, you can use QuickBooks advanced inventory settings if you would like the flexibility to work in FIFO costing in addition to average costing for tracking inventory. In addition, QuickBooks advanced inventory settings provide even more options for tracking inventory, including allowing for multiple inventory locations and entering serial numbers and lots at the time of purchase, transfer, or sale.

9. Click

The Preferences window closes. Now, you can add your product to the Item List.

10. Click in the Company area of the Home page

The Item List opens:

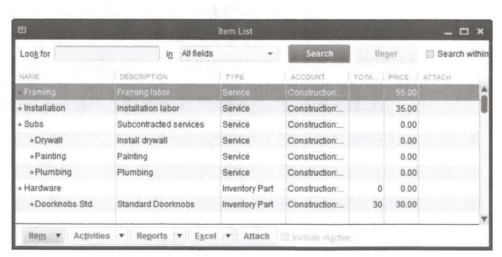

Note: The size of your Item List may be different. You may resize and move the window as necessary.

11. Click at the bottom of the window

A drop-down menu displays.

12. Select   New   from the drop-down menu

The New Item window opens:

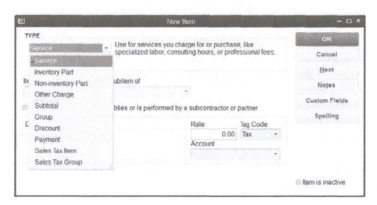

The New Item window allows you to select the type of item you want to enter. QuickBooks will then display fields based on the particular type of item selected.

13. Select   **Inventory Part**   from the Type drop-down menu

The New Item window is updated to display information for an inventory part:

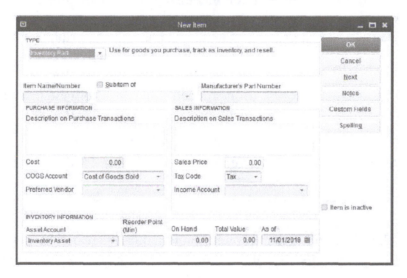

Note: In QuickBooks Premier, a Reorder Point Max field also displays.

Notice a description of what an inventory part is used for displays next to the Type field.

14. Type   **Cab 2015**   in the Item Name/Number field (2015 is the style number)

15. Type   **Kitchen Cabinet #2015**   in the Description on Purchase Transactions field

16. Press | Tab | to move to the Cost field

QuickBooks fills in the Description on Sales Transactions field with the same data you entered for the purchase description.

17. Type **169** in the Cost field

18. Press 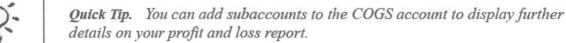 to move to the COGS Account field

QuickBooks assigns this item to the Cost of Goods Sold account, which is automatically created by QuickBooks when you set up your first inventory item. This account allows you to easily track the cost to you for the items you have sold. On a profit and loss report, QuickBooks subtracts the total cost of goods sold from your total income to provide a gross profit report before expenses.

Quick Tip. *You can add subaccounts to the COGS account to display further details on your profit and loss report.*

19. Select Joshua Hardware Supplies from the Preferred Vendor drop-down menu

20. Click in the Description on Sales Transactions field

If you want the description that displays on the invoice to be different from the description that displays on the purchase order, type the invoice description in this field. In this exercise, you will keep the same description for both.

21. Type **225** in the Sales Price field

22. Select Construction : Materials from the Income Account drop-down menu

The Income Account field allows you to link the item to an account, so that when the item is used on a form, it will post an entry to that account.

23. Press 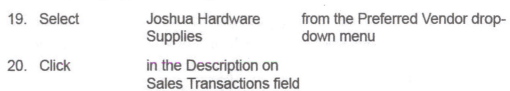 to move to the Asset Account field

The Inventory Asset account is automatically created by QuickBooks when you set up your first inventory item. This account tracks the current value of your inventory. You will leave this default selection.

24. Press Tab

25. Type **15** in the Reorder Point (Min) field

The Reorder Point (Min) is the minimum quantity of an inventory item that you want to have in stock. When the quantity reaches the minimum reorder point, you will want to order more of the item.

Quick Tip. *You can set up the Reminders list so that QuickBooks reminds you when it's time to reorder an item.*

26. Press Tab to move to the On Hand field

Note: If you are using QuickBooks Premier, you will need to press Tab twice.

27. Type   **20**   in the On Hand field

This indicates that you have 20 cabinets in your inventory.

28. Press to move to the Total Value field

QuickBooks has calculated the value of your item automatically by multiplying the quantity on hand (On Hand) by the cost:

You can add custom fields to the Item List the same way you can add them to the Customers & Jobs, Vendor, and Employees lists. Custom fields provide a way to track item information specific to your business, such as colors or serial numbers.

29. Click

The Custom Fields for Cab 2015 window opens:

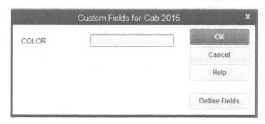

30. Click

The Set Up Custom Fields for Items window opens:

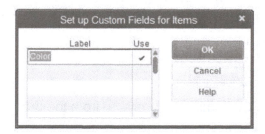

31. Type   **Finish**   in the second Label row (below Color)

32. Click   in the Use column

A check mark displays in the Use column. This indicates that this custom field will be available for use by all items in the Item List.

33. Click   to close the Set up Custom Fields for Items window

The Custom Fields for Cab 2015 window displays the new Finish field:

34. Type   **Natural Oak**   in the Finish field

35. Click   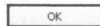   to close the Custom Fields for Cab 2015 window

36. Click   OK   to save the item and close the New Item window

QuickBooks updates the Item List to include the new cabinet item:

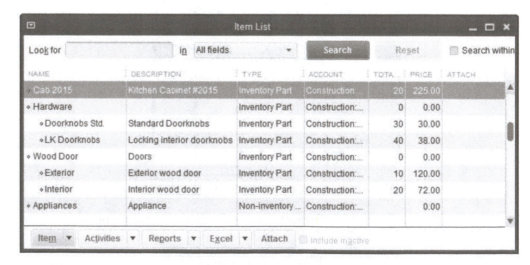

To add the Finish column to the Item List,

37. Click   Item

38. Select   Customize Columns   from the drop-down menu

A Customize Columns - Item List window opens:

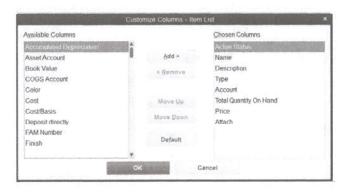

39. Select   Finish   in the Available Columns list

40. Click

Finish is added to the Chosen Columns list:

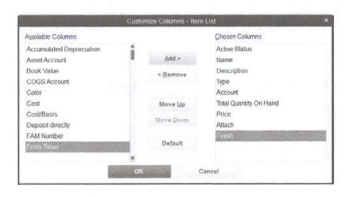

41. Click   OK

The Finish column is added as the last column in the Item List:

When you add customized fields for items, you must also add these fields to a template in order for them to display on forms. For example, if you want the Finish information for the kitchen cabinet item to display on a purchase order form, you must add the Finish field to a customized template. In the next exercise, you will see the Finish field displayed on a purchase order.

42. Click to close the Item List and return to the Home page

Ordering Inventory

After you enter inventory items into the Item List, and vendors in to the Vendor list, you can order items to keep your inventory stocked.

Creating a Purchase Order

In this exercise, you will create a purchase order to order an item you stock in inventory from a vendor — a wood door from Fellows Windows & Doors.

1. Click in the Vendors area of the Home page

Note: If inventory and purchase orders were not made active in the Preferences window, the Purchase Orders icon would not be displayed.

The Create Purchase Orders window opens:

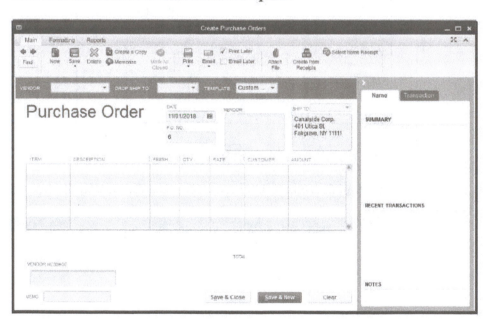

The Create Purchase Orders window allows you to enter the product you want to order, the quantity you want to order, and the vendor from which you want to purchase the product. As you fill in this information, QuickBooks automatically calculates a purchase order number, item cost, and total cost.

Notice that QuickBooks has already entered today's date and a sequential purchase order number (P.O. No. 6).

2. Select Fellows Windows & Doors from the Vendor drop-down menu

QuickBooks fills in the purchase order with information about Fellows Windows & Doors:

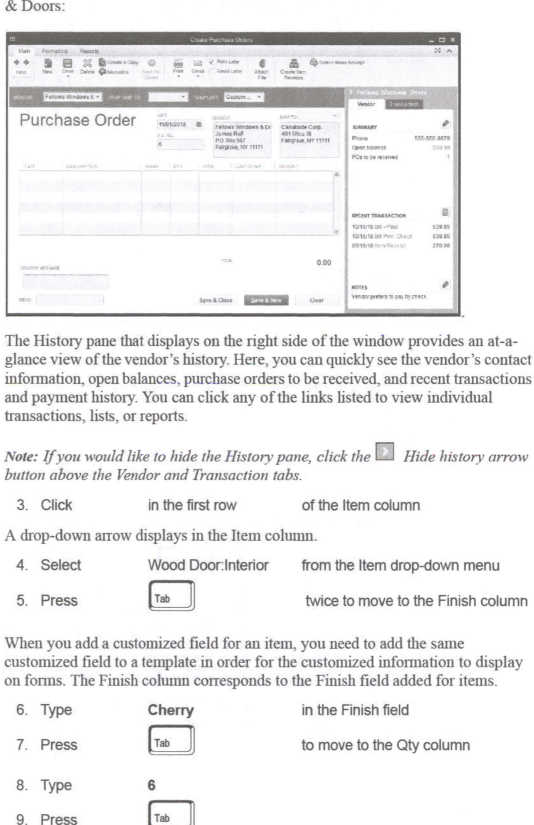

The History pane that displays on the right side of the window provides an at-a-glance view of the vendor's history. Here, you can quickly see the vendor's contact information, open balances, purchase orders to be received, and recent transactions and payment history. You can click any of the links listed to view individual transactions, lists, or reports.

Note: If you would like to hide the History pane, click the ▶ *Hide history arrow button above the Vendor and Transaction tabs.*

3. Click   in the first row   of the Item column

A drop-down arrow displays in the Item column.

4. Select   Wood Door:Interior   from the Item drop-down menu

5. Press   [Tab]   twice to move to the Finish column

When you add a customized field for an item, you need to add the same customized field to a template in order for the customized information to display on forms. The Finish column corresponds to the Finish field added for items.

6. Type   **Cherry**   in the Finish field

7. Press   [Tab]   to move to the Qty column

8. Type   **6**

9. Press   [Tab]

QuickBooks automatically calculates the total amount of this purchase order by multiplying the quantity by the rate.

Quick Tip. If you are purchasing an item for a specific customer, you can select the customer's name from the Customer drop-down menu.

10.	Click	in the Vendor Message field	at the bottom of the Purchase Order

11.	Type	**Please rush ship this order**	in the Vendor Message field

The Purchase Order should resemble the figure below:

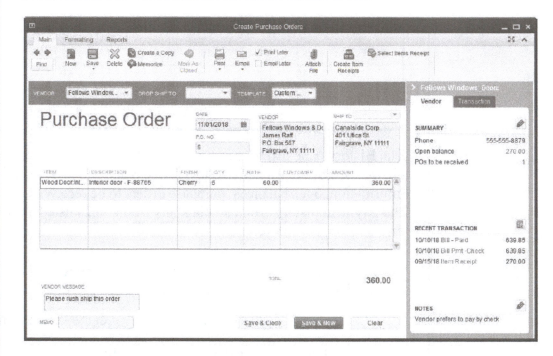

12.	Click		to record the Purchase Order

The Create Purchase Orders window closes and the Home page is displayed. After you have created a purchase order, QuickBooks adds an account to the Chart of Accounts called Purchase Orders. This is a non-posting account and does not affect your balance sheet or income statement.

Generating a Purchase Orders Report

The Purchase Orders account can be used to produce a QuickReport that shows all of your purchase orders, so that you are always aware of what is on order.

To generate a report of all the purchase orders you have written,

Chart of
Accounts

1.	Click	in the Company area of the Home page

The Chart of Accounts opens:

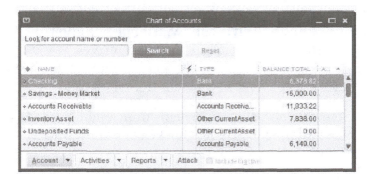

Note: You may resize and move the Chart of Accounts as necessary.

2. Click   Purchase Orders   to select it (scroll down to the bottom of the list)

3. Click   Reports ▼   at the bottom of the window

A drop-down menu displays.

4. Select   QuickReport: Purchase Orders   from the drop-down menu

The Account QuickReport opens.

5. Select   All   from the Dates drop-down menu

The Account QuickReport is updated to display all purchase orders:

Note: If you did not change your computer's date as recommended in the Before You Get Started lesson, the dates that display on your screen will be different.

Because purchase orders are listed chronologically, notice the purchase order you just created is listed last in the report, below all previous purchase orders.

6. Close the Account QuickReport window

7. Close the Chart of Accounts to return to the Home page

Receiving Inventory

When you receive the items you have purchased, you should enter them into inventory. You may receive items with a bill or without a bill attached. When you receive an item before the bill for the items arrives, you use an item receipt to receive the items into inventory. An item receipt can be converted into a bill in QuickBooks after you receive the bill from the vendor.

In this exercise, you will receive items from a purchase order without a bill. You will create an item receipt to let QuickBooks know you received the items. You will enter the bill later when it arrives.

To receive inventory without a bill attached,

1. Click   Receive Inventory   in the Vendors area of the Home page

A drop-down menu displays:

> Receive Inventory with Bill
> Receive Inventory without Bill

2. Select   **Receive Inventory without Bill**   from the drop-down menu

The Create Item Receipts window opens:

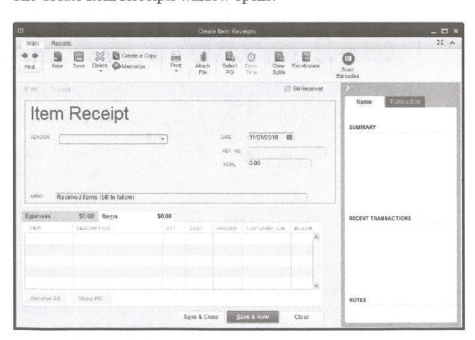

The Create Item Receipts window is used for receiving items into inventory before the bill for the items arrives.

3. Select   **Fellows Windows & Doors**   from the Vendor drop-down menu

An Open POs Exist dialog box displays informing you there are open purchase orders for this vendor and asking if you want to receive against one or more of these orders:

4. Click

The Open Purchase Orders window for Fellows Windows & Doors displays with two purchase orders listed:

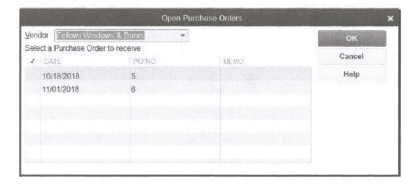

5. Click   6   in the PO No. column to select the purchase order you just created

QuickBooks places a check mark in the left-most column to indicate the item is selected.

6. Click to transfer the purchase order information to the item receipt

The purchase order information is transferred to the Create Item Receipts window:

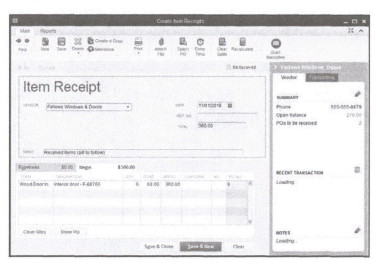

Note: If necessary, the quantity of the item received can be adjusted on this window.

7. Click   Save & Close   to close the Create Item Receipts window and return to the Home page

QuickBooks processes the items and adds them to your inventory. If you display the Item List, you will see that you now have six additional wood interior doors on hand - a total of 26 doors in inventory.

Paying for Inventory

When you receive an invoice for the items you purchased, you should enter the bill into QuickBooks. You can enter the bill and pay later, or enter the bill and pay at the same time.

In this exercise, you will enter a bill and pay at the same time.

1. Click   **Enter Bills Against Inventory**   in the Vendors area of the Home page

The Select Item Receipt window opens, allowing you to select the vendor and the receipted item for which to enter the bill:

2. Select   Fellows Windows & Doors   from the Vendor drop-down menu

QuickBooks populates the Date and Memo fields with information that corresponds to the items you have received from Fellows Windows & Doors:

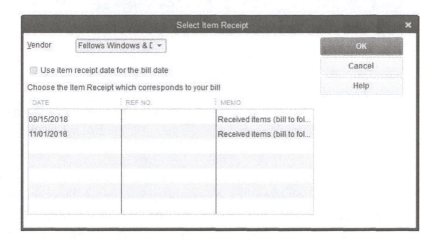

3. Click **11/01/2018** in the Date column to select that item receipt

4. Click

The Enter Bills window is updated with information about the inventory received:

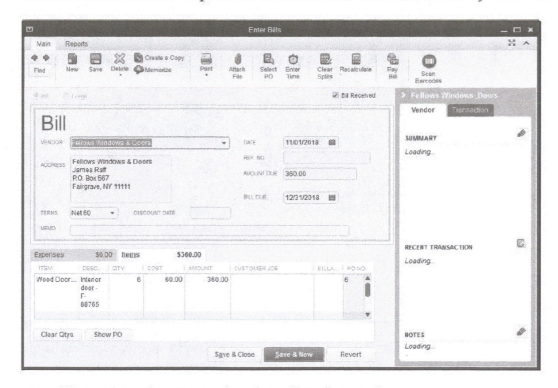

Note: If necessary, the cost can be adjusted on this window.

5. Click

A Recording Transaction dialog box displays:

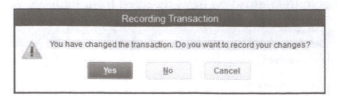

6. Click to record the transaction, close the Enter Bills window, and return to the Home page

QuickBooks automatically updates the Accounts Payable account in the Chart of Accounts to mark the bill for Fellows Windows & Doors as received. If you look at the Accounts Payable account in the Chart of Accounts, it will display a balance increase of $360.00, based on the bill entered for Fellows Windows & Doors.

To pay the bill,

7. Click **Pay Bills** in the Vendors area of the Home page

The Pay Bills window opens:

The Pay Bills window allows you to specify which bills to pay and the payment method (check or credit card) to use to pay the bills.

8. Select the check box to the left of the Fellows Windows & Doors bill

QuickBooks places a check mark in the check box next to the bill to show that it has been selected.

9. Click the To be printed button in the Payment Method area to select it

10. Click  to close the Pay Bills window

QuickBooks creates a check in your Checking account to Fellows Windows & Doors for $360.00 and a Payment Summary window opens:

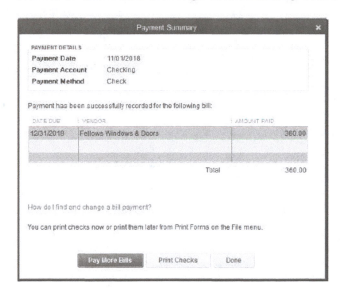

This window displays a summary of payments and allows you to choose whether to pay more bills or to print checks now. If you choose not to print checks now, you can print them at a later time by selecting File : Print Forms : Checks from the menu bar.

11. Click   Print Checks

The Select Checks to Print window opens:

The Select Checks to Print window allows you to select which checks to print from a list of checks to be printed. The check to Smith's Construction Rental displays because it was previously selected to print.

If the correct check number is not displayed in the First Check Number text box, you can change the check numbers that will print. Notice that all the checks in the list are already selected to print.

Note: For more information about the types of checks and the check styles QuickBooks supports, refer to the QuickBooks Help.

12.   Press   Tab   to move to First Check Number

The number 1 becomes selected.

13.   Type   **151**   as the first check number to be printed

14.   Click   OK   to print the checks

The Print Checks window opens:

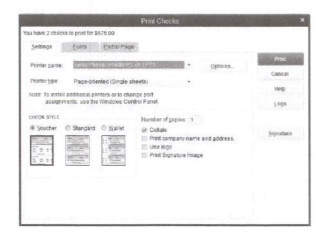

The Print Checks window allows you to select the check style and whether you want your company name and address or logo printed on the checks.

Note: You must have a printer driver and printer installed on your computer or network to print checks. If your computer is not set up to print, click the Cancel button to close the Print Checks window and click the Cancel button to close the Select Checks to Print window. To open the Select Checks to Print window at a later time, you can select File : Print Forms : Checks from the menu bar.

You will accept the default settings.

15.   Click   Print   to print the checks

When the checks have printed, QuickBooks displays a Print Checks - Confirmation window asking if the check(s) printed correctly:

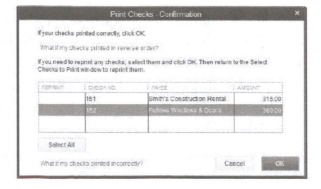

For the purpose of this exercise, you will assume that the checks printed correctly.

16. Click to close the Print Checks - Confirmation window

Manually Adjusting Inventory

When you take a physical count of your inventory items and your physical inventory count does not match QuickBooks inventory quantities, you can adjust the inventory manually.

To adjust the inventory manually,

1. Click in the Company area of the Home page

A drop-down menu displays:

Adjust Quantity/Value On Hand...
Learn about serial #/lots and more

Note: If you are using the QuickBooks Premier or Accountant version, the drop-down menu displays additional options for Inventory Center and Build Assemblies.

2. Select Adjust Quantity/Value On Hand

The Adjust Quantity/Value on Hand window opens:

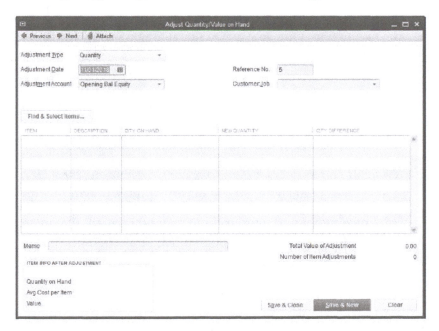

This window allows you to select the adjustment type, adjustment account, the item to adjust, and either the new quantity or the quantity difference.

3. Press to move to Adjustment Account

4. Type **Inventory Ad**

QuickBooks completes the field with Inventory Adjustment.

5. Click in the first row of the Item column

A drop-down arrow displays in the Item field.

6. Select Wood Door:Interior from the Item drop-down menu

7. Click in the New Quantity in the same row
column

When you conduct a physical inventory, you find there are 24 interior wood doors.

8. Type **24** (the number of doors in inventory)

9. Press

QuickBooks automatically calculates the quantity difference and places a -2 in the Qty Difference column:

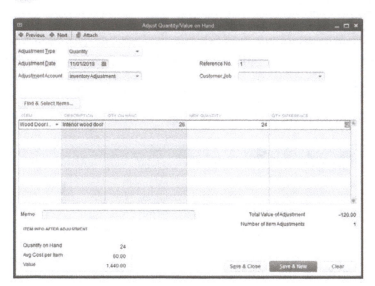

Note: If you did not change your computer's date, type 11/1/2018 in the Adjustment Date field. Otherwise, your quantity difference will be different.

Because two wood interior doors were damaged, the inventory account has been adjusted to remove two doors. Notice at the bottom right of the window the Total Value of Adjustment is -120.00.

10. Click Save & Close to close the window and display the Home page

QuickBooks adjusts the inventory. If you display the Item List, you will see the new inventory total for Interior wood doors.

Review

In this lesson, you have learned how to:

☑ Enter inventory

☑ Order inventory

☑ Receive inventory

☑ Pay for inventory

☑ Manually adjust inventory

Practice:

1. Enter a new part into inventory using the following information:

Item Name/Number:	Counter
Purchase Description:	Kitchen Counter
Cost:	280.00
COGS Account:	Cost of Goods Sold
Preferred Vendor:	Joshua Hardware Supplies
Sales Description:	Same as Purchase Description
Sales Price:	340.00
Income Account:	Construction:Materials
Asset Account:	Inventory Asset
Reorder Point:	5
On Hand:	6

2. Order 20 standard doorknobs from Joshua Hardware Supplies.

3. Receive the 20 standard doorknobs without a bill.

4. Process the bill by entering it against inventory and then pay for the 20 standard doorknobs.

5. Generate a Purchase Orders report to view the recent purchase order to Joshua Hardware Supplies.

6. Adjust the inventory so that there is a new quantity of 7 wood exterior doors.

7. Close the company file.

Notes:

Selling Your Product

In this lesson, you will learn how to:

- ❑ Create product invoices
- ❑ Apply credit to invoices
- ❑ Email invoices
- ❑ Set price levels
- ❑ Create sales receipts

Concept

QuickBooks allows you to easily keep track of income you receive from inventory item sales. When you sell products from inventory, you need to enter the products on a sales form so QuickBooks can properly decrease inventory quantities. QuickBooks allows you to use different forms, such as invoices and sales receipts to record sales.

Product invoices are used when you sell a product and the customer does not pay in full at the time of the sale. Sales receipts are used when full payment is received at the point of sale.

Scenario

Canalside Corp. does new construction, remodeling, and repairs and also has a small mail-order business for custom wood doors and hardware, which it keeps in stock. In this lesson, you will create a product invoice for products sold by the business, noting how this invoice affects the item inventory and the Chart of Accounts in QuickBooks. You will then create a credit memo for a customer and apply the credit to a product invoice. After applying the credit, you will learn how to email the invoice to a customer from within QuickBooks and will also learn how to edit your email provider. You will then learn how to create a price level, associate the price level with a customer, and use the price level on a sales form. As a final step, you will enter a cash sale and check its affect on the Chart of Accounts.

Practice Files: B18_Selling_Your_Product.qbw

Creating Product Invoices

A product invoice allows you to record a sale you made and track the amount your customer owes to you. Invoicing customers for goods sold allows the customer to pay later, at which time you can process the payment received.

In this exercise, you will create a product invoice for James Wilson DDS, who purchased three interior wood doors with hardware for part of the expansion work you are doing on his dental office.

1. Open   B18_Selling_Your   using the method described in
                              Product.qbw   Before You Get Started

The QuickBooks Login dialog box displays:

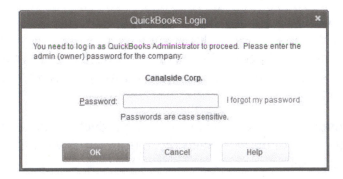

This dialog box informs you that you must login as a QuickBooks Administrator in order to open the company file.

2. Type   **Canalside2**   in the Password field

Note: Passwords are case-sensitive.

3. Click

QuickBooks opens the file.

4. Click   to close the Reminders window

QuickBooks displays the Home page:

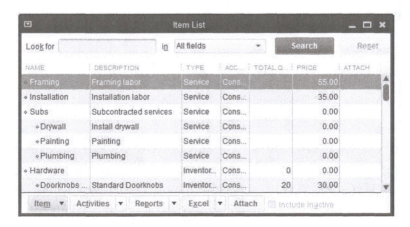

When you create an invoice, the items on the invoice are deducted from inventory. Therefore, you will look at the Item List before creating your invoice to see how many locking interior doorknobs and interior wood doors you have on hand (in inventory).

To open the Item List,

5. Click [Items & Services] in the Company area of the Home page

The Item List opens:

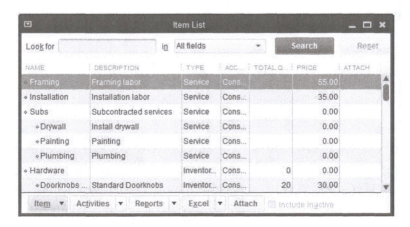

Note: You may resize and move the Item List window as necessary.

The Item List is used to record information about the products and services you buy and sell and for items that perform calculations, such as discounts and sales tax.

6. Scroll down the list so that you can view both Hardware and Wood Door in the Name column

Notice the total quantity on hand for locking interior doorknobs is 40 and the total quantity on hand for interior wood doors is 20.

7. Click to close the Item List and return to the Home page

Now, you will create a product invoice to sell your products out of your inventory.

To create an invoice,

8. Click **Create Invoices** in the Customers area of the Home page

The Create Invoices window opens displaying the Intuit Service Invoice.

9. Select **Intuit Product Invoice** from the Template drop-down menu

The Create Invoices window displays the Intuit Product Invoice:

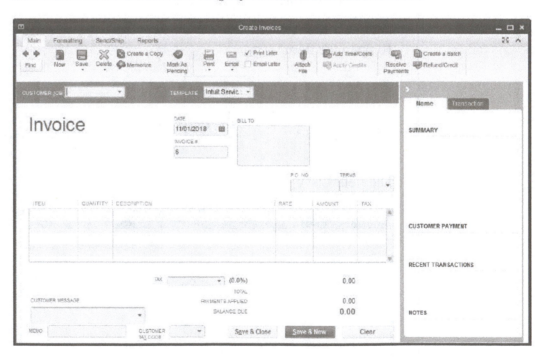

The Create Invoices window allows you to enter all information necessary to sell a product out of inventory, including customer name, bill to address, ship to address, P.O. number, shipping date and method, quantity, item code, taxes, and total cost values.

10. Select **James Wilson DDS : Dental office** from the Customer : Job drop-down menu

QuickBooks fills in the invoice with information about this customer:

Note: If your window does not display the History pane, click the  *Show history arrow.*

The History pane on the right side of the window provides an at-a-glance view of the customer's history. Here, you can quickly see the customer's phone number and preferred delivery method, as well as their open balances, active estimates, unbilled time and expenses, customer expenses, and recent transactions. You can click any of the links to view individual transactions, lists, or reports.

Note: If you would like to close the History pane, click the  *Hide history arrow.*

11. Type **2345** in the P.O. No. field

12. Click [▾] next to the Via field

A list of shipping methods used to send products to customers displays:

```
<Add New>

Airborne
DHL
Federal Express
UPS
US Mail
```

You will now add a new shipping method to the product invoice.

13. Select <Add New> from the drop-down menu

The New Shipping Method window opens:

This window allows you to enter other shipping companies you may use, such as local shipping companies.

14.	Type	**Common Carrier**	in the Shipping Method field
15.	Click	OK	to close the New Shipping Method window

The new shipping method is added to the Via drop-down list and displays in the Via field. This new shipping method will now be available whenever you create a product invoice.

16.	Type	**3**	in the first row of the Quantity column
17.	Press	Tab	to move to the Item Code field
18.	Type	**Int (for Interior Wood Doors)**	in the Item Code field
19.	Press	Tab	

QuickBooks automatically fills in the item name with **Wood Door:Interior**.

Notice that QuickBooks fills in the rest of the fields on the first row for interior wood doors based on the information entered for this item.

20.	Type	**3**	in the second row of the Quantity column
21.	Press	Tab	to move to the Item Code field
22.	Type	**LK (for Locking Interior Doorknobs)**	in the Item Code field
23.	Press	Tab	

QuickBooks automatically fills in the rest of the information for the locking interior doorknobs based on the information entered for this item.

24.	Click	in the Customer Message field	
25.	Type	**T (for the message Thank you for your business.)**	in the Customer Message field
26.	Press	Tab	

QuickBooks completes the rest of the message, **Thank you for your business**:

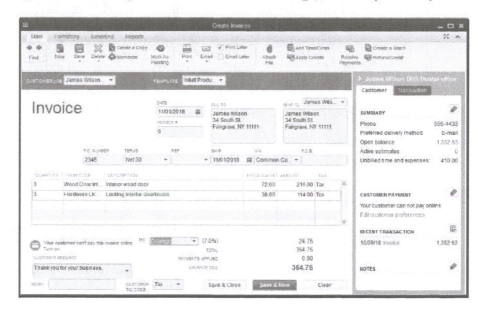

QuickBooks automatically calculates the sales tax amount based on the default sales tax entered in the customer record for James Wilson DDS.

27. Click   Save & Close   to record the invoice and return to the Home page

QuickBooks automatically updates the on hand amounts for interior wood doors and locking interior doorknobs in the Item List.

To view the new on hand amounts,

28. Click   Items & Services   in the Company area of the Home page

The Item List opens:

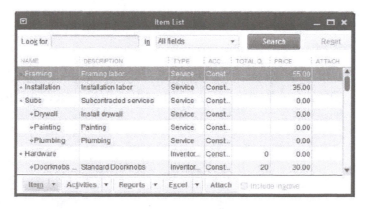

29. Scroll down the list so that you can view both Hardware and Wood Door in the Name column

Notice the total quantity on hand for locking interior doorknobs has been reduced to 37 and the on hand amount of interior wood doors is down to 17.

To view an Inventory Item QuickReport for interior wood doors,

30. Select   Interior wood door   in the Item List

31. Click   Reports ▼   at the bottom of the window

A drop-down menu displays.

32. Select   QuickReport: Interior   from the drop-down menu

An Inventory Item QuickReport for interior wood doors opens:

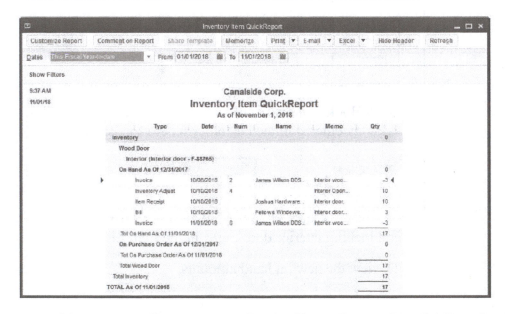

Note: If your report does not resemble the figure above, select All from the Dates drop-down menu.

This report displays the history of purchases and sales for the interior wood door inventory item for this fiscal year-to-date.

33. Close the Inventory Item QuickReport

34. Close the Item List

QuickBooks also updates the Accounts Receivable account for the amount of this invoice. QuickBooks uses an Accounts Receivable account to track the money owed to you.

To view the Accounts Receivable register,

1. Click   Chart of Accounts   in the Company area of the Home page

The Chart of Accounts opens:

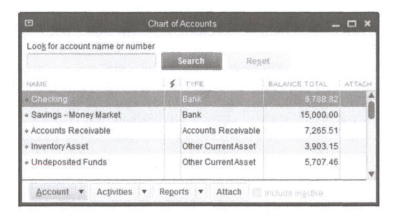

Note: You may resize and move the Chart of Accounts window as necessary

2. Select   Accounts Receivable   from the list of accounts

3. Click   at the bottom of the window

A drop-down menu displays.

4. Select   Use Register   from the drop-down menu

Quick Tip. *You can also double-click Accounts Receivable in the list to open the register.*

The Accounts Receivable register opens:

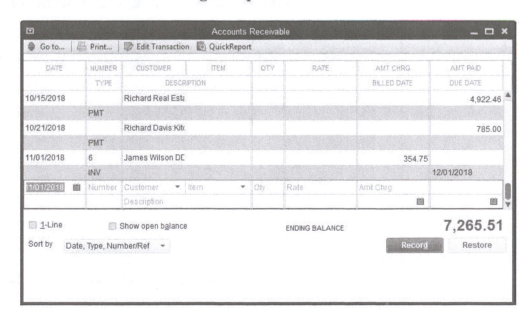

Notice the invoice for James Wilson DDS has been posted to the register.

5. Close the Accounts Receivable window

6. Close the Chart of Accounts to return to the Home page

Applying Credit to Invoices

A credit memo can be created when a customer returns items for which you have already recorded an invoice, customer payment, or sales receipt. Examples of credit memos are when a customer cancels a sale, returns an item, or overpays. After you have created a credit memo for a customer, you can apply the amount of the credit to any unpaid invoices and billing statements for that customer.

In this exercise, you will create a credit memo for Richard Davis and then apply the credit to a new product invoice you create for the purchase of a kitchen appliance.

First, you will view the original invoice for Richard Davis.

1. Click in the Customers area of the Home page

The Create Invoices window opens.

2. Click  (the Previous button) in the toolbar of the Create Invoices window until the invoice for Richard Davis:Kitchen displays

The invoice for Richard Davis:Kitchen displays:

You will create a credit memo for the two plumbing fixtures displayed on this invoice that were purchased by Richard Davis. Richard returned these items because they were the wrong size for his kitchen remodeling project.

3. Close the Create Invoices window

You will now create a credit memo.

4. Select   **Customers : Create**   from the menu bar
                                         Credit Memos/Refunds

The Create Credit Memos/Refunds window opens:

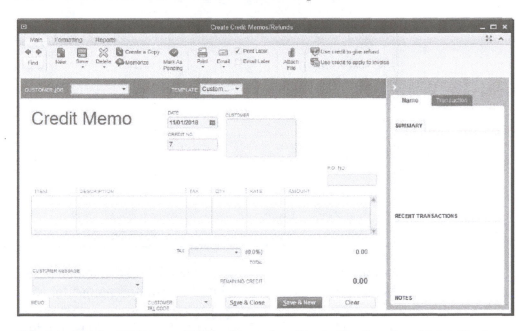

The Create Credit Memos/Refunds window is similar to other QuickBooks windows in that it allows you to enter all of the information necessary to create a credit memo for a customer.

5. Select   **Richard Davis :**   from the Customer : Job drop-down
                                       Kitchen   menu

QuickBooks automatically fills in information on the credit memo for Richard Davis based on the information entered for this customer.

6. Type   **Fix (for Fixtures)**   in the first row of the Item column

7. Press

QuickBooks automatically fills in the item name with **Fixtures**.

Notice that QuickBooks fills in the rest of the fields on the first row based on the information entered for this item.

8. Type   **2**   in the Qty field

9. Press

The Amount, Total, and Remaining Credit fields are automatically updated:

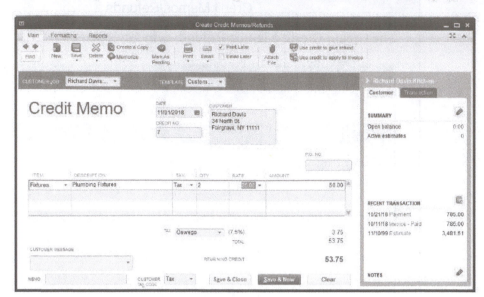

QuickBooks automatically calculated the sales tax amount to be credited based on the default sales tax entered in the customer record for Richard Davis.

10. Click to record the credit memo

An Available Credit window opens:

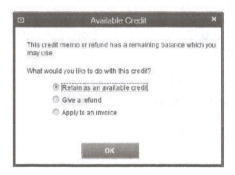

This window allows you to specify how you would like to use the credit; either retain it as an available credit, give a refund, or apply it to an existing invoice.

In this exercise, you will retain the amount as an available credit and then apply it to a new invoice you create for Richard Davis.

With the Retain as an available credit option selected,

11. Click   OK   to return to the Home page

After you have created a credit memo for a customer, you can apply the amount of the credit to unpaid invoices and billing statements for that customer. Because Richard Davis is purchasing an appliance from you for his kitchen remodeling work, you will now create a new invoice and apply the available credit to the invoice.

12. Click   in the Customers area of the Home page

The Create Invoices window opens.

13. Select   Richard Davis : Kitchen   from the Customer:Job drop-down menu

QuickBooks fills in the invoice with Richard Davis' information.

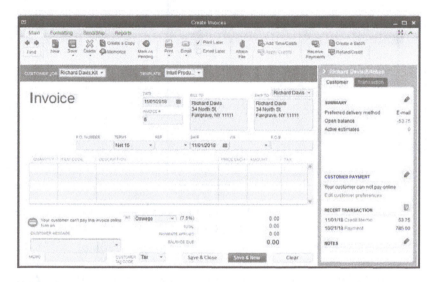

14. Type   1   in the first row of the Quantity column

15. Type   **App (for Appliances)**   in the Item Code field

16. Press   Tab

QuickBooks automatically fills in the Item Code field with **Appliances**.

QuickBooks fills in the rest of the fields in the first row based on the information entered for the Appliances item.

17. Click   in the toolbar at the top of the window

A Recording Transaction dialog box displays:

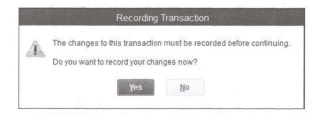

This dialog box informs you that you must record changes to the transaction before continuing.

18. Click to record changes to the transaction

The Apply Credits window opens:

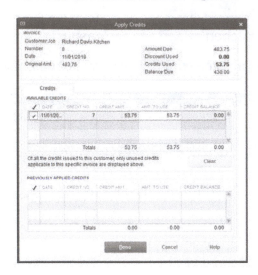

This window displays all available credits for a customer, as well as any previously applied credits. Because Richard Davis only has one credit memo for $53.75, that amount will be applied to the invoice.

Quick Tip. *You do not have to apply the entire amount of the credit at one time. You can change the amount of credit to use in the Amt. to Use column.*

19. Click

The Create Invoices window is updated with the credit:

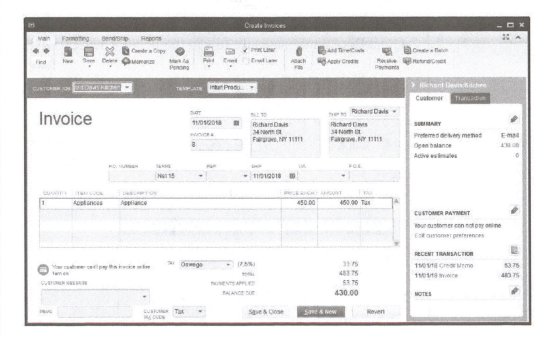

A credit amount of $53.75 now displays in the Payments Applied area and the new Balance Due ($430.00) displays below the applied payment.

Notice the Print Later check box in the toolbar at the top of the window is selected, indicating that this invoice will be printed later. The Email Later check box is not selected. You will now learn how to email an invoice to a customer.

Emailing Invoices

QuickBooks allows you to email forms and reports to vendors, customers, and employees, directly from within the QuickBooks application.

If you have Microsoft® Outlook®, Outlook Express, or Windows mail installed as your default email program with a properly configured profile, QuickBooks will use it when it sends email. In this exercise, Microsoft® Outlook® is used.

Note: If you are not using one of these email programs, you will not be able to complete this exercise in it's entirety, but you can follow along with the steps.

To email an invoice to a customer,

1.	Select	the Email Later check box	in the toolbar
2.	Deselect	the Print Later check box	in the toolbar

3. Click   in the toolbar

A drop-down menu displays:

```
Invoice
Invoice and Attached Files
Batch
```

You can choose to email just this invoice or a batch of invoices.

4.	Select	Invoice	from the drop-down menu

An Information Missing or Invalid dialog box displays:

This dialog box informs you that the customer's email address is missing. In order to email an invoice to a customer, you must provide QuickBooks with your company's email address, as well as the customer's email address.

Quick Tip. *If you need to enter an email address for your company, select Company : Company Information from the menu bar. When the Company Information window opens, enter the email address in the Email field.*

For this exercise, you will enter your personal email address.

5. Type   **[your email address]**   in the Email address(es) field

Quick Tip. *You can email the invoice to multiple customers by entering their email addresses separated by semicolons.*

6. Click   OK

A Recording Transaction dialog box displays:

7. Click   Yes   to record the transaction

A Sending Email Using Outlook dialog box displays informing you that QuickBooks supports Outlook:

Note: If you have Outlook installed as your email program, but your profile has not been configured, a No Profiles have been created dialog box or an Outlook Profile Does Not Exist dialog box displays indicating you must create a profile first to use Outlook to send email. If you do not have Outlook or Windows mail installed as your default email program, a dialog box displays allowing you to choose your email method. Selecting the Setup my email now option displays the Preferences window. You can then select Send Forms from the list of preferences and specify the service you use to send emails. The next exercise, Integrating with Web Mail, covers this in further detail.

8. Click   Close

The email message displays:

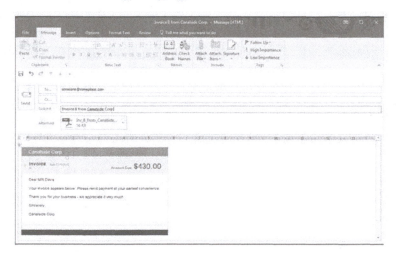

Note: Your email may look slightly different depending on the email application you are using.

Notice that QuickBooks automatically populates the To line with the recipient's email address and the Subject line with the subject of the email. QuickBooks also creates a message to the recipient and attaches the invoice.

9. Click 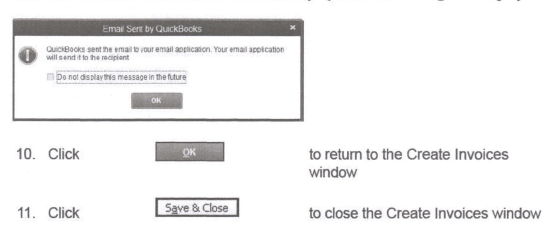 to send the email

Note: Your window may display a different Send button.

After the email has been sent, an Email Sent by QuickBooks dialog box displays:

Email Sent by QuickBooks ✕
QuickBooks sent the email to your email application. Your email application will send it to the recipient
☐ Do not display this message in the future
OK

10. Click   OK   to return to the Create Invoices window

11. Click   Save & Close   to close the Create Invoices window

You return to the Home page.

Integrating with Web Mail

In addition to Microsoft Outlook, QuickBooks allows you to send invoices and other forms and documents using web mail services, such as Hotmail, Yahoo, and Gmail. To specify the service you use to send emails, you must edit your preferences in QuickBooks.

1. Select   Edit : Preferences   from the menu bar

The Preferences window opens with the General category selected:

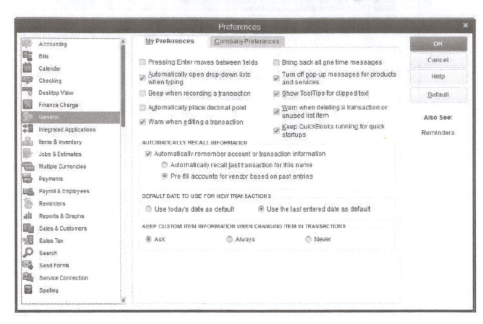

Note: Your window may display a different selection.

2. Select   Send Forms   from the list of preferences in the left pane

The My Preferences tab for sending forms displays:

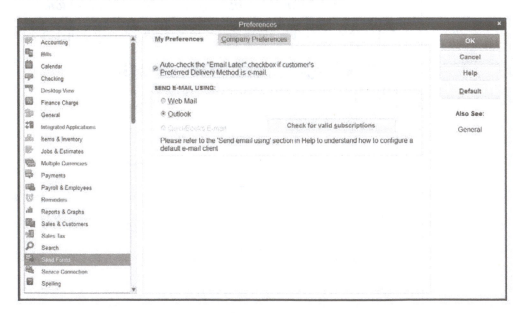

Note: If you do not have Microsoft® Outlook® installed or you have not created a profile to use Outlook to send email, the Outlook option will not display in the Send E-mail Using area.

3. Select   Web Mail   in the Send E-Mail Using area

The My Preferences tab is updated with Web Mail settings:

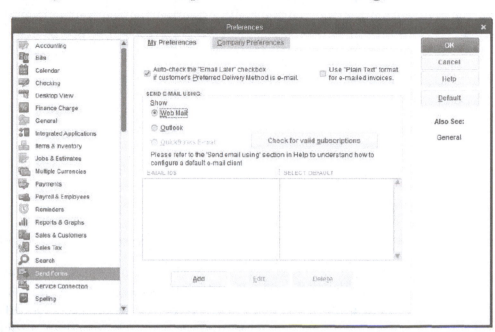

4. Click Add

Quick Tip. *To edit email settings, you click the Edit button.*

The Add Email Info window opens:

For this exercise, you will enter information for a fictitious Hotmail account.

The Email Id field is where you enter your email address.

5.	Type	**abc@hotmail.com**	in the Email Id field
6.	Select	**Outlook/Hotmail/Live**	from the Email Provider drop-down menu

The Add Email Info window updates:

7. Verify the Use enhanced security (Recommended) check box is selected

QuickBooks no longer uses SMTP, since most web mail providers recommend to not use it. The new web mail with enhanced security uses the latest industry standard to send emails. This allows you to authorize QuickBooks with full account access to your web mail provider. By using this feature, you won't need to enter your web mail password each time you use web mail. Instead, you enter your credentials one time as part of the initial set up.

8. Click

The Login window opens:

From this window, you enter your email or Intuit User ID and your password to authorize QuickBooks to access your web mail account. QuickBooks will then send you a verification code. You will need to enter this verification code along with additional personal information to complete the set up.

You will not complete the set up at this time.

9. Close   the Login window   to return to the Add Email Info window

10. Click   to return to the My Preferences tab

11. Click to close the Preferences window

The Preferences window closes and you return to the Home page.

Setting Price Levels

If you sell products or services that have varying prices per sale, you will want to set up price levels. Price levels allow you set custom pricing for different customers and jobs. After you create a price level, you can associate it with one or more customers or jobs. Then, every time you create an invoice, sales receipt, or other type of sales form for that customer or job, QuickBooks will automatically apply the appropriate price to the sale.

Canalside Corp. has completed multiple jobs for James Wilson DDS and is now completing work at his dental office. In this exercise, you will set up a price level to offer a 10% discount for all materials purchased for the dental office work.

Note: You must have the price levels preference enabled to create or edit price levels. To verify it is enabled, select Edit : Preferences from the menu bar. When the Preferences window opens, select the Sales & Customers preference, select the Company Preferences tab, verify that the Enable price levels option is selected, and click the OK button.

To create a price level,

1. Select   Lists : Price Level List   from the menu bar

The Price Level List window opens:

The Price Level List stores all of the price levels you create.

2. Click

A drop-down menu displays:

3. Select **New** from the drop-down menu

The New Price Level window opens:

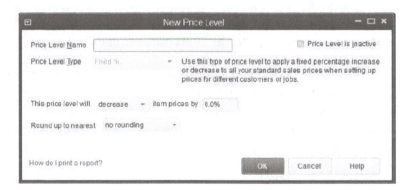

4. Type **Dental Office Discount** in the Price Level Name field

5. Verify that Fixed % displays in the Price Level Type field

Note: If you are using the QuickBooks Premier version, Per Item may be displayed in the Price Level Type field and you will need to select Fixed % from the drop-down menu.

Fixed percentage price levels allow you to increase or decrease prices of all items for a particular customer or job by a fixed percentage. In this example, you will use a fixed percentage price level to offer James Wilson a 10% discount on all products and services you sell.

Quick Tip. Per item price levels allow you to set the exact dollar amount for items associated with different customers and jobs. For example, you may lower the price of one of your items for a preferred customer, but charge a standard rate for all other customers. For fixed priced items, you will need to enter the price in the Custom Price column or choose one or more items from the list and then adjust the selected prices in bulk. Per item price levels are based on currency, while fixed percentage price levels are not. The Per Item price level is only available if you are using the QuickBooks Premier version or higher.

6. Verify that decrease is selected from the This price level will drop-down menu

7. Type **10%** in the item prices by field

This indicates that the price for all products and services set to this price level should be decreased by 10%.

8. Select   from the Round up to the nearest drop-down menu

This will round up all prices to the nearest penny.

9. Click   OK

The Price Level List displays the new price level:

10. Close the Price Level List window

To associate the Dental Office Discount price level with James Wilson's Dental Office job,

11. Click   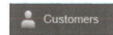   on the Icon Bar

The Customer Center opens with James Wilson DDS selected in the Customers & Jobs list:

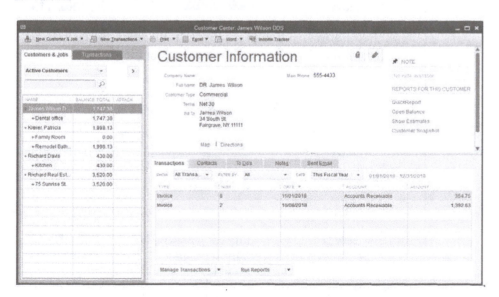

12. Select   Dental office   in the Customers & Jobs list

13. Click in the Job Information area

The Edit Job window opens with the Address Info tab displayed.

14. Select

The Payment Settings tab displays:

15. Select   Dental Office   from the Price Level drop-down
                    Discount   menu

16. Click to return to the Customer Center

You can now use this price level on all sales forms associated with the James Wilson DDS Dental office job to adjust the price of products and services sold for this job.

To use this price level on an invoice,

17. Click  on the Customer Center toolbar

A drop-down menu displays.

18. Select   Invoices   from the drop-down menu

19. Select   James Wilson DDS :   from the Customer:Job drop-down
                    Dental office   menu (if necessary)

20. Press

QuickBooks populates the invoice with information about this customer:

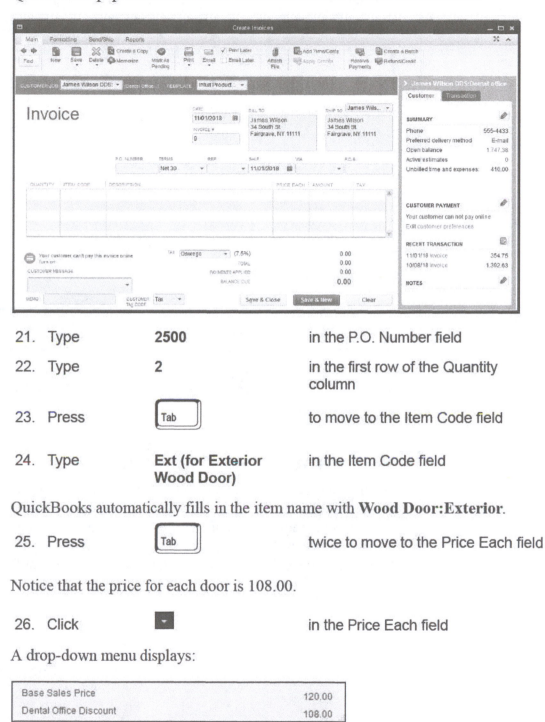

21.	Type	**2500**	in the P.O. Number field
22.	Type	**2**	in the first row of the Quantity column

23.	Press		to move to the Item Code field

24.	Type	**Ext (for Exterior Wood Door)**	in the Item Code field

QuickBooks automatically fills in the item name with **Wood Door:Exterior**.

25.	Press	Tab	twice to move to the Price Each field

Notice that the price for each door is 108.00.

26.	Click	▼	in the Price Each field

A drop-down menu displays:

Base Sales Price	120.00
Dental Office Discount	108.00

The drop-down menu shows that the Base Sales Price of this item is 120.00 and the price with the Dental Office Discount is 108.00. Based on the customer and job selection, QuickBooks automatically applied a 10% discount to the sale of this item.

27.	Press	Tab	

Your Create Invoices should resemble the figure below:

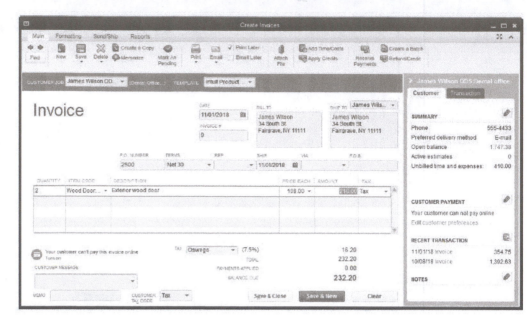

28. Click to record the invoice

29. Click on the Icon Bar

You return to the Home page.

Creating Sales Receipts

When you receive full payment at the time of a sale, you can use a sales receipt, rather than an invoice, to record the sale. Sales receipts can include payments by cash, check, credit card/debit card, e-check, and more. These sales do not require an invoice because you have already received payment. Sales receipts allow you to track each sale, calculate any sales tax, and print a receipt for the sale.

To create a sales receipt,

1. Click in the Customers area of the Home page

The Enter Sales Receipts window opens:

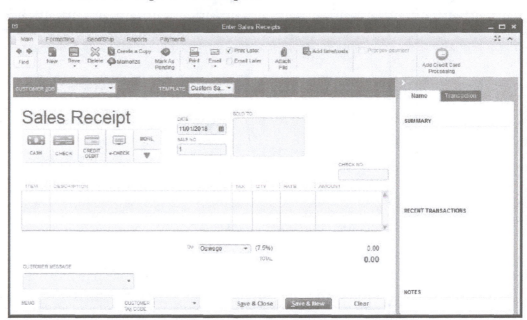

The Enter Sales Receipts window allows you to enter information for a sale with immediate payment. By using this window, you can enter a sale for a customer without having to enter any additional information for that customer.

2. Click   in the Sold To field

3. Type   **Fred Joseph**   in the Sold To field

Caution. *Be sure to enter the name Fred Joseph in the Sold To field; not the Customer: Job field, so that you do not need to use the Quick Add feature.*

4. Click   below the Sales Receipts heading

5. Type   **201**   in the Check No. field

6. Type   **Ext (for Exterior)**   in the first row of the Item column

7. Press   Tab

QuickBooks automatically fills in the field with Wood Door:Exterior.

8. Type   **1**   in the Qty field

Your window should resemble the figure below:

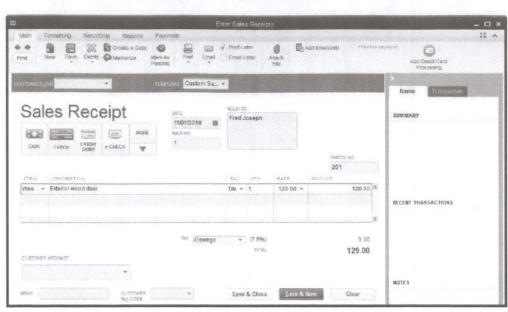

9. Click to record the cash sale and return to the Home page

 Quick Tip. *If you wanted to print the sales receipt for a customer, you would click the print icon on the toolbar.*

The Inventory Asset account tracks the current value of your inventory. Each time you create an inventory part item, QuickBooks preselects Inventory Asset as the asset account for the new item. Therefore, when you sell inventory items, the Inventory Asset account is automatically updated.

To see how the sale of the exterior wood door affected your Inventory Asset account, you can open the Chart of Accounts.

10. Click in the Company area of the Home page

The Chart of Accounts opens:

11. Double-click   Inventory Asset

The Inventory Asset account register opens:

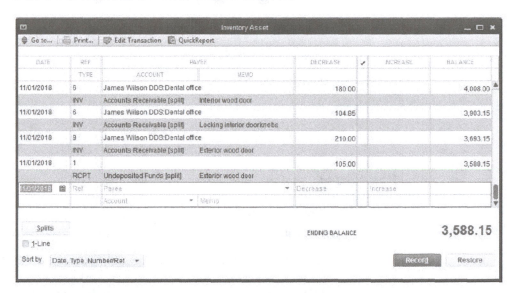

QuickBooks automatically updates the Inventory Asset account to account for the inventory item sold.

12. Close the Inventory Asset account register and the Chart of Accounts

You return to the Home page.

Review

In this lesson, you have learned how to:

☑ Create product invoices

☑ Apply credit to invoices

☑ Email invoices

☑ Set price levels

☑ Create sales receipts

Practice:

1. Create a credit memo for the 75 Sunrise St. job for Richard Real Estate for one locking interior doorknob and retain it as an available credit.

2. Create a product invoice for the 75 Sunrise St. job for Richard Real Estate for two exterior wood doors and two standard doorknobs. Select UPS as the shipping method and enter the customer message "We appreciate your prompt payment".

3. Apply the credit for the locking interior doorknob and process the invoice.

4. Create a cash sales receipt for Janet R. Titan for one non-inventory item, fixture plumbing.

5. Close all open windows and close the company file.

Invoicing for Services

In this lesson, you will learn how to:

- ❑ Set up a service item
- ❑ Change the invoice format
- ❑ Create a service invoice
- ❑ Edit an invoice
- ❑ Void an invoice
- ❑ Delete an invoice
- ❑ Enter statement charges
- ❑ Create billing statements

Concept

Typically, service businesses differ significantly from product businesses both in the way they are organized and in the way they conduct business. In QuickBooks, however, selling a service is very similar to selling a product: you can send an invoice when a service is provided, or you can send a billing statement for a service provided over a period of time.

Invoicing for a service simply requires you to set up a service item in the Item List. When the service item is used on an invoice, QuickBooks automatically enters the service item description and rate. QuickBooks also makes it easy to display and use the service format invoice, which provides you with the fields typically used to sell a service.

Billing statements list the charges a customer has accumulated over a period of time. You can enter the charges when they occur, then send a statement at your regular billing time.

Scenario

In this lesson, you will add a new service item to your Item List. After you change between the various predefined invoice formats, you will create a service invoice for the new service item. You will then edit an invoice, void an invoice, and delete an invoice. Next, you will enter statement charges that reflect ongoing repairs and maintenance for a customer you bill monthly. Finally, you will create and print the billing statement for the ongoing repairs and maintenance.

Practice Files: B18_Invoicing_for_Services.qbw

Setting Up a Service Item

Before you can invoice a customer for performing a service, you must create a service item in the Item List. A service item includes all the information QuickBooks needs to complete a Service invoice, including service description and rate.

In this exercise, you will create a service item and subitem for Canalside Corp. services.

Note: For this lesson, be sure to change your computer's date to 11/1/2018 before opening the QuickBooks file, as recommended in the Before You Get Started lesson. This will ensure that the dates you see on your screen match the dates in this lesson.

To set up a service item,

1. Open	B18_Invoicing_for Services.qbw	using the method described in Before You Get Started

The QuickBooks Login dialog box displays:

This dialog box informs you that you must login as a QuickBooks Administrator in order to open the company file.

2. Type	**Canalside2**	in the Password field

Note: Passwords are case-sensitive.

3. Click

QuickBooks opens the file.

4. Click to close the Reminders window

QuickBooks displays the Home page:

To open the Item List,

5. Click   **Items & Services**   in the Company area of the Home page

The Item List opens:

Note: You may resize and move the Item List window as necessary.

The Item List is used to record information about the products and services you buy and sell and for items that perform calculations, such as discounts and sales tax.

6. Click   **Item ▼**   at the bottom of the window

A drop-down menu displays.

7. Select   **New**   from the drop-down menu

The New Item window opens:

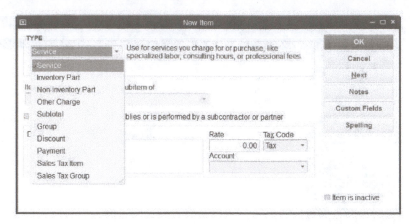

When the New Item window opens, a drop-down menu displays and the Service selection appears in the Type field.

8.	Press	Tab	to accept the default selection of Service
9.	Type	**Repair**	in the Item Name/Number field
10.	Type	**Repair Labor**	in the Description field
11.	Select	Non	from the Tax Code drop-down menu

This selection indicates that this is a non-taxable service.

12.	Press	Tab	to move to the Account field

This field allows you to link the item to an account, so that when the item is used on a form, it will post an entry to that account.

13.	Type	**Labor**	
14.	Press	Tab	to select the Construction:Labor account

The New Item window should resemble the figure below:

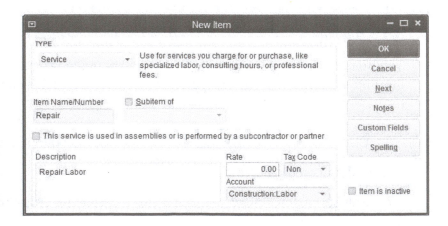

15. Click OK

QuickBooks creates the new service item and adds it to the Item List:

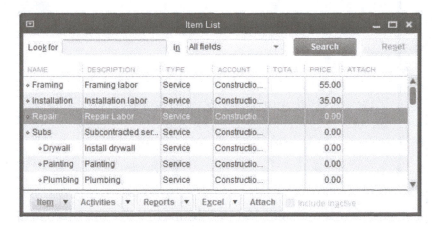

To add a Plumbing subitem to Repair,

16. Click   Item ▼   at the bottom of the window

A drop-down menu displays.

17. Select   New   from the drop-down menu

QuickBooks displays the New Item window with Service in the Type field.

18. Press   Tab   to move to the Item Name/Number field

19. Type   **Plumbing**   in the Item Name/Number field

20. Select   the Subitem of check box

21. Type   **Repair**   in the Subitem of field

22. Type   **Plumbing repairs and maintenance**   in the Description field

23. Press   Tab   to move to the Rate field

24. Type   **55**   in the Rate field

25. Select   Non   from the Tax Code drop-down menu

26. Press   Tab   to move to the Account field

27. Type   **Labor**

28. Press   Tab   to select the Construction:Labor account

The New Item window should resemble the figure below:

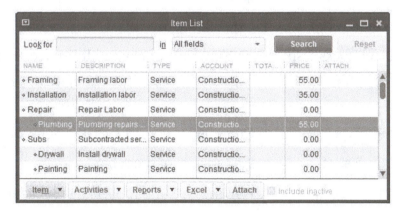

Note: If you are using the QuickBooks Premier version, the New Item window will also include a Unit of Measure option.

29. Click   OK

QuickBooks updates the Item List:

Notice that the Plumbing subitem is indented under the Repair item.

Note: You may need to scroll up the list to view the Repair item.

30. Close the Item List

Changing the Invoice Format

QuickBooks provides various preset formats for your sales forms. The three main formats are Product, Service, and Professional invoices. Product invoices allow you to enter all information necessary to sell a product out of inventory. Although you can create invoices for services using the Product format, the Service and Professional formats have been tailored to the different types of data required for invoicing services. QuickBooks allows you to easily switch between the three Intuit invoice templates or your own custom templates; simply select the template directly on the invoice form.

Service Format

Although Service format invoices are used for billing customers for time spent performing a certain task, they can also be used to handle products. For example, a garage or service station charges for labor time and for specific parts needed for the repairs.

To view a service invoice,

◆ Click in the Customers area of the Home page

The Create Invoices window opens, displaying the Intuit Service Invoice:

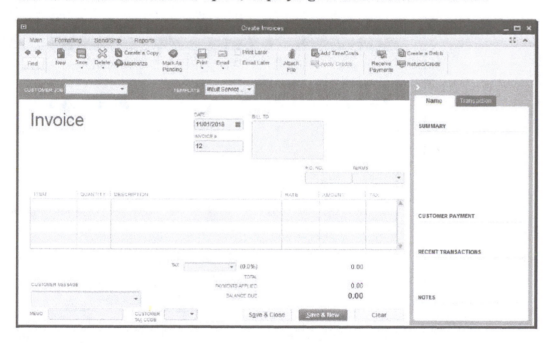

Note: If your window displays the Intuit Product Invoice, select the Intuit Service Invoice from the Template drop-down menu.

For a service invoice, shipping-related fields that display in the product invoice are eliminated.

Professional Format

The Professional format is most often used for services in which extra room is required for a description of services rendered. For example, a consultant or lawyer providing varying services in different situations would need to thoroughly describe each item on the invoice.

To view a professional invoice,

1. Click next to the Template field in the Create Invoices window

A drop-down menu displays:

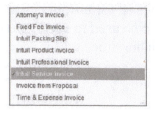

Note: Depending on the version of QuickBooks you are using, your drop-down menu may display different invoices.

2. Select   Intuit Professional   from the drop-down menu
                      Invoice

The invoice on your screen should resemble the figure below:

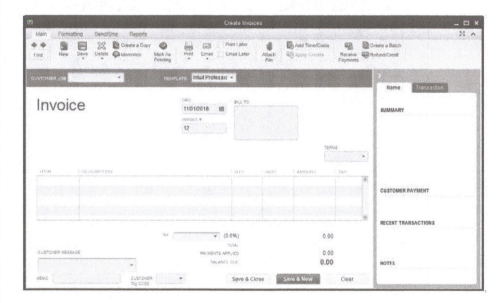

Notice that the Professional invoice looks similar to the Service invoice.

Creating a Service Invoice

Creating a Service invoice is similar to creating a Product invoice. In this exercise, you will create an invoice for kitchen plumbing repair work that was completed for Richard Davis.

To create a service invoice,

1. Select   Intuit Service   from the Template drop-down menu
                      Invoice

The Create Invoices window displays the Intuit Service Invoice.

2. Select   **Richard Davis**   from the Customer:Job drop-down menu

3. Type   **100**   in the P.O. No. field

4. Press   [Tab]   twice to move to the Item field

5. Select   Repair:Plumbing   from the Item drop-down menu

When you create invoices, you use items from the Item List. Items provide a quick means of data entry, but more importantly, they handle the behind-the-scenes accounting.

6. Press   [Tab]   to move to the Quantity field

7. Type   **4**   for the number of hours

8. Press   [Tab]   to accept the quantity

The Amount field is updated to reflect the total of the quantity entered multiplied by the rate charged for the service. Your invoice should resemble the figure below:

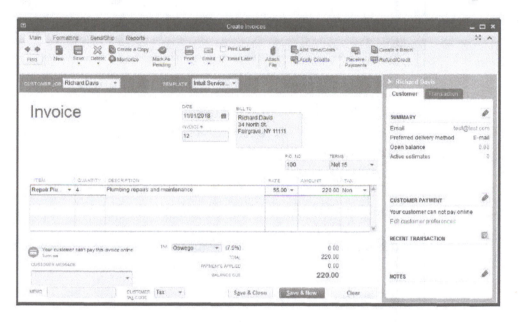

9. Click   [Save & Close]   to record the invoice

You return to the Home page.

Editing an Invoice

If you made a mistake on an invoice, you can correct the mistake by editing the invoice. For example, you may have billed an incorrect quantity to a customer or accidentally omitted a charge for a service or product.

In this exercise, you will edit an invoice to James Wilson to correct the quantity of hours he was billed. You will use the Customer Center to locate the invoice.

1. Click   [Customers]   on the Icon bar

Quick Tip. *If you need to edit an invoice for which you do not know the customer's name, you can select Edit : Search from the menu bar and search by invoice number, amount, or date. You can also use the search field in the Icon Bar.*

The Customer Center opens with the customer James Wilson selected:

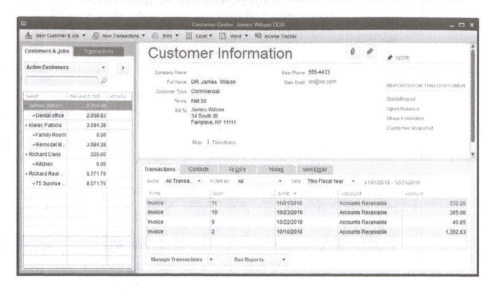

Notice that James Wilson has four invoices listed.

Note: If you did not change your computer's date as recommended in the Before You Get Started lesson, select All from This Fiscal Year on the Transactions tab in the Customer Information area.

2. Double-click   Invoice 10   in the list of invoices

The Create Invoices window opens displaying the invoice for James Wilson:

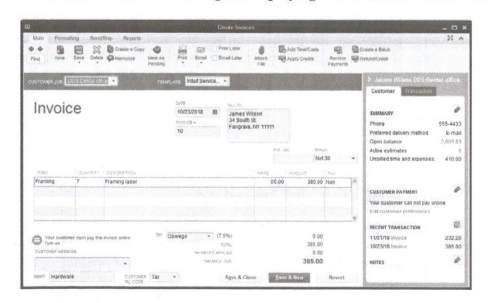

3. Type   **6**   to replace 7 in the Quantity field

4. Press   to accept the new quantity

The Amount field is updated to reflect the new total:

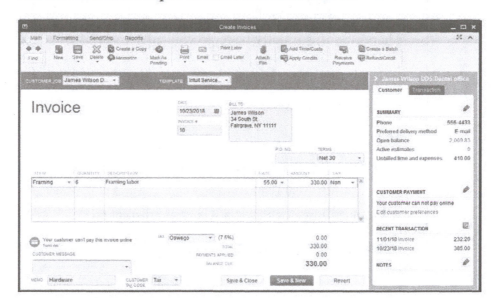

5. Click  to record the invoice

A Recording Transaction dialog box displays informing you that you have changed the transaction:

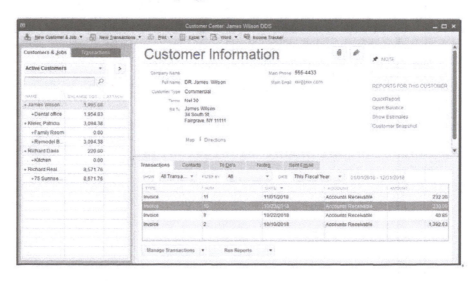

6. Click to record changes to the transaction

The Customer Center displays:

Notice the updated total for Invoice 10.

Voiding an Invoice

You should always keep a record of all transactions, including invoice numbers. Therefore, it is usually better to void an invoice, than delete it.

Caution. *If you have already received payment for an invoice, you will not be able to void the invoice. Instead, you should issue a credit memo or refund in order to adjust the transaction.*

To void an invoice,

1. Select Kleier, Patricia on the Customers & Jobs tab of the Customer Center

All transactions for Patricia Kleier are displayed:

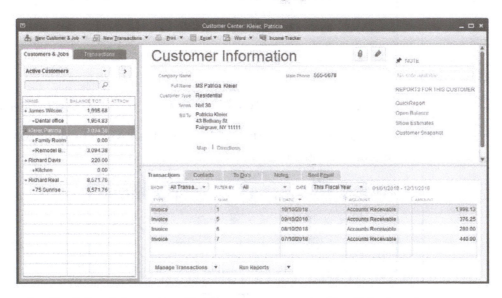

2. Double-click Invoice 5 in the list of invoices

The Create Invoices window opens displaying the invoice for Patricia Kleier:

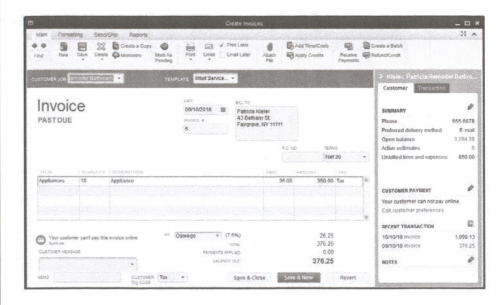

3. Click in the toolbar of the Create Invoices window

A drop-down menu displays allowing you to choose whether to delete or void the invoice:

Delete

Void

4. Select   Void   from the drop-down menu

The invoice amounts are changed to zeros and the memo in the invoice is marked as VOID:

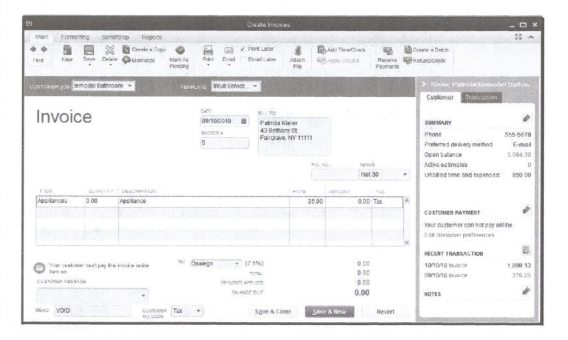

5. Click to record the invoice

A Recording Transaction dialog box displays informing you that you have changed the transaction:

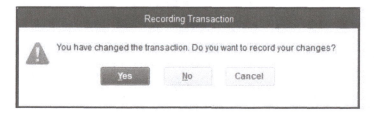

6. Click to record changes to the transaction

The Customer Center displays:

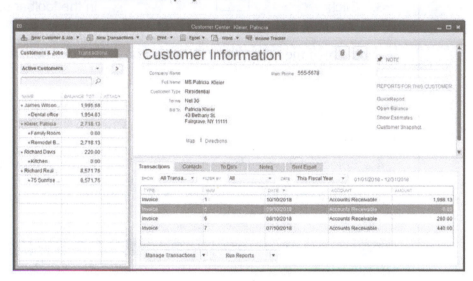

Notice the amount for Invoice 5 is now $0.00.

Deleting an Invoice

You should only delete an invoice if you have not printed it, saved it, or sent it to the customer.

Caution. *If you delete an invoice with a payment applied to it, the payment remains in your records, the money remains in your bank account, and a credit balance is created for the customer, but the payment is no longer linked to an invoice.*

To delete an invoice,

1. Select **Richard Real Estate** on the Customers & Jobs tab of the Customer Center

All transactions for Richard Real Estate are displayed:

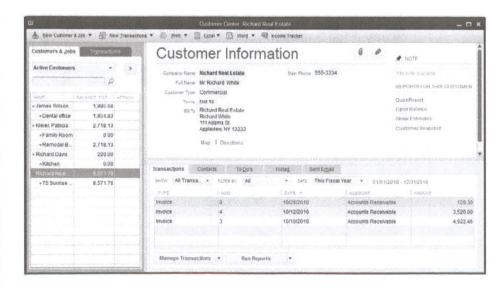

2. Double-click   Invoice 8   in the list of invoices

The Create Invoices window opens displaying the invoice for Richard Real Estate:

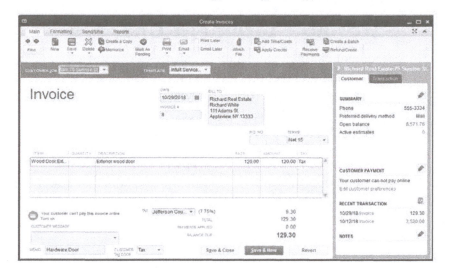

3. Click   in the toolbar of the Create Invoices window

A Delete Transaction dialog box displays:

4. Click   OK   to delete the invoice

5. Click   Save & Close   in the Create Invoices window

You return to the Customer Center:

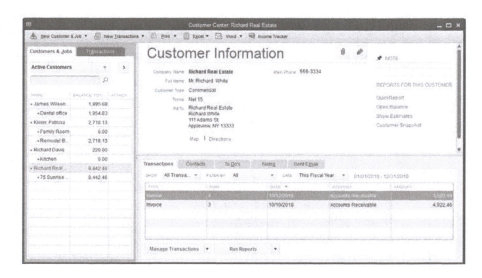

Notice Invoice 8 no longer displays in the list of invoices.

6. Close the Customer Center to return to the Home page.

Entering Statement Charges

Statement charges are useful to businesses that want to accumulate charges from customers before requesting payment. You enter statement charges one by one, as you perform services for customers. This allows you to track the amount your customers owe you (accounts receivable) and then bill periodically for all services performed in a set period of time.

Canalside Corp. does ongoing repairs and maintenance for Richard Real Estate's apartment complex on 75 Sunrise St. and bills them on a monthly basis.

To enter a statement charge for Richard Real Estate's apartment complex,

1. Click in the Customers area of the Home page

The Accounts Receivable register for James Wilson DDS opens:

2. Select Richard Real Estate: 75 Sunrise St. from the Customer : Job drop-down menu

The register changes to reflect the Richard Real Estate account.

3. Press `Tab` to move to the Item field

4. Select **Repair** from the Item drop-down menu

5. Press `Tab` to move to the Qty field

6. Type **6** (the number of hours)

7. Press 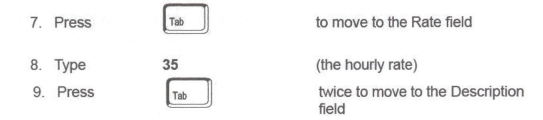   to move to the Rate field

8. Type   **35**   (the hourly rate)

9. Press   twice to move to the Description field

QuickBooks highlights Repair Labor. You will replace this text with a more detailed description.

10. Type   **Repaired broken window, Unit 2B**

11. Click   Record   to record the statement charge

Your register should resemble the figure below:

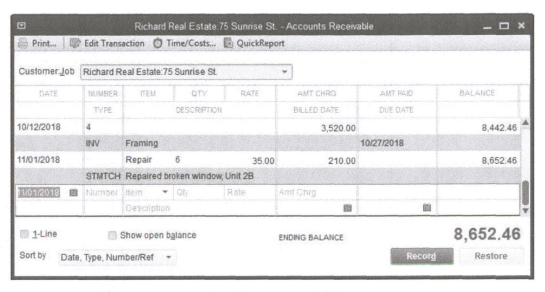

12. Close the Richard Real Estate: 75 Sunrise St. Accounts Receivable register to return to the Home page.

Creating Billing Statements

When you enter statement charges, you are accumulating charges that will eventually be included on a billing statement. Billing statements enable a customer to view their account activity history, including charges, payments, and balances for a specified time period.

When you send a billing statement to a customer, QuickBooks does the following:

- Enters the statement date in the Billed field of the customer register for each item on the statement.

- Calculates when the payment is due based on the terms for that customer, and fills in the Due field of the customer register with the appropriate due date.

When you are ready to bill your customers, you can print the statement on statement forms, company letterhead, or blank paper.

To create a billing statement,

1. Click in the Customers area of the Home page

The Create Statements window opens:

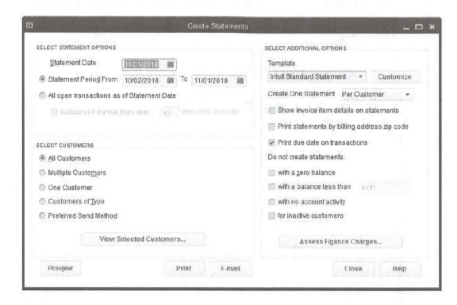

The Create Statements window allows you to select the dates for which you want to print statements, the customers for whom you want to print statements, and additional options, such as printing due dates on transactions or printing statements in order by billing address zip code.

2. Select 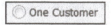 in the Select Customers area

A blank field appears with a drop-down menu allowing you to select the customer and job for whom you want to print statements.

3. Select   **Richard Real Estate:**   from the drop-down menu
                     75 Sunrise St.

Note: If you did not change your computer's date as recommended in the Before You Get Started lesson, type 12/1/2018 in the Statement Date field and select the All Open Transactions as of Statement Date option.

To view the statement on-screen before you print it,

4. Click at the bottom of the window

The Print Preview window opens:

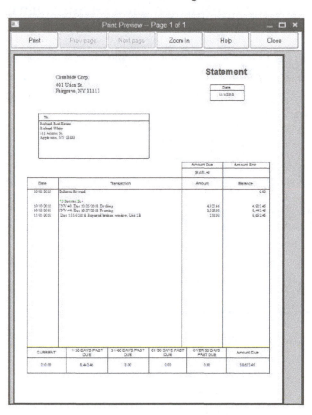

You can zoom in to take a closer look at the statement by moving the magnifying tool and clicking over the statement image.

When you are through viewing the statement,

5. Click | Close | to return to the Create Statements window

6. Click | Print | in the Create Statements window

The Print Statement(s) window opens:

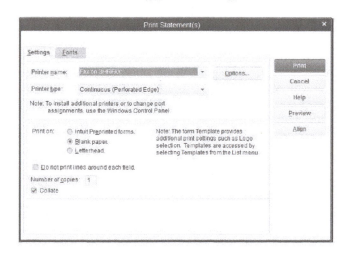

This window allows you to specify print settings, such as the material to print on and the number of copies to print. For this exercise, you will accept the default selections.

Note: You must have a printer driver and printer installed on your computer or network in order to print statements. If your computer is not set up to print, click Cancel to close the Print Statement(s) window and then close the Create Statements window.

7. Click   Print

The following message displays asking if each statement printed correctly:

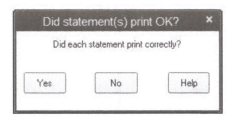

Assume the statement printed correctly.

8. Click   Yes

9. Click   Close   to close the Create Statements window

You return to the Home page.

Review

In this lesson, you have learned how to:

☑ Set up a service item

☑ Change the invoice format

☑ Create a service invoice

☑ Edit an invoice

☑ Void an invoice

☑ Delete an invoice

☑ Enter statement charges

☑ Create billing statements

Practice:

1. Create a service item using the data below:

Item Name:	Electrical
Subitem of:	Repair
Description:	Electrical repair
Rate:	$50.00
Tax Code	Not taxable
Account:	Construction: Labor

2. Open the Create Invoices window and change the invoice format to the Intuit Product Invoice and the Intuit Professional Invoice.

3. Create a Service invoice for Kleier, Patricia : Family Room; P.O. number 101; for 4 hours of electrical repair work.

4. Update the number of hours spent on installation in Invoice 6 for Patricia Kleier to 10 hours.

5. Void Invoice 12 for Richard Davis. *(Hint: Deselect the Email Later check box to save and close the Create Invoices window)*

6. Delete Invoice 6 for Patricia Kleier.

7. Create a statement charge to Richard Real Estate: 75 Sunrise St. for 2.5 hours of electrical repair work in Unit 3C.

8. Preview the billing statement for Patricia Kleier's family room.

9. Close the company file.

Notes:

Processing Payments

In this lesson, you will learn how to:

- ❑ Display the Open Invoices report
- ❑ Use the Income Tracker
- ❑ Receive payments for invoices
- ❑ Make deposits
- ❑ Handle bounced checks

Concept

Payments on invoices can be processed as soon as a payment is received. When a payment is received, QuickBooks allows you to process the payment immediately with easy-to-use forms.

After payments are received from invoices or cash sales, you can deposit them into your bank account.

Scenario

In this lesson, you have received payment from a customer towards one of their invoices. First, you will display the Open Invoices report to see how many invoices are still unpaid. You will then use the Income Tracker to view overdue invoices. Next, you will apply the payment received toward an open invoice and deposit it into the company's checking account. And finally, you will learn how to handle a bounced check received from a customer due to insufficient funds.

Practice Files: B18_Processing_Payments.qbw

Displaying the Open Invoices Report

If your customers don't pay you in full at the time you provide them with a service or product, you need to track how much they owe you. Using an invoice helps you keep track of what customers owe you. And, you can easily view all invoices for which you have not received payment using the Open Invoices Report.

Note: For this lesson, change your computer's date to 11/1/2018 before opening the QuickBooks file, as recommended in the Before You Get Started lesson. This will ensure that the dates you see on your screen match the dates in this lesson.

To display the Open Invoices report,

1.	Open	B18_Processing Payments.qbw	using the method described in Before You Get Started

The QuickBooks Login dialog box displays:

This dialog box informs you that you must login as a QuickBooks Administrator in order to open the company file.

2.	Type	**Canalside2**	in the Password field

Note: Passwords are case-sensitive.

3.	Click	

QuickBooks opens the file.

4.	Click		to close the Reminders window

QuickBooks displays the Home page:

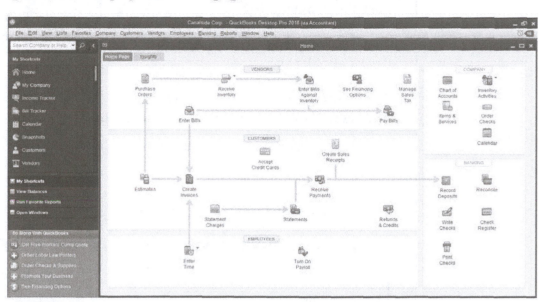

5. Select   Reports : Customers   from the menu bar
                     & Receivables :
                     Open Invoices

The Open Invoices report displays:

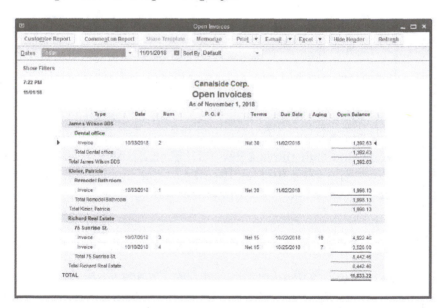

Note: If you did not change your computer's date as recommended in the Before You Get Started lesson, you will need to select All from the Dates drop-down menu in order to view all open invoices.

The Open Invoices report lists unpaid invoices and statement charges as of the current date, grouped and subtotaled by customer and job. Notice there is one open invoice for the James Wilson Dental Office job, one open invoice for Patricia Kleier's bathroom remodel job, and two open invoices for the Richard Real Estate 75 Sunrise St. job.

To view detailed information for any transaction in this report, you simply double-click the transaction.

6. Position   the mouse pointer   over the number 4 in the Num column

The mouse pointer changes to a magnifying glass with the letter Z 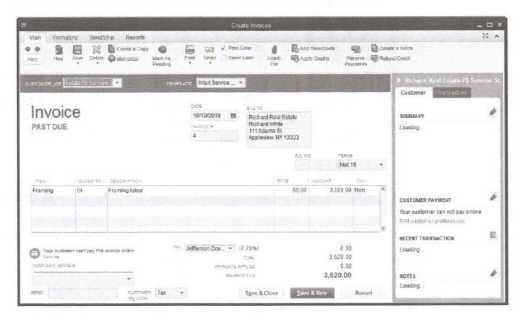 for Zoom. The zoom feature allows you to quickly look at the specifics of a transaction.

7. Double-click   the left mouse button   to zoom in on Invoice 4 for the Richard Real Estate 75 Sunrise St. job

The Create Invoice window opens displaying Invoice 4:

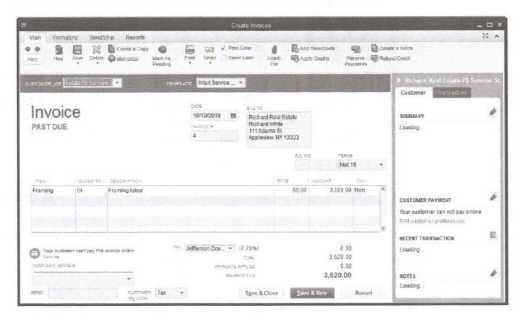

QuickBooks displays a PAST DUE stamp on invoices that are past due. This allows you to easily identify all past due invoices, as well as remind customers they have exceeded their payment terms.

Note: If you did not change your computer's date as recommended in the Before You Get Started lesson, the PAST DUE stamp will not display.

Quick Tip. To display the Past Due Stamp on printed or emailed invoices, click Formatting on the toolbar and select Manage Templates on the Formatting toolbar. In the Manage Templates window, click OK, and then select the Print Past Due Stamp check box in the Basic Customization window.

8. Close the Create Invoices window to return to the Open Invoices report

9. Close the Open Invoices report to return to the Home page

Note: If a dialog box displays informing you that you have modified settings for this report and asks if you want to memorize the report, select the Do not display this message in the future check box and click the No button.

Using the Income Tracker

Another method to quickly display all invoices for which you have not received payment is to use the Income Tracker. The Income Tracker allows you to view all of your income-producing transactions in one location, including overdue invoices, so you can easily manage collecting payments from your customers.

Note: When you set up a company file, only the QuickBooks Administrator has access to the Income Tracker. If another user needs access, the Administrator must edit that user's particular role to include full access to the Income Tracker.

To view overdue invoices using the Income Tracker:

1. Select   Customers :   from the menu bar
    Income Tracker

Quick Tip. You can also click the Income Tracker shortcut in the Icon bar to open the Income Tracker.

The Income Tracker opens:

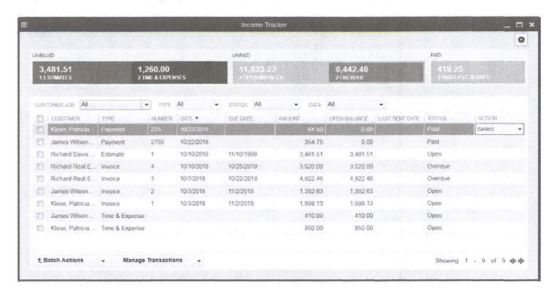

Note: If you did not change your computer's date as recommended in the Before You Get Started lesson, your window will be slightly different.

When you open the Income Tracker, it displays all unbilled items (estimates, sales orders, and time and expenses), all unpaid sales (open and overdue invoices), and all paid sales (payments and sales receipts). The totals for all unbilled, unpaid, and paid sales are displayed at the top of the window in colored blocks.

Each row displays an individual transaction and the column at the end of the row allows you to perform actions on the transaction.

2. Click   1   in the Number column for the
    Richard Davis estimate

The estimate for Richard Davis is selected.

3. Click   the drop-down arrow   in the Action column for the selected estimate

Options to convert the estimate to an invoice, mark it as inactive, print the row, and email the row display.

4. Click   4   in the Number column for the Richard Real Estate invoice

Invoice 4 for Richard Real Estate is selected.

5. Click   the drop-down arrow   in the Action column for the selected invoice

Options for receiving payment for the invoice, printing the invoice, and emailing the invoice display.

6. Click

> **8,442.46**
> 2 OVERDUE

The Income Tracker is updated to display only the two overdue invoices:

Quick Tip. *You can use the Customer:Job, Type, Status, and Date drop-down arrows to filter the transactions even further.*

From here, you can see that the two open invoices for the Richard Real Estate 75 Sunrise St. job are overdue. The Aging column displays exactly how many days each invoice is overdue.

7. Close the Income Tracker to return to the Home page

Receiving Payments for Invoices

After you send out invoices, your customers should send you payment for the goods or services they purchased. You can then apply these payments to the open invoices.

To receive payments,

1. Click in the Customers area of the Home page

The Receive Payments window opens:

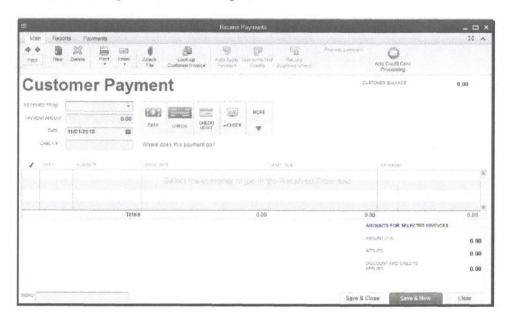

The Receive Payments window allows you to match payments with open invoices.

2. Select   Richard Real Estate: from the Received From drop-down
             75 Sunrise St.   menu

QuickBooks fills out the form with the outstanding invoices for the Richard Real Estate: 75 Sunrise St. job:

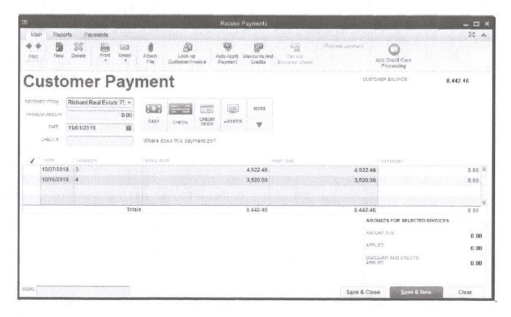

3. Type   **7520**   in the Payment Amount field (the payment you received from Richard Real Estate)

4. Click

5. Type   **123**   in the Check # field

Your Receive Payments window should resemble the figure below:

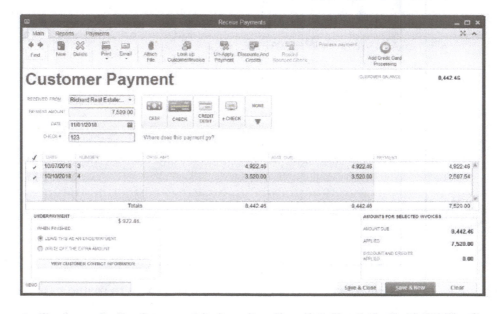

A check mark displays next to Invoices 3 and 4. By default, QuickBooks applies payment to the oldest invoice first, then to the next oldest, and so on.

Quick Tip. If QuickBooks does not automatically apply payments to invoices, check your preferences by selecting Edit : Preferences from the menu bar. When the Preferences window opens, select the Payments preference, click the Company Preferences tab, and select the Automatically apply payments check box.

In this exercise, you want to pay the most recent invoice first. To distribute the payment to different invoices,

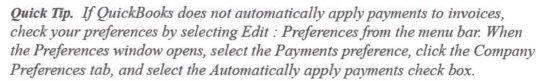

6. Click   in the Receive Payments window toolbar

QuickBooks removes the check marks from the left of Invoices 3 and 4.

7. Click   in the column   to the left of invoice 4

QuickBooks displays the amount to be applied to the invoice (3520.00) in the Payment column.

8. Click   in the column   to the left of invoice 3

The remaining amount to be applied to the invoice (4000.00) displays in the Payment column. When the undistributed amount is less than amount due, QuickBooks applies the entire amount to the invoice, leaving a balance due on the invoice.

9. Verify the Leave this as an underpayment option is selected in the Underpayment section at the bottom of the window to indicate that $922.46 is still due on the invoice

Your Receive Payments window should resemble the figure below:

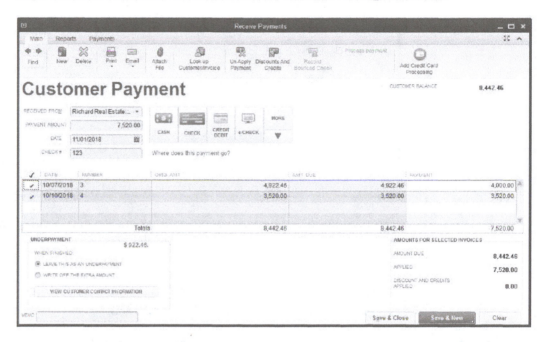

10. Click   [Save & Close]   to process the payment and return to the Home page

The Open Invoices report should no longer display Invoice 4 for the Richard Real Estate 75 Sunrise St. job and should display a balance of $922.46 still due on Invoice 3.

To view the Open Invoices report,

11. Select   Reports : Customers   from the menu bar
                      & Receivables :
                      Open Invoices

The Open Invoices report opens:

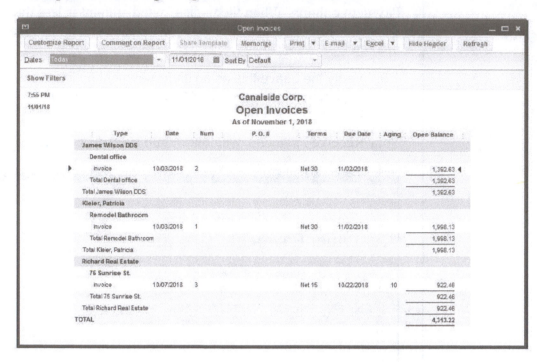

Note: If you did not change your computer's date as recommended in the Before You Get Started lesson, select All from the Dates drop-down menu to view all open invoices.

Notice that Invoice 3 is now the only open invoice for the Richard Real Estate 75 Sunrise St. job and there is a balance of $922.46.

Quick Tip. *The Open Invoices report allows you to determine if there are any payments or credits that have not been applied to an invoice. When payments or credits are not applied to an invoice, the Open Invoices report displays the invoice and payment or credit as open, although the customer's balance may be zero.*

You can now view Invoice 4 again to see that it has been paid. After an invoice has been paid, it is marked with a PAID stamp.

To view the paid invoice for the Richard Real Estate 75 Sunrise St. job,

12. Position   the mouse pointer   over the number 3 in the Num column

The mouse pointer changes to a magnifying glass with the letter Z 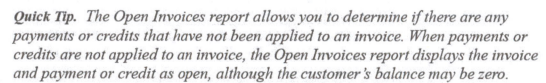 for Zoom.

13. Double-click   the left mouse button   to zoom in on Invoice 3

Invoice 3 displays in the Create Invoices window with a PAST DUE stamp:

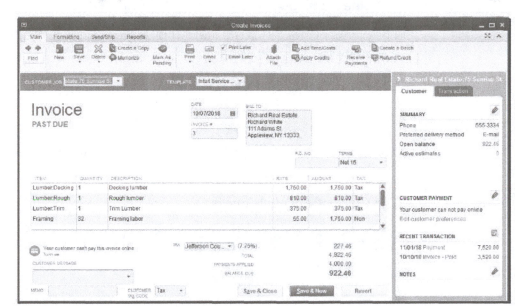

14. Click (the Next button) in the top left corner of the window until 4 displays in the Invoice # field

Invoice 4 for the Richard Real Estate 75 Sunrise St. job displays:

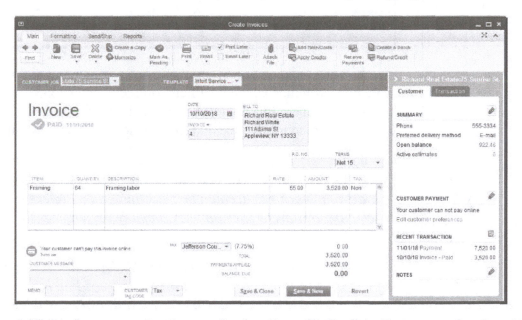

A PAID stamp now displays on the invoice with the date that was entered on the Receive Payments form. By including the date with the stamp, QuickBooks allows you to quickly determine when a payment was received.

Quick Tip. *You can check the payment history for an invoice by pressing the Ctrl and H keys simultaneously. QuickBooks will display a Transaction History - Invoice window listing the payment history. You can also click the Transaction tab in the History pane of the Create Invoices window.*

15. Close the Create Invoices window and the Open Invoices report to return to the Home page

The payments for $3520.00 and $4000.00 are also reflected in the Chart of Accounts.

To view the updates in the Chart of Accounts,

16. Click   in the Company area of the Home page

The Chart of Accounts opens:

QuickBooks reduces the Accounts Receivable account and increases the Undeposited Funds account. When you record a customer payment, QuickBooks holds the payment in a default account called Undeposited Funds until you deposit it in a bank account. Notice that the balance in the Undeposited Funds account is 7,520.00.

Quick Tip. *You can choose whether or not to use the Undeposited Funds account as a default deposit to account by selecting Edit : Preferences and selecting or deselecting this preference on the Company Preferences tab under the Payments category.*

Caution. *All payments are added to the Undeposited Funds account until they are deposited. A growing balance in the Undeposited Funds account commonly occurs when you receive a payment, enter it correctly for a customer, but then you look in your check register and do not see the payment you just recorded. Because you do not see the payment, it is a common mistake to re-enter the payment and post it to an Income account. The way to avoid this mistake is to always make a deposit after receiving a payment from a customer following the steps in the next section - Making Deposits. This will automatically move the funds from the Undeposited Funds account to the appropriate deposit account.*

17. Close the Chart of Accounts to return to the Home page

Making Deposits

After you have received payment on invoices and cash sales, you can deposit the payments into your bank account.

To process a deposit,

1. Click in the Banking area of the Home page

Notice a 1 displays on the Record Deposits icon indicating there is one payment to deposit.

The Payments to Deposit window opens:

The Payments to Deposit window allows you to select the payments you want to deposit.

2. Click the payment from Richard Real Estate

QuickBooks places a check mark to the left of the payment to indicate it is selected.

3. Click to record the deposit

Quick Tip. If you are holding a check and do not want to deposit it yet, you can delete the line for that check in the Make Deposits window. The undeposited check will remain in the Undeposited Funds account.

The Make Deposits window opens:

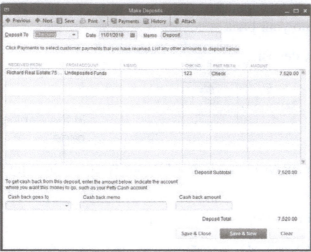

 Quick Tip. *Clicking the Print button at the top of the window allows you to print a deposit summary that lists the payments being deposited. You can also print a preprinted deposit slip that can be submitted to the bank. The preprinted deposit slip also prints a deposit summary for your records.*

You can deposit funds to any of the accounts listed in the Deposit To drop-down menu. In this exercise, you will leave the default selection of Checking.

4. Click to make the deposit to the Checking account and update the Chart of Accounts

In the Chart of Accounts, QuickBooks reduces the Undeposited Funds account and increases the Checking account for the amount of the deposit.

To view the updates,

5. Click in the Company area of the Home page

The Chart of Accounts opens:

The Checking account has increased by $7,520.00 to $14,728.07 and the Undeposited Funds account has decreased by $7,520.00 to $0.

6. Double-click   Checking   in the Name column

The Checking account register opens:

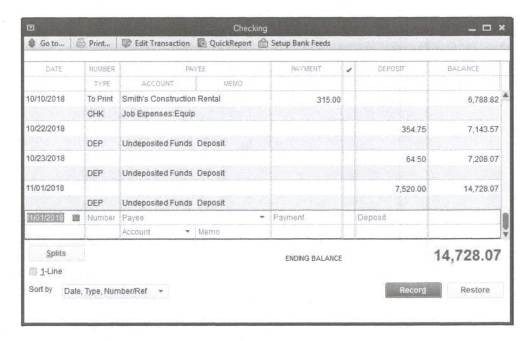

The deposit of $7,520.00 is listed for the current date.

7. Close the Checking account register and Chart of Accounts to return to the Home page.

Handling Bounced Checks

A bounced check is a check that a bank returns because it is not payable due to insufficient funds. When a customer's check is returned for insufficient funds, you will want to record it in QuickBooks in order to balance your books and account for the bounced check amount.

QuickBooks will automatically mark the original invoice as unpaid and create a new invoice for the fee you want to charge your customer. You can then send your customer a statement, or the original invoice, along with the new invoice for the bounced check fee.

In this exercise, a check from James Wilson has been returned due to insufficient funds. You will need to re-invoice the customer for the amount owed, as well as for any fees you were charged by your bank for the returned check.

1. Click   in the Customers area of the Home page

The Receive Payments window opens:

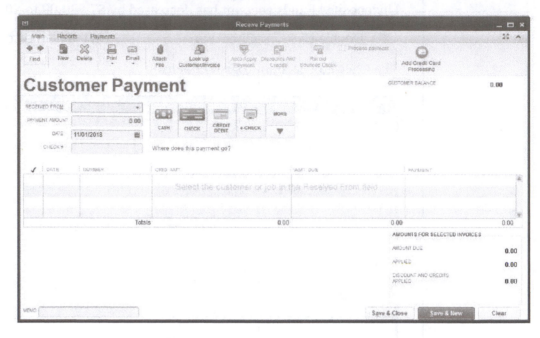

2. Click   ⬅ (the Previous   in the top left corner of the window
                                  button)   until the payment of 354.75 displays

                                                    for the James Wilson DDS:Dental
                                                    Office job

Your Receive Payments window should resemble the figure below:

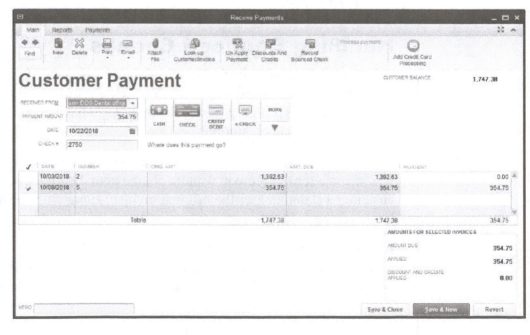

3. Click   in the toolbar

The Manage Bounced Check window opens:

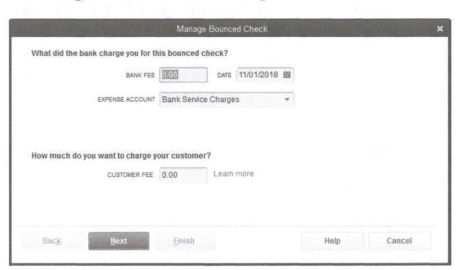

The top portion of this window allows you to specify the amount the bank charged you for the bounced check.

4. Type **25.00** in the Bank Fee field

5. Leave the default date in the Date field

6. Verify that Bank Service Charges is selected from the Expense Account drop-down menu

The lower portion of this window allows you to specify the amount you want to charge the customer for bouncing the check. This amount is typically greater than the amount the bank charged.

7. Type **35.00** in the Customer Fee field

8. Click [Next]

The Bounced Check Summary screen displays:

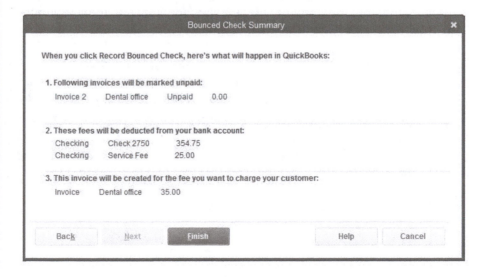

This window informs you that Invoice 2 will be marked as unpaid and that the fee for Check 2750 (354.75), as well as the 25.00 bank service fee, will be deducted from your Checking account. In addition, an invoice for 35.00 will be created for the fee you want to charge the customer.

9. Click to record the bounced check

You return to the Receive Payments window:

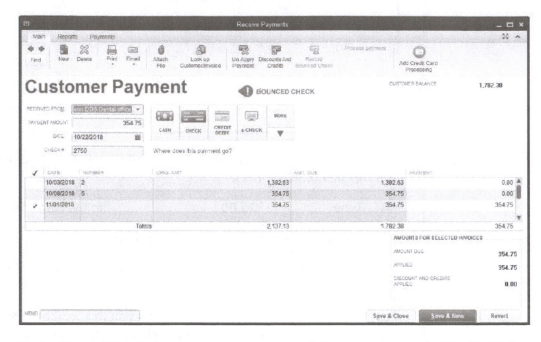

Note: If you did not change your computer's date as recommended in the Before You Get Started lesson, your window will appear slightly different.

A line entry has been created for the bounced check and a BOUNCED CHECK stamp displays on the window. In addition, an invoice was created for the $35.00 bounced check fee you are charging the customer.

10. Click to return to the Home page

Quick Tip. If you receive a bounced check on a sales receipt or when you are making a deposit for the check, you will need to create an Other Charge item named Bounced Check and a second Other Charge item called Bad Check Charge for the service charge you assess customers for bounced checks. You will then use these Other Charge items to re-invoice the customer for the bounced check, as well as any bank fees you want to recover. This will back out the original transaction on your books. The income for the original sale will be recorded when you receive the new customer payment. Refer to the QuickBooks Help for detailed steps.

To view the invoice created for the bounced check charge,

11. Click in the Customers area of the Home page

The Create Invoices window opens:

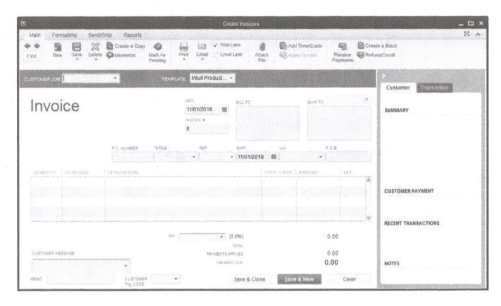

12. Click ⬅ (the Previous button) in the top left corner of the window until Invoice 7 displays

Invoice 7 displays in the Create Invoices window:

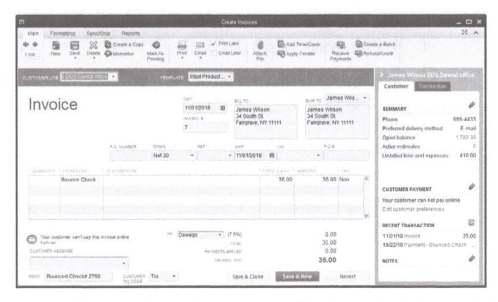

You would now want to send your customer this invoice for the bounced check fee along with the original invoice.

Quick Tip. *QuickBooks includes a bounced check letter you can send to the customer with the invoice when a check has been returned for insufficient funds. To create the letter, select Company : Prepare Letters with Envelopes : Customer Letters from the menu bar and follow the instructions in the Letters and Envelopes wizard for a bounced check letter.*

13. Click to return to the Home page

To view the new checking account balance,

14. Click [Chart of Accounts] in the Company area of the Home page

The Chart of Accounts opens:

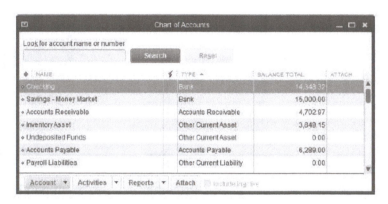

The Checking account has been reduced by $379.75 ($354.75 plus $25.00) to $14,348.32.

15. Double-click Checking in the Name column

The Checking account register opens:

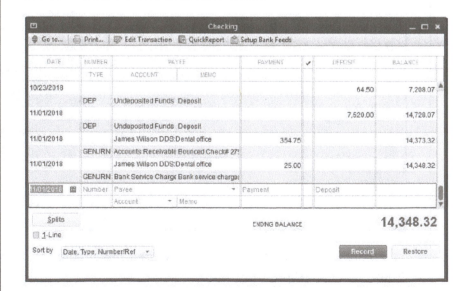

The last two transactions listed are the payment withdrawals for the returned check amount of $354.75 and 25.00 for the returned check bank service charge.

Caution. *The bank charges issued by the bank will appear on the bank statement along with any other bank charges, if applicable. When you reconcile your checking account, be sure to enter the bounced check charge of $25.00 in the Service Charge field and assign it to the appropriate expense account, such as Bank Service Charge.*

16. Close the Checking account register and Chart of Accounts to return to the Home page

When you receive full payment from the customer, as well as payment for the fees you charged the customer for insufficient funds, you should apply the payment to the open invoice.

You will now receive payment from James Wilson for $354.75, the amount of the original invoice, and the $35.00 for the customer charge.

17. Click   in the Customers area of the Home page

The Receive Payments window opens:

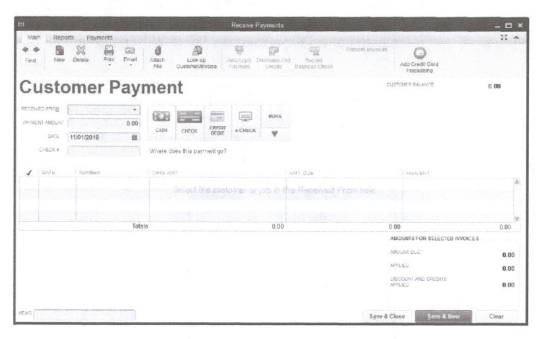

18. Select   James Wilson DDS: Dental office   from the Received From drop-down menu

QuickBooks fills out the form with the outstanding invoices for the James Wilson Dental Office job:

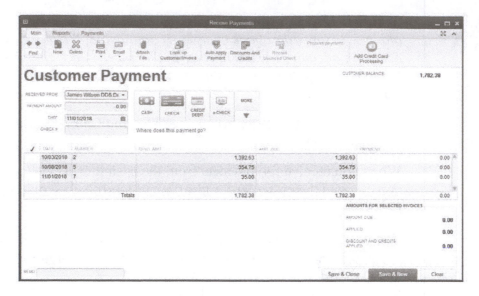

19. Type   **389.75**   in the Payment Amount field (the payment received for the original invoice and the customer fee for insufficient funds)

When a customer payment has been returned for insufficient funds, QuickBooks recommends that the customer send a money order or cashier's check for the new amount due. In this exercise, James Wilson has sent his payment via a cashier's check.

20. Click

A Payment Method window opens:

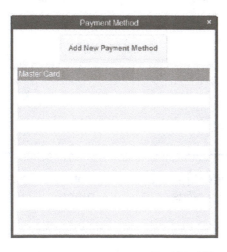

21. Click

The New Payment Method window opens:

22. Type   **Cashier's Check**   in the Payment Method field

23. Select   Check   from the Payment Type drop-down menu

24. Click   [OK]   to return to the Receive Payments window

25. Click   [MORE ▼]

The Payment Method window displays the new Cashier's Check payment method:

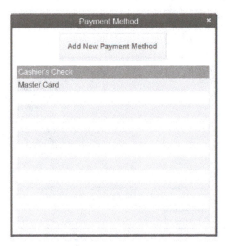

26. Select   Cashier's Check

You return to the Receive Payments window.

27. Type   **11030**   in the Check # field

Notice that QuickBooks automatically places a check mark to the left of Invoice 2, indicating that the $389.75 payment will be applied to this invoice.

Note: If you did not change your computer's date as recommended in the Before You Get Started lesson, the payment amounts may already be correctly applied and you can skip steps 28-30.

Because you do not want this payment applied to Invoice 2,

28. Click   in the Receive Payments window toolbar

QuickBooks removes the check mark from the left of Invoice 2.

29. Click   in the column   to the left of Invoice 5 for 354.75

QuickBooks places a check mark to the left of Invoice 5 and displays the amount to be applied to the invoice (354.75) in the Payment column.

30. Click   in the column   to the left of Invoice 7 for 35.00

QuickBooks places a check mark to the left of Invoice 7 and displays the remaining amount to be applied to the invoice (35.00) in the Payment column.

Your window should resemble the following:

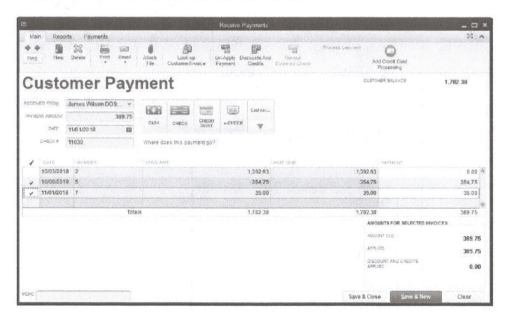

31. Click   Save & Close   to process the payment and return to the Home page

To deposit the payment,

32. Click   in the Banking area of the Home page

The Payments to Deposit window opens:

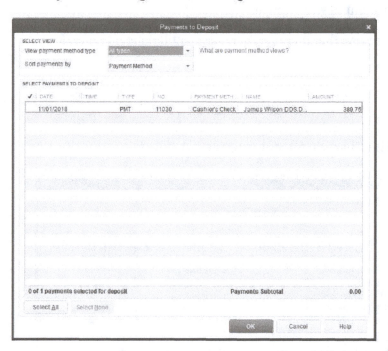

33. Click   the payment   to select it

QuickBooks places a check mark to the left of the payment.

34. Click   [OK]   to record the deposit

QuickBooks displays the Make Deposits window:

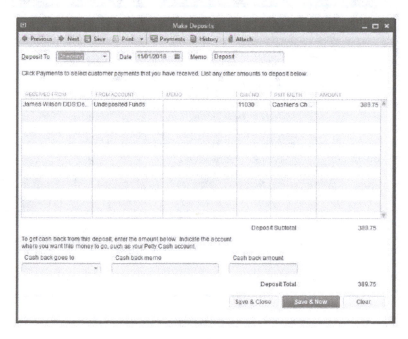

35. Click   [Save & Close]   to make the deposit to the Checking account

In the Chart of Accounts, QuickBooks increases the Checking account for the amount of the deposit.

To view the new checking account balance,

36. Click in the Company area of the Home page

The Chart of Accounts opens:

The Checking account has increased by $389.75 to $14,738.07.

37. Double-click Checking in the Name column

The Checking account register opens:

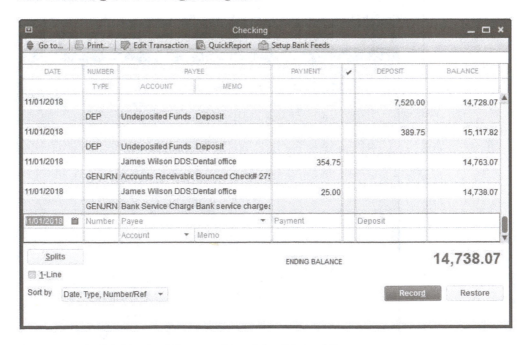

The deposit for $389.75 is now listed in the register.

38. Close the Checking account register and Chart of Accounts to return to the Home page

Review

In this lesson, you have learned how to:

- ☑ Display the Open Invoices report
- ☑ Use the Income Tracker
- ☑ Receive payments for invoices
- ☑ Handle a bounced check
- ☑ Make deposits

Practice:

1. Receive a payment (check number 2346 in the amount of $500.00) from Patricia Kleier for invoice 1 for remodeling the bathroom. Leave the amount still due as an underpayment.

2. Display the Open Invoices report and zoom in to display Invoice 1 in the Create Invoices window and to see the $500 payment applied.

3. View the Undeposited Funds amount in the Chart of Accounts.

4. Process a deposit to the Checking account for the payment.

5. View the new Checking account and Undeposited Funds totals in the Chart of Accounts.

6. Use the Manage Bounced Check window to process a returned check for Patricia Kleier's family room job in the amount of $564.50 with a $25.00 returned check fee. Charge a customer fee of 35.00.

7. View the Checking account register to ensure the $589.50 (564.50 and 25.00) has been deducted from the balance.

8. Use the Income Tracker to view all open invoices.

9. Close the company file.

Notes:

Working with Bank Accounts

In this lesson, you will learn how to:

- ❑ Write a QuickBooks check
- ❑ Void a QuickBooks check
- ❑ Use bank account registers
- ❑ Enter a handwritten check
- ❑ Transfer funds between accounts
- ❑ Reconcile checking accounts

Concept

QuickBooks makes writing checks and working in bank account registers easy. Writing a check in QuickBooks is similar to writing a paper check. Balance sheet accounts, such as checking and savings accounts, have account registers that resemble your own bank registers. Each register shows every transaction for that account, as well as the account balance. For example, if you enter a check or void a check, QuickBooks lists it in the check register. Or, if you transfer money from a checking account to a savings account, the transaction will be listed in both account registers.

Scenario

In this lesson, you will work in the QuickBooks account registers. First, you will write a QuickBooks check to pay for a utilities bill. Then, you will void a QuickBooks check. Next, you will enter a handwritten check into your checking account register to record a spur-of-the-moment purchase. To cover the checks for your quarterly taxes, you will transfer money from your savings account to your checking account. Finally, you will reconcile your checking account with the most recent statement from your bank.

Practice Files: B18_Working_with_Bank_Accounts.qbw

Writing a QuickBooks Check

You can enter checks directly into the check register by using the QuickBooks Write Checks window. This window allows you to write checks for an expense that you have not entered as a bill in QuickBooks or to record a cash transaction.

Note: For this lesson, set your computer's date to 11/1/2018 before opening the QuickBooks file, as recommended in the Before You Get Started lesson. This ensures that the dates you see on your screen match the dates in this lesson.

To write a QuickBooks check,

1. Open   B18_Working_with   using the method described in
                       Bank_Accounts.qbw   Before You Get Started

The QuickBooks Login dialog box displays:

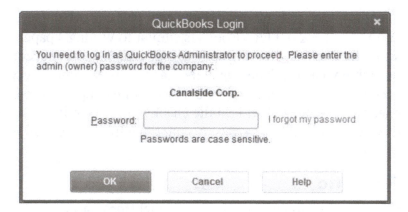

This dialog box informs you that you must login as a QuickBooks Administrator in order to open the company file.

2. Type   **Canalside2**   in the Password field

Note: Passwords are case-sensitive.

3. Click

QuickBooks opens the file.

4. Click   to close the Reminders window

QuickBooks displays the Home page:

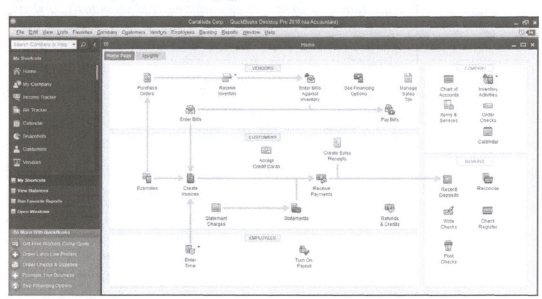

To open the Write Checks window,

5. Click in the Banking area of the Home page

The Write Checks - Checking window opens:

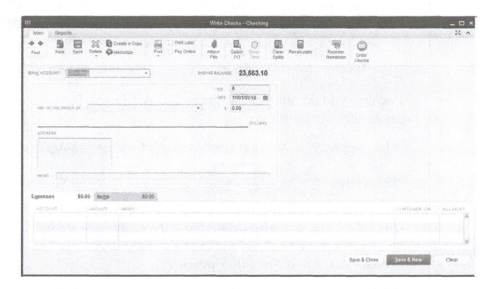

The Write Checks window allows you to view a payee's address information and allocate a check between multiple accounts, as well as use multiple memo fields.

Notice the Bank Account field displays Checking, the account from which you are writing this check, and the ending balance of the checking account is displayed to the right of the Bank Account field. The Date field is automatically populated with today's date. For this exercise, you will leave the default account and date.

Caution. *Do not use the Write Checks window to pay sales tax, payroll taxes and liabilities, or bills that you have entered previously. Instead, you should use the Pay Sales Tax window to pay sales tax, the Pay Payroll Taxes and Liabilities window to pay scheduled payroll liabilities, and the Pay Bills window for paying A/P bills.*

6.	Type	**F (for Fairgrave)**	in the Pay to the Order of field
7.	Press	Tab	

QuickBooks fills in the field with **Fairgrave Gas & Electric**.

Quick Tip. *QuickBooks has an autorecall feature that will automatically fill in the amount from the last transaction with this payee. This is convenient when you have recurring payments of the same amount. You can turn the autorecall feature on by selecting Edit : Preferences, clicking the General category, and selecting the Automatically recall last transaction for this name option.*

8.	Type	**256.91**	in the $ field (the amount of the gas and electric bill)

Notice that QuickBooks has automatically added two lines to the Account column on the Expenses tab at the bottom of the window. The Expenses tab allows you to assign the amount of the check to one of the expense accounts in your companies Chart of Accounts. QuickBooks suggests assigning this check to the Utilities:Gas and Electric and Utilities:Water accounts.

9.	Highlight	0.00	in the Amount column to the right of the Utilities:Gas and Electric account
10.	Type	**256.91**	to replace 0.00

Because you do not pay Fairgrave Gas & Electric for your water service, you will delete this account.

11.	Highlight	the Utilities:Water text	in the Account column
12.	Press	Delete	to delete the text

Quick Tip. *You can also delete the text by highlighting the Utilities: Water account and pressing the Ctrl and Delete keys simultaneously. This deletes both the account name and the dollar amount.*

13.	Highlight	0.00	in the Amount column
14.	Press	Delete	to delete the text

Your Write Checks - Checking window should resemble the figure below:

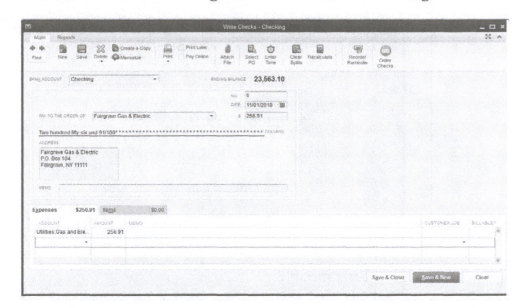

Notice the amount displayed on the Expenses tab equals the check amount (256.91). If you break down the check into multiple expenses, the total on the Expenses tab still needs to equal the check amount or QuickBooks will display a warning when you try to save the transaction that the transaction is not in balance and it is unable to record the transaction.

Note: The Items tab is only used when purchasing items you plan to stock in inventory.

15. Click  Save & Close

QuickBooks records the check in the register. To open the Checking account register and view the check you just wrote,

16. Click  in the Banking area of the Home page

Canalside Corp. has more than one type of bank account, so the Use Register dialog box displays allowing you to select the account register to open:

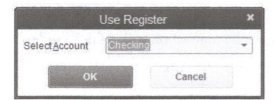

With the Checking account selected,

17. Click OK

The Checking account register opens:

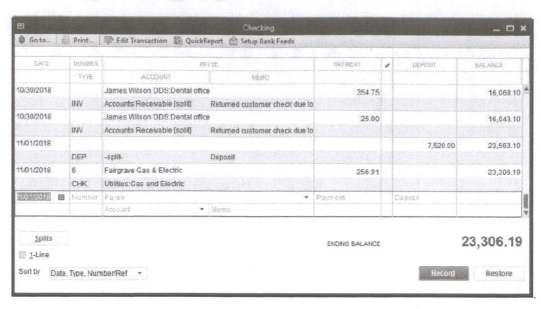

Note: The size of your Checking account register may be different. You may resize and move the window as necessary.

The check you just wrote is listed as the last transaction in the register.

Voiding a QuickBooks Check

If you need to cancel out the amount of a check, you can void the check or delete it. Voiding a check changes the amount to zero and keeps the empty transaction in QuickBooks (other information remains unchanged, such as the name of the payee, address, and date). When you void a check, you are able to reverse the void.

Deleting a check irreversibly removes the transaction from QuickBooks and cannot be undone. For complete records, you should void a transaction, rather than delete it.

Caution. *You should never void checks or transactions that have already been cleared.*

With the Checking account register displayed,

1. Select the transaction to Smith's Construction Rental for $315.00 (scroll up in the register)

QuickBooks highlights the transaction with a thick border

2. Select Edit : Void Check from the QuickBooks menu bar

Quick Tip. *You can also right-click on the selected transaction and select Void Check from the drop-down menu.*

The amount in the payment column is changed to 0.00 and VOID displays in the Memo column:

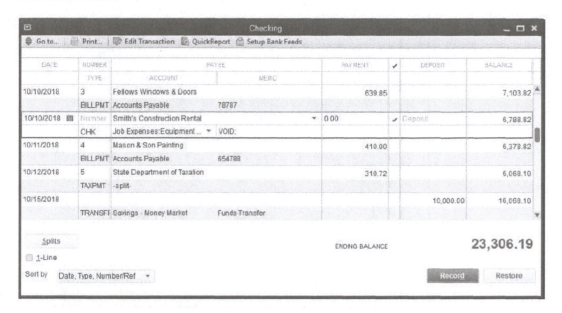

3. Click 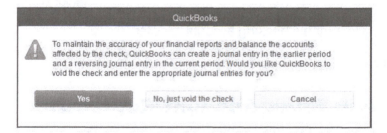 Record

The Recording Transaction dialog box displays:

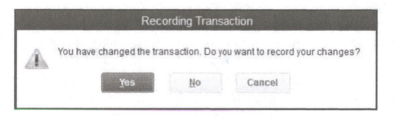

Recording Transaction

You have changed the transaction. Do you want to record your changes?

Yes   No   Cancel

4. Click   Yes   to record the voided transaction

A QuickBooks dialog box displays asking about recording journal entries:

QuickBooks

To maintain the accuracy of your financial reports and balance the accounts affected by the check, QuickBooks can create a journal entry in the earlier period and a reversing journal entry in the current period. Would you like QuickBooks to void the check and enter the appropriate journal entries for you?

Yes   No, just void the check   Cancel

You will not be recording journal entries in this lesson.

5. Click   No, just void the check

6. Double-click   in the Balance column   of the voided transaction to Smith's Construction Rental

The Write Checks - Checking window opens with the check to Smith's Construction Rental displayed:

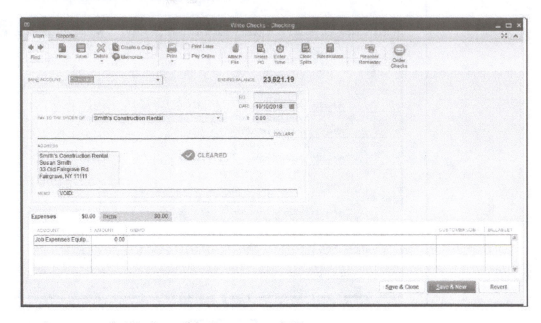

Notice VOID is displayed in the Memo field.

Quick Tip. *When you void a transaction, QuickBooks zeroes all amounts that display in the transaction, however the transaction is not removed. Instead, the transaction displays in the account register as voided. You can reverse the voided transaction by reentering the original amount of the transaction in the Payment column of the account register, deleting the word Void in the Memo column, clearing the check mark in the check mark column, and saving the transaction. When doing this, the Voided and Deleted Transactions reports will display the original state of the transaction, the state after voiding, and the state after reversing the voiding.*

7. Click   [Save & Close]   to close the Write Checks - Checking window

8. Close the Checking account register

You return to the Home page.

Using Bank Account Registers

When you work in QuickBooks, you often use forms, such as checks or invoices, to enter information. Behind the scenes, QuickBooks records your entries in the appropriate account register. Each balance sheet account listed on the Chart of Accounts has a register associated with it, except for Retained Earnings.

1. Click   Chart of Accounts   in the Company area of the Home page

The Chart of Accounts opens:

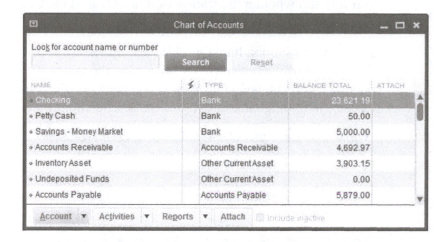

2. Double-click   Savings - Money Market

The register for the Savings - Money Market account opens:

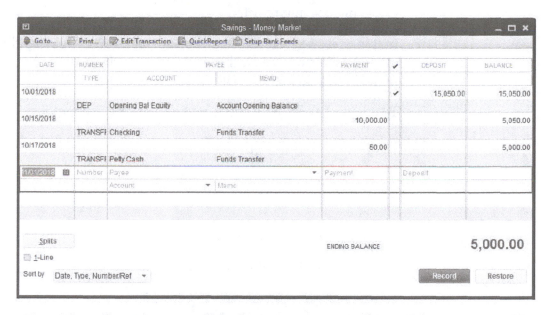

All QuickBooks registers work in the same way, regardless of the accounts with which they are associated. Some common features of all registers include:

• The register shows every transaction that affects an account's balance, listed in chronological order. For example, in a checking account, the register shows checks you have written (either with QuickBooks or by hand), deposits to the account, and withdrawals from the account.

• The columns in the register give specific information about the transaction. The first column is the date. The second column shows a reference number (for example, a check number or DB for debit) and a type (to tell you whether the transaction represents a check or a bill payment or a deposit, for example). The next column lists the payee, the account to which you have assigned the transaction, and any descriptive memo you choose to include. The final columns for a bank account show the transaction amount (either in the Payment or Deposit column) and whether the transaction has cleared the bank (indicated by a check mark in the column).

- On every transaction line, QuickBooks shows the account's running balance. The bottom of the register window shows the account's ending balance—the balance when QuickBooks takes into account all the transactions entered in the register, including checks you have not yet printed.

3. Close the Savings - Money Market account register

4. Close the Chart of Accounts

You return to the Home page.

Entering a Handwritten Check

Sometimes you need to write a check on the spot for items you did not plan to purchase. QuickBooks allows you to write the check, then enter it later in the Checking account register.

In this exercise, you decide to stop at Bayshore Office Supply and purchase some office products. Because this is an unplanned purchase, you write a check immediately and enter it into QuickBooks later.

To enter a handwritten check in the Checking account register,

1. Click in the Banking area of the Home page

Quick Tip. *You can also enter a handwritten check in the Write Checks window.*

The Use Register dialog box opens:

2. Click to accept Checking

The register for the Checking account opens:

DATE	NUMBER	PAYEE		PAYMENT	✓	DEPOSIT	BALANCE
	TYPE	ACCOUNT	MEMO				
10/30/2018		James Wilson DDS:Dental office		354.75			16,383.10
	INV	Accounts Receivable [split]	Returned customer check due to				
10/30/2018		James Wilson DDS:Dental office		25.00			16,358.10
	INV	Accounts Receivable [split]	Returned customer check due to				
11/01/2018						7,520.00	23,878.10
	DEP	-split-	Deposit				
11/01/2018	6	Fairgrave Gas & Electric		256.91			23,621.19
	CHK	Utilities:Gas and Electric					
11/01/2018	Number	Payee		Payment		Deposit	
		Account	Memo				

Splits

☐ 1-Line

ENDNG BALANCE   **23,621.19**

Sort by   Date, Type, Number/Ref ▾

Record   Restore

3. Press   [Tab]   to move to the Number field

QuickBooks automatically populates the Number field with the next check number.

4. Press   [Tab]   to move to the Payee field

5. Type   **Bayshore Office Supply**

6. Press   [Tab]   to move to the Payment field

A Name Not Found dialog box displays:

Name Not Found

Bayshore Office Supply is not in the Name list.

To automatically add Bayshore Office Supply to the Name list, click QuickAdd. You can enter more detailed information later.

To enter the detailed information now, click Set Up (usually not required).

[Quick Add]   [Set Up]   [Cancel]

This dialog box informs you that Bayshore Office Supply is not in the Name list. You can choose to set up detailed information about Bayshore Office Supply now or enter more detailed information at a later time.

For this exercise, you will automatically add Bayshore Office Supply to the Name list without entering detailed information.

7. Click   [Quick Add]

The Select Name Type window opens:

This window allows you to select the type of name you are adding, such as a vendor's name or a customer's name. Vendor is selected by default.

8. Click   OK

QuickBooks adds the new vendor to the Vendors list and you return to the Checking account register.

9. Type   **99.95**   in the Payment field

10. Press   Tab   to move to the Account field

11. Type   **O (for Office Supplies)**

12. Press   Tab

QuickBooks automatically completes the entry with Office Supplies.

13. Type   **Paper and toner cartridges**   in the Memo field

14. Click   Record

The transaction is recorded in the account register and the Ending Balance decreases by $99.95:

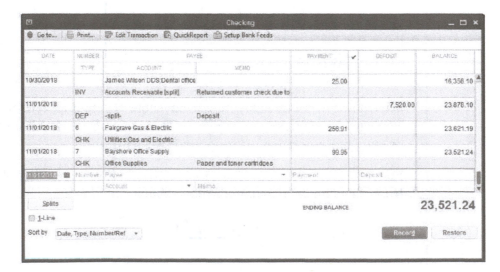

15. Close the Checking account register to return to the Home page

Transferring Funds Between Accounts

QuickBooks allows you to easily move funds between accounts using the Transfer Funds Between Accounts window. Canalside Corp. needs to transfer $5,000.00 from the Savings account to the Checking account to cover a quarterly income tax payment.

To transfer funds,

1. Select   Banking : Transfer   from the menu bar
                   Funds

The Transfer Funds Between Accounts window opens:

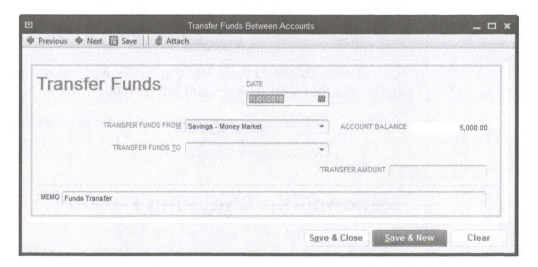

Notice that Savings - Money Market already displays in the Transfer Funds From field and the Savings account balance is displayed in the Account Balance field.

2. Press   twice to move to Transfer Funds To

3. Type   **C (for Checking)**   in the Transfer Funds To field

4. Press   Tab

QuickBooks automatically fills in Checking and displays the account balance for the Checking account.

5. Type   **5000.00**   in the Transfer Amount field

The Transfer Funds Between Accounts window should resemble the figure below:

	Transfer Funds Between Accounts	_ □ ✕
← Previous	➡ Next	🖫 Save		📎 Attach		

Transfer Funds   DATE
11/01/2018 📅

TRANSFER FUNDS FROM Savings - Money Market   ▼   ACCOUNT BALANCE   5,000.00

TRANSFER FUNDS TO Checking   ▼   ACCOUNT BALANCE   23,521.24

TRANSFER AMOUNT   5000.00

MEMO Funds Transfer

Save & Close   Save & New   Clear

6. Click   Save & Close

QuickBooks decreases the balance in the Savings account and increases the balance in the Checking account by $5,000.00.

Caution. *Transferring money between accounts in QuickBooks does not transfer money between your actual bank accounts. You will still need to transfer the same amount of money between your bank accounts.*

Reconciling Checking Accounts

Reconciling is the process of verifying that your checking account record matches the bank's record. When you manually reconcile your checking account, you need to open and work in a register.

An Overview of Reconciliation

When you keep your records with QuickBooks, you do not have to worry about addition or subtraction errors like you do when you are using a manual check register. Even so, it is important to get in the habit of reconciling your QuickBooks bank accounts on a monthly basis. This helps you avoid overdraft charges for bad checks, enables you to detect possible bank errors, and helps you keep more accurate financial records.

Your bank sends you a statement for each of your accounts each month. The statement shows all the activity in your account since the previous statement, including:

*   The opening balance for your bank account (amount in your account as of the previous statement)

*   The ending balance for your bank account (amount in your account as of the closing date for the statement)

*   The amount of interest, if any, you have received for this statement period

- Any service charges assessed by the bank for this statement period

- Checks that have cleared the bank

- Deposits you have made to the account

- Any other transactions that affect the balance of your account (for example, automatic payments or deposits, or automatic teller machine [ATM] withdrawals or deposits)

When you receive a statement from your bank or from a credit card company, you can reconcile the statement with your QuickBooks records. You can reconcile any QuickBooks bank account, including accounts for savings and money market funds. The goal of reconciling is to make sure that your QuickBooks records and the bank's statement agree on the account balance.

Reconciling an Account

In this exercise, you will reconcile the Checking account using the statement below:

Great Statewide Bank
123 4th Street
Bayshore, NY 12345

Opening Balance: 9,000.00

Date	Description/Transaction	Debits	Credits
10/09/2018	Check 1	1,100.00	
10/09/2018	Check 2	156.33	
10/10/2018	Check 3	639.85	
10/11/2018	Check 4	410.00	
10/12/2018	Check 5	310.72	
10/15/2018	Transfer from Savings		10,000.00
10/22/2018	Deposit		354.75
10/30/2018	Returned Check	354.75	
10/30/2018	Insufficient Funds Fee	25.00	
11/01/2018	Deposit		7,520.00
11/01/2018	Check 6	256.91	
11/01/2018	Check 7	99.95	
11/01/2018	Transfer from Savings		5000.00
11/01/2018	Interest		2.75
11/01/2018	ATM Withdrawal	20.00	
11/01/2018	Debit Card	30.00	

Service Charge: 14.00

Ending Balance: 28,459.99

To reconcile the Checking account,

1. Click in the Banking area of the Home page

The Begin Reconciliation window opens.

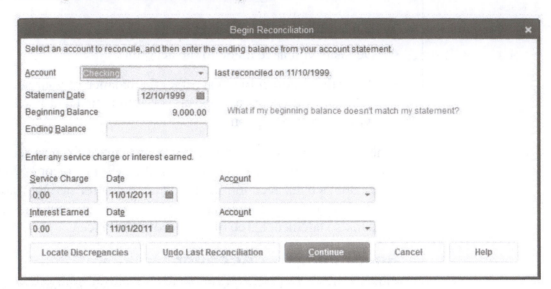

Notice the default account displayed is Checking.

2.	Press	Tab	to move to the Statement Date field
3.	Type	**11/1/2018**	for the date of the statement
4.	Press	Tab	to move to the Ending Balance field
5.	Type	**28,459.99**	in the Ending Balance field
6.	Press	Tab	to move to the Service Charge field
7.	Type	**14**	in the Service Charge field
8.	Press	Tab	to move to the Date field
9.	Type	**11/1/2018**	for the date of the service charge
10.	Select	Bank Service Charges	from the Account drop-down menu
11.	Click	Continue	

The Reconcile - Checking window opens:

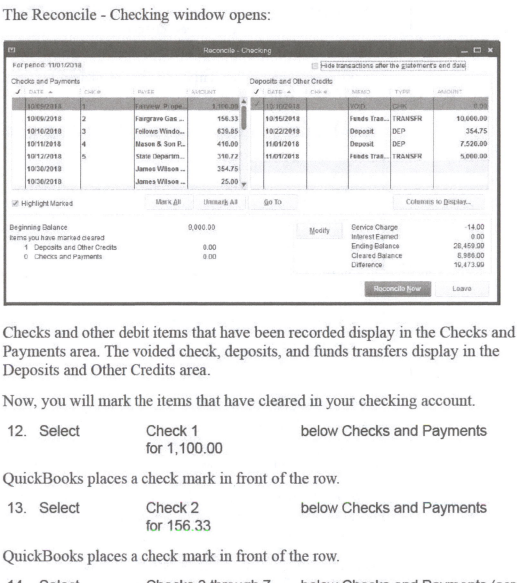

Checks and other debit items that have been recorded display in the Checks and Payments area. The voided check, deposits, and funds transfers display in the Deposits and Other Credits area.

Now, you will mark the items that have cleared in your checking account.

12. Select   Check 1 for 1,100.00   below Checks and Payments

QuickBooks places a check mark in front of the row.

13. Select   Check 2 for 156.33   below Checks and Payments

QuickBooks places a check mark in front of the row.

14. Select   Checks 3 through 7   below Checks and Payments (scroll down to view all checks)

QuickBooks places a check mark in front of each of the rows.

15. Select   the Funds Transfer for 10,000   below Deposits and Other Credits

16. Select   the Deposit for 354.75   below Deposits and Other Credits

17. Select   the Deposit for 7,520.00   below Deposits and Other Credits

18. Select   the Funds Transfer for 5,000   below Deposits and Other Credits

19. Select   the debit for 354.75 (a returned check from James Wilson)   below Checks and Payments

20. Select   the debit for 25.00   below Checks and Payments
                                 (a returned check
                                 fee)

QuickBooks places a check mark in front of each of the rows. Your window should resemble the figure below:

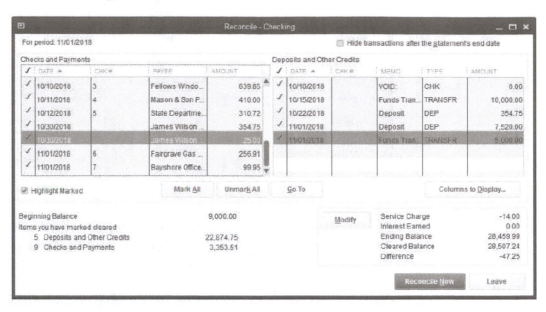

Notice the amount of the difference displayed in the bottom right corner is -47.25. Because the difference is not 0.00 yet, you will not reconcile the account and should not close this window.

Caution. *If the amount of the Difference is not 0, your account does not balance for the period of time covered by the statement. You should locate the error and correct the difference before reconciling the account.*

There is a difference of 47.25 because there are transactions you made that were not automatically recorded in QuickBooks, including an ATM withdrawal, a debit card purchase, and a deposit of interest income. You will now add these transactions to the checking account, so that you can correctly reconcile the account.

When you use an ATM machine or debit card to get cash for your business, you need to record the transaction as a transfer in QuickBooks.

To record an ATM withdrawal from the checking account,

21. Select   Banking : Transfer   from the menu bar
                                 Funds

The Transfer Funds Between Accounts window opens:

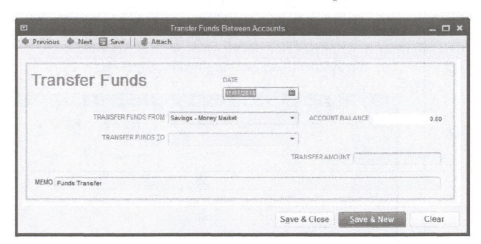

22.	Select	Checking	from the Transfer Funds From drop-down menu
23.	Select	Petty Cash	from the Transfer Funds To drop-down menu
24.	Type	**20.00**	in the Transfer Amount field
25.	Type	ATM Withdrawal	to replace Funds Transfer in the Memo field

Your Transfer Funds Between Accounts window should resemble the figure below:

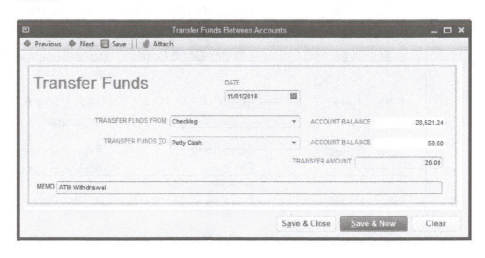

26.	Click	Save & Close	to record the transfer and return to the Reconcile - Checking window

Now, you will record a debit card purchase for gas. You can use the Write Checks window to record purchases made using debit cards or other forms of electronic payment. When recording a debit using the Write Checks window, you enter a code that indicates the payment form, such as DB for debit card, in place of the check number.

To record a debit card purchase,

| 27. | Select | Banking : Write Checks | from the menu bar |

The Write Checks - Checking window opens:

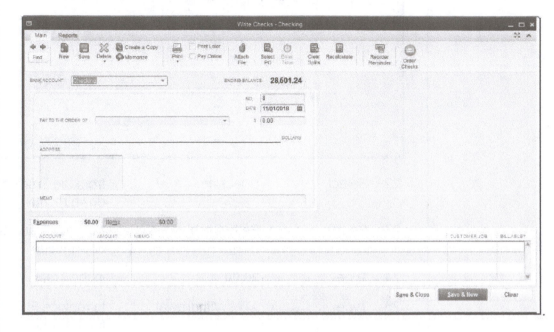

Notice the Bank Account field displays Checking, the account from which you are deducting this debit transaction.

28.	Select	Bayshore Automotive	from the Pay to the Order of drop-down menu
29.	Type	**DB** (for Debit Card)	to replace the number 8 in the No. field
30.	Type	**30.00**	in the $ field (the amount of the gas purchase)
31.	Select	Automobile Expense	from the Account drop-down menu on the Expenses tab
32.	Press	Tab	to move to the Amount column

QuickBooks automatically fills in **30.00**:

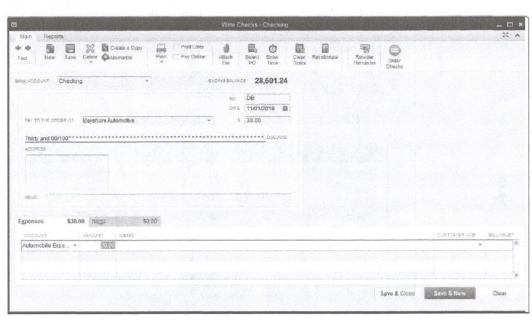

33. Click   Save & Close

QuickBooks records the debit card transaction and returns you to the Reconcile - Checking window.

Now, you will record an interest deposit in the checking account.

34. Click   to the left of the Service Charge and Interested Earned amounts in the Reconcile - Checking window

The Begin Reconciliation window opens displaying the reconciliation data that you entered previously.:

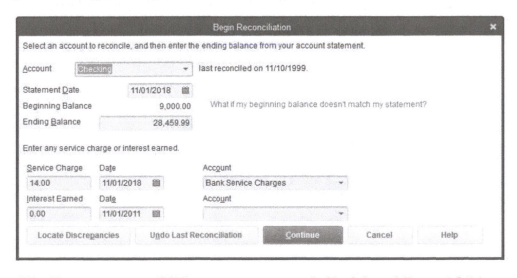

35. Type   **2.75**   in the Interest Earned field

36. Type **11/01/2018** in the Date field (for the date the interest was debited to your account)

37. Select Interest Income from the Account drop-down menu

38. Click [Continue]

The Reconcile - Checking window opens:

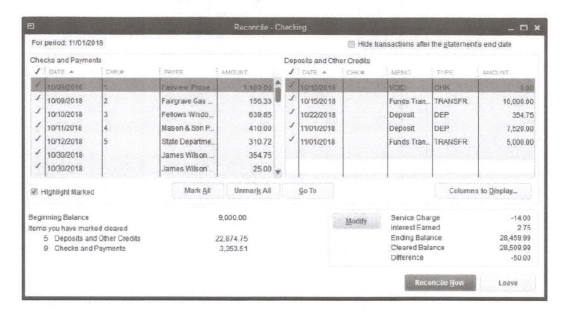

The ATM withdrawal and debit card purchase display in the Checks and Payments area. The interest income you just entered displays in the Interest Earned field below the Service Charge field.

Note: You may need to scroll down to view the ATM withdrawal and debit card purchase.

Now, you will mark the ATM withdrawal and debit card purchase as cleared in your checking account.

39. Select the ATM withdrawal for 20.00 below Checks and Payments

QuickBooks places a check mark in front of the row.

40. Select the debit card purchase for 30.00 below Checks and Payments

QuickBooks places a check mark in front of the row.

The Reconcile - Checking window should resemble the figure below:

Notice the amount of the difference displayed in the bottom right corner is 0.00. You can now finish reconciling your account.

Quick Tip. *Selecting a transaction and clicking the Go To button displays the actual transaction so that you can view further details about that transaction.*

41. Click   Reconcile Now

Note: If an Information dialog box about online banking appears, click the OK button.

When the reconciliation is complete, a Select Reconciliation Report window opens:

You can choose to display a summarized reconciliation report, a detailed report, or both reports.

42. Select   Detail

43. Click

The Reconciliation Report dialog box displays:

44. Click OK

The Reconciliation Detail report opens:

Canalside Corp.						
Reconciliation Detail						
Checking, Period Ending 11/01/2018						
Type	Date	Num	Name	Clr	Amount	Balance
Beginning Balance						9,000.00
Cleared Transactions						
Checks and Payments - 12 items						
Check	10/09/2018	1	Fairview Properties	✓	-1,100.00	-1,100.00
Check	10/09/2018	2	Fairgrave Gas & E...	✓	-156.33	-1,256.33
Bill Pmt -Check	10/10/2018	3	Fellows Windows...	✓	-639.85	-1,896.18
Bill Pmt -Check	10/11/2018	4	Mason & Son Pain...	✓	-410.00	-2,306.18
Sales Tax Paym...	10/12/2018	5	State Department o...	✓	-310.72	-2,616.90
Invoice	10/30/2018	6	James Wilson DDS...	✓	-354.75	-2,971.65
Invoice	10/30/2018	6	James Wilson DDS...	✓	-25.00	-2,996.65
Check	11/01/2018	6	Fairgrave Gas & E	✓	-256.91	-3,253.56
Check	11/01/2018	7	Bayshore Office S...	✓	-99.95	-3,353.51
Check	11/01/2018	DB	Bayshore Automo...	✓	-30.00	-3,383.51
Transfer	11/01/2018			✓	-20.00	-3,403.51
Check	11/01/2018			✓	-14.00	-3,417.51
Total Checks and Payments					-3,417.51	-3,417.51
Deposits and Credits - 6 items						
Check	10/10/2018		Smith's Constructio...	✓	0.00	0.00
Transfer	10/15/2018			✓	10,000.00	10,000.00
Deposit	10/22/2018			✓	354.75	10,354.75
Deposit	11/01/2018			✓	2.75	10,357.50
Transfer	11/01/2018			✓	5,000.00	15,357.50

After you have reviewed the report,

45. Close the Reconciliation Detail window

QuickBooks returns you to the Home page.

Quick Tip. *QuickBooks Premier or higher give you access to 120 previous reconciliation reports. QuickBooks Pro only allows you to access the last reconciliation report created. If you would like to undo your last reconciliation, click the Reconcile icon in the Banking area of the Home page or select Banking : Reconcile from the menu bar. When the Begin Reconciliation window opens, select the appropriate account from the Account drop-down list and click the Undo Last Reconciliation button.*

Next, you will open the Checking account register to view the cleared checks.

46. Click in the Banking area of the Home page

The Use Register dialog box opens:

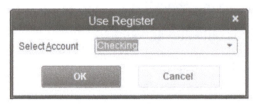

47. Click OK to accept Checking

The Checking account register opens:

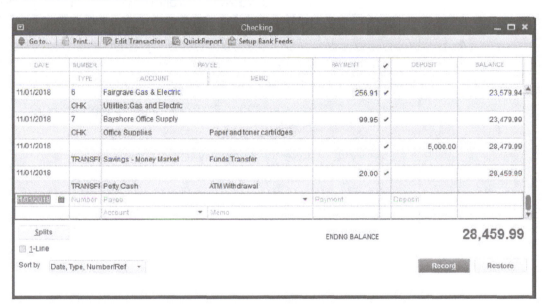

DATE	NUMBER	PAYEE		PAYMENT	✓	DEPOSIT	BALANCE
	TYPE	ACCOUNT	MEMO				
11/01/2018	6	Fairgrave Gas & Electric		256.91	✓		23,579.94
	CHK	Utilities:Gas and Electric					
11/01/2018	7	Bayshore Office Supply		99.95	✓		23,479.99
	CHK	Office Supplies	Paper and toner cartridges				
11/01/2018					✓	5,000.00	28,479.99
	TRANSFR	Savings - Money Market	Funds Transfer				
11/01/2018				20.00	✓		28,459.99
	TRANSFR	Petty Cash	ATM Withdrawal				
11/01/2018	Number	Payee		Payment		Deposit	
		Account	Memo				

| Splits | | ENDING BALANCE | 28,459.99 |

☐ 1-Line

Sort by Date, Type, Number/Ref ▾   Record   Restore

All cleared items will have a check mark in the ✓ column.

48. Scroll to the top of the register to view all cleared items

49. Close the Checking account register

Caution. *You should never edit or delete a reconciled transaction. If you attempt to do so, a Transaction Reconciled window will display, warning you that the transaction has already been reconciled and that recording changes will impact your reconciliation balance.*

Review

In this lesson, you have learned how to:

- ☑ Write a QuickBooks check
- ☑ Void a QuickBooks check
- ☑ Use bank account registers
- ☑ Enter a handwritten check
- ☑ Transfer funds between accounts
- ☑ Reconcile checking accounts

Practice:

1. Use the Checking account register to enter a handwritten check for $76.95. Date it using today's date, use the next check number, and make it payable to Carolyn's Express Delivery Service. Charge the check to the Miscellaneous Expense account and add a memo for delivery of a new sign.

2. Write a QuickBooks check to Cal Telephone for $143.87 for this month's phone bill. Assign it to the Telephone account.

3. Transfer $2000.00 from the Checking account to the Petty Cash account.

4. Close the company file.

Entering and Paying Bills

In this lesson, you will learn how to:

❑ Handle expenses

❑ Use QuickBooks for accounts payable

❑ Use the Bill Tracker

❑ Enter bills

❑ Pay bills

❑ Enter vendor credit

Concept

Processing your expenses is just as important as processing your income. QuickBooks provides multiple ways to handle expenses, including providing an Accounts Payable register, which helps track the money you owe to others. This is the best way to keep track of your cash flow.

Scenario

In this lesson, you will open the Accounts Payable register to see how QuickBooks keeps track of all your bills and payments. You will also use the Bill Tracker to view both unpaid and paid bills. You will enter a bill that you owe to an advertising agency, splitting the bill between two accounts to better track your expenses. Then, you will pay the bill with a check and see how the Accounts Payable and Checking account registers record the transactions. Finally, you will enter credit you have received from a vendor for the return of two items and then apply this credit to a bill.

Practice Files: B18_Entering_and_Paying_Bills.qbw

Handling Expenses

Whether your expenses are personal or for your business, you can handle them in one of the following ways:

- You can write a handwritten check now and enter the information into a QuickBooks check register later. While this does not take advantage of Quick-Books's timesaving features, sometimes it is necessary. For example, if you purchase supplies at a retail store, payment is usually expected on the spot, and you may not know the exact amount in advance.

- You can use QuickBooks to write and print a check. When you receive a bill for which you want to make immediate payment, you can write a QuickBooks check quickly and accurately, and you receive an additional advantage: QuickBooks makes the entry into your checking account register for you automatically.

- You can use QuickBooks's accounts payable to track the amounts you owe. This is the best way to keep track of your cash flow needs and to handle bills you want to pay later.

- You can pay for the expense by credit card and enter the credit card receipt into QuickBooks later.

Using QuickBooks for Accounts Payable

Some business owners, especially those who own smaller, home-based businesses, pay their bills when they receive them. Other business owners find it more convenient to pay bills less often. (They also like keeping the cash in the company for as long as possible.) If you do not plan on paying your bills right away, QuickBooks can help you keep track of what you owe and when you owe it.

The money you owe for unpaid bills is called your Accounts Payable. QuickBooks uses the Accounts Payable account to track all the money you owe. Like any QuickBooks balance sheet account, the Accounts Payable account has a register where you can view all of your bills at once.

Note: For this lesson, set your computer's date to 11/1/2018 before opening the QuickBooks file, as recommended in the Before You Get Started lesson. This will ensure that the dates and amounts you see on your screen match the dates and amounts in this lesson.

To view an Accounts Payable register for Canalside Corp.,

1. Open   B18_Entering_and   using the method described in
                              _Paying_Bills.qbw   Before You Get Started

The QuickBooks Login dialog box displays:

This dialog box informs you that you must login as a QuickBooks Administrator in order to open the company file.

2. Type   **Canalside2**   in the Password field

Note: Passwords are case-sensitive.

3. Click

QuickBooks opens the file.

4. Click   to close the Reminders window

QuickBooks displays the Home page:

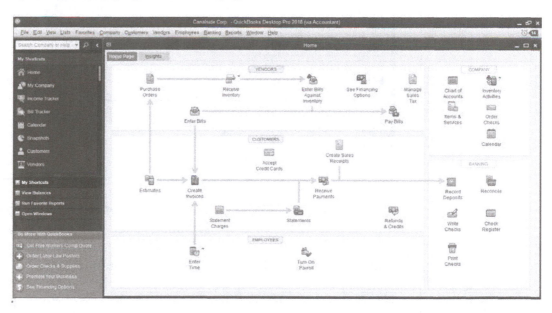

To open the Chart of Accounts,

5. Click   in the Company area of the Home page

The Chart of Accounts opens:

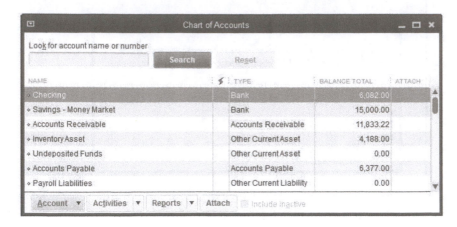

Note: You may resize and move the Chart of Accounts as necessary.

6. Double-click   Accounts Payable   to open the register

The Accounts Payable register opens:

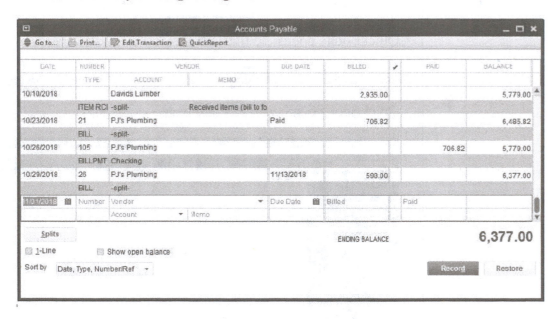

The Accounts Payable register keeps track of each bill you have entered, shows you the due date, and keeps a running balance of all the bills you owe. As a business owner, this helps you forecast your cash flow, and the QuickBooks reminder system helps you pay your bills on time.

Quick Tip. The Sort by field in the lower-left corner allows you to change the sort order of the register.

7. Close the Accounts Payable window and Chart of Accounts to return to the Home page

Using the Bill Tracker

Another method to track and manage your bills is to use the Bill Tracker. The Bill Tracker allows you to easily view all of your vendor-related payables, such as bills and purchase orders.

Note: When you set up a company file, only the QuickBooks Administrator has access to the Bill Tracker. If another user needs access, the Administrator must edit that user's particular role to include full access to the Bill Tracker.

To view bills using the Bill Tracker:

1. Select   Vendors : Bill Tracker   from the menu bar

Quick Tip. You can also click the Bill Tracker shortcut in the Icon bar to open the Bill Tracker.

The Bill Tracker opens:

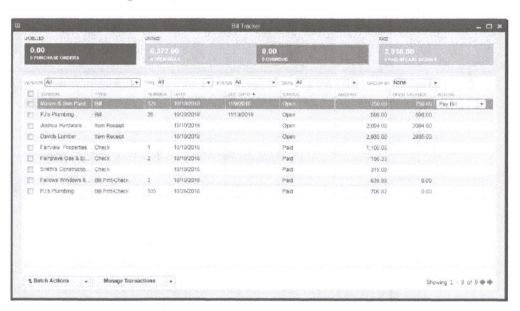

Note: If you did not change your computer's date as recommended in the Before You Get Started lesson, your window will be slightly different.

When you open the Bill Tracker, it displays all unbilled purchases (purchase orders), all unpaid bills (open and overdue bills), and all bills paid within the last 30 days. The totals for all unbilled, unpaid, and paid bills are displayed at the top of the window in colored blocks.

Each row displays an individual transaction and the column at the end of the row allows you to perform actions on the transaction. For example, for a row displaying a bill, you have the option of paying the bill, copying the bill, or printing the bill. For a row displaying a check, you have the option to print the check.

Quick Tip. You can use the drop-down arrows below the totals to filter the transactions even further.

2. Click

The Bill Tracker is updated to display the four open bills:

To view an individual transaction,

3. Double-click   the PJ's Plumbing bill

The bill for PJ's Plumbing opens in the Enter Bills window:

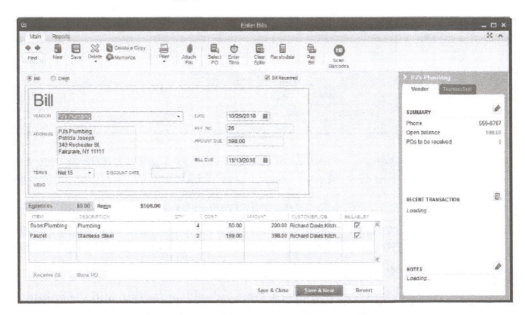

4. Close the PJ's Plumbing bill to return to the Bill Tracker

5. Close the Bill Tracker to return to the Home page

Entering Bills

When you receive a bill from a vendor, you should enter it into QuickBooks as soon as possible. This keeps your cash flow forecast reports up-to-date and lets you avoid setting aside and forgetting about a bill.

Canalside Corp. received a bill from the company that created its new brochures. Canalside does not plan to pay the bill until close to its due date, but the company wants to keep an eye on the accounts payable total, so it enters the bill now.

To enter a bill,

1. Click in the Vendors area of the Home page

The Enter Bills window opens:

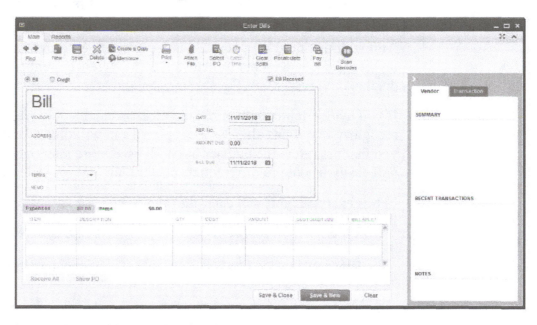

The top half of the window is where you enter the bill. The bottom half is the detail area, where you can assign the bill amount to different expense accounts, customers, or jobs. The pane on the right side of the window provides an at-a-glance view of a vendor's history when a vendor is selected from the Vendor drop-down menu.

Notice that the Bill Received check box displayed at the top of the window has a check mark in it. The only time the Bill Received check box should be cleared is if you are using QuickBooks for inventory and you want to record items that you have received, but have not actually been billed for yet.

2. Type   **Bristol Advertising**   in the Vendor field

3. Press

A Vendor Not Found dialog box displays informing you that Bristol Advertising is not in the Vendor list:

Clicking the Quick Add button allows you to set up the vendor with the minimum amount of data that QuickBooks needs to continue. In this exercise, you will use the Quick Add feature.

4.	Click	Quick Add	to add Bristol Advertising to the Vendor list
5.	Press	Tab	to move to the Ref. No. field

Although this field is optional, it is important to enter reference numbers for bills, invoices, and statements. When you use a reference number, the number will display in the Accounts Payable register and other windows.

If you inadvertently enter a bill, invoice, or statement twice, QuickBooks will recognize that it has already been entered and will display a dialog box warning you that the reference number has been used more than once. If this happens, you will easily be able to differentiate one bill, invoice, or statement from another.

In this exercise, you will enter the invoice number associated with this bill.

6.	Type	**442**	in the Ref. No. field
7.	Press	Tab	to move to the Amount Due field
8.	Type	**1500.00**	

QuickBooks automatically supplies a date in the Bill Due field. If you do not have payment terms entered for this vendor, the default date displayed in the Bill Due field is ten days later than the date entered in the Date field. If you had entered payment terms for this vendor, QuickBooks would have used those terms to calculate the bill's due date.

Because you just set up the vendor during this transaction, you have not yet specified any payment terms. You will specify payment terms now.

9.	Select	1% 10 Net 30	from the Terms drop-down menu

This selection specifies that you are expected to pay the net amount (the total outstanding on the invoice) within 30 days of receiving this bill. If you pay within 10 days of receipt of the bill, you will receive a 1% discount. Notice that the Bill Due field now displays a date 30 days from the current date.

Notice also that a Discount Date field has been added to the right of the Terms field. This vendor's payment terms include a discount for early payment, so QuickBooks has automatically populated this field with the date you would need to pay the bill by in order to receive the discount.

10.	Click	the Expenses tab	
11.	Click	in the first row of the Account column	on the Expenses tab
12.	Type	**Pr (for Printing)**	
13.	Press	Tab	to accept Printing and Reproduction

QuickBooks allows you to assign your transactions to more than one account, so you can keep close track of where your company spends its money. Canalside Corp. wants to assign the majority of this bill to a Printing and Reproduction expense account and the rest to an Office Supplies expense account.

14.	Type	**1450.00**	to change the amount from 1,500.00 to 1,450.00
15.	Click	in the Account column below Printing and Reproduction	to display a drop-down arrow
16.	Select	Office Supplies	from the Account drop-down menu (scroll down)

QuickBooks automatically assigns the remainder of the bill amount ($50.00) to Office Supplies:

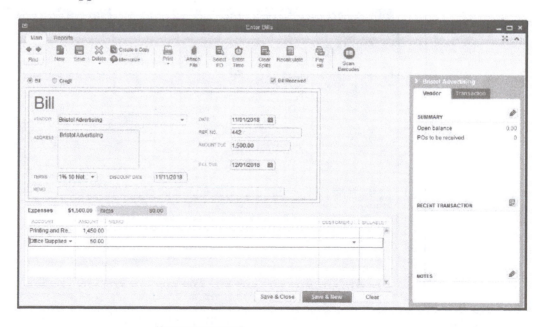

17.	Click	Save & Close	to record the bill

Because you changed the payment terms for Bristol Advertising, an Information Changed dialog box displays:

18. Click to make the change permanent

The next time you enter a bill for the Bristol Advertising vendor, the same payment terms will be used (1% 10 Net 30).

Paying Bills

You can use the Pay Bills window to pay outstanding bills you have already entered into QuickBooks. When you open QuickBooks, a Reminders window displays informing you if you have transactions to complete, such as bills to pay.

To pay a bill,

1. Click in the Vendors area of the Home page

The Pay Bills window opens:

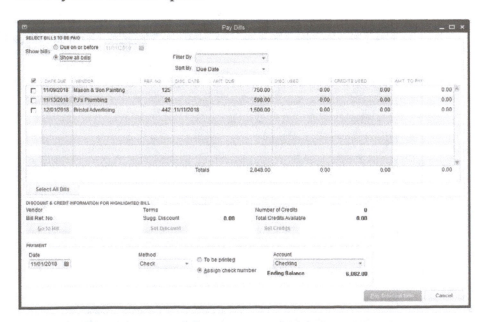

 Quick Tip. If the bill you want to pay is not displayed on the screen, use the scroll bar to locate it, or select the Show all bills option at the top of the window.

The Pay Bills window displays your unpaid bills as of any date you enter. To pay the bills, simply check off the bills you want to pay. You can pay by check or credit card. In this exercise, you will pay a bill using a check printed by QuickBooks.

2. Verify   Check   is selected from the Method drop-down menu

Note: If you select Credit Card from the Method drop-down menu and do not have a credit card set up, QuickBooks will prompt you to set up the account.

3. Click   in the Payment Method area at the bottom of the window to select it

Quick Tip. *If you paid a bill with a handwritten check and want to reference the check number used, select the Assign check number option. When you click the Pay Selected Bills button, an Assign Check Number dialog box displays allowing you to assign the check number.*

If you have multiple accounts, select the one you want to use to pay the bill from the Account drop-down menu.

4. Verify   Checking   is selected from the Account drop-down menu

5. Click   the check box   to the left of the Bristol Advertising bill to select it

QuickBooks displays a check mark next to the bill and decreases the amount in the checking account Ending Balance field to reflect a payment of $1,500.00.

Notice the suggested 1% discount of $15.00 for early payment displays on the Pay Bills window, but has not yet been applied to the payment.

To apply the discount,

6. Click

The Discount and Credits window opens with the Discount tab displayed:

The payment terms and discount amount are displayed on the Discount tab. You can now select the account you use to track income from this discount.

7. Select **Printing and Reproduction** from the Discount Account drop-down menu (scroll down)

The Printing and Reproduction expense is now reduced by $15.00 and the discount will be recorded in the Printing and Reproduction account.

8. Click Done

The Pay Bills window should resemble the figure below:

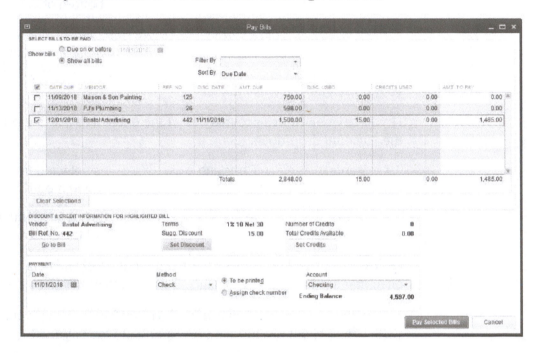

The Disc. Used column for the Bristol Advertising row now displays 15.00, the amount of the discount, and the amount to pay has been reduced by 15.00 to 1,485.00. The ending balance of the checking account has also increased by 15.00.

Quick Tip. *To automatically apply discounts and credits when you pay bills, select Edit : Preferences from the menu bar. When the Preferences window opens, select Bills from the list of preferences and click the Company Preferences tab. Select the Automatically use credits check box, select the Automatically use discounts check box, select a default discount account for tracking the discounts you apply, and click the OK button. Now, when you pay bills, discounts and credits will be automatically deducted from the amount of the bill.*

9. Click Pay Selected Bills

A Payment Summary window opens:

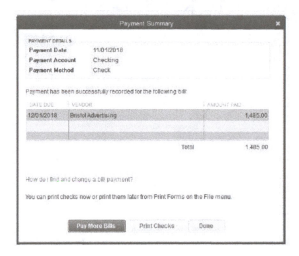

This window displays the total amount of the payment to Bristol Advertising and allows you to continue paying more bills, to print a check for the bill now, or to complete the pay bills transaction.

10. Click   Done

QuickBooks makes an entry in the Accounts Payable register, showing a decrease of $1,485 in the total amount of payables, and a check is created in your Checking account.

To see how the $15.00 affected the Printing and Reproduction expense account,

11. Click   in the Company area of the Home page

The Chart of Accounts opens:

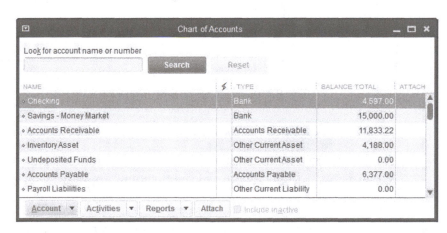

12. Double-click   the Printing and Reproduction Expense account (scroll down)

The Account QuickReport window displays a QuickReport of printing and reproduction expenses for this fiscal year-to-date:

Note: Select This Fiscal Year-to-date from the Dates drop-down menu if necessary.

Notice that the expense account has been reduced by $15.00, which reflects the discount taken for early payment.

13. Close the Account QuickReport

To view the Accounts Payable register,

14. Double-click   Accounts Payable   in the Chart of Accounts (scroll up)

The Accounts Payable register opens:

DATE	NUMBER	VENDOR		DUE DATE	BILLED	✓	PAID	BALANCE
	TYPE	ACCOUNT	MEMO					
10/29/2018	26	PJ's Plumbing		11/13/2018	598.00			6,377.00
	BILL	-split-						
11/01/2018		Bristol Advertising					1,485.00	4,892.00
	BILLPMT	Checking [split]						
11/01/2018		Bristol Advertising					15.00	4,877.00
	DISC	Checking [split]						
11/01/2018	442	Bristol Advertising		Paid	1,500.00			6,377.00
	BILL	-split-						
11/01/2018	Number	Vendor		Due Date	Billed		Paid	
		Account	Memo					

Splits   ENDING BALANCE   **6,377.00**

1-Line   Show open balance

Sort by Date, Type, Number/Ref

Record   Restore

The last three entries in the register show the bill and the bill payment for Bristol Advertising, and the amount of the discount applied.

 Quick Tip. *Another method for viewing bills to be paid in your Accounts Payable register is to generate an A/P Aging Summary report. To generate this report, select Reports : Vendors & Payables : A/P Aging Summary from the menu bar.*

At the same time QuickBooks recorded the entry in the Accounts Payable account, it made an entry in the Checking account.

To view this entry,

15. Close the Accounts Payable register to return to the Chart of Accounts

16. Double-click   Checking   in the Chart of Accounts

The Checking account register opens:

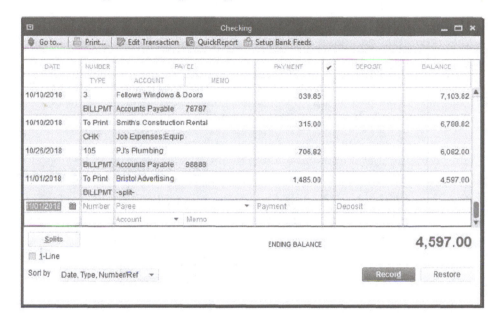

The last entry in the register is for the bill payment to Bristol Advertising. The Number/Type column indicates the bill payment check still needs to be printed.

Note: If you did not change your computer's date as recommended in the Before You Get Started lesson, the bill payment to Bristol Advertising will be listed at the top of the register.

17. Click   Bristol Advertising   in the Account column

QuickBooks highlights the Bristol Advertising transaction with a thick border.

18. Click      at the top of the Checking register

The Bill Payments(Check) - Checking window opens:

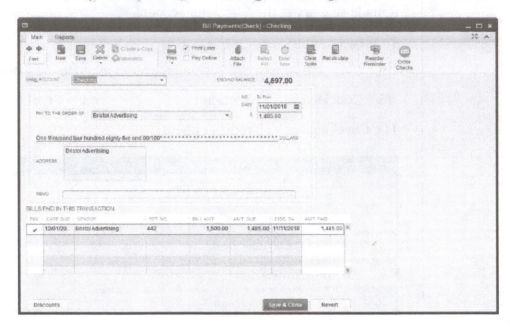

This check is called a Bill Payment Check. It differs from the check used to enter checks directly into the Checking account, because it shows expenses directly on the check.

19. Click   Save & Close

20. Close the Checking account register and the Chart of Accounts

You return to the Home page.

Entering Vendor Credit

Vendor credit is money that is owed to you from a vendor. The credit may be for the return of items you purchased, for damaged items you received, from overpayment of a previous bill, or for a variety of other reasons. When you are owed credit, you must enter the credit for the vendor and save it before you can apply it to a bill.

In this exercise, you will enter a credit from PJ's Plumbing for the return of two plumbing fixtures. Before entering the credit, you'll look at the flow of transactions prior to returning the plumbing fixtures.

1. Click   Vendors   on the Icon Bar

The Vendor Center opens:

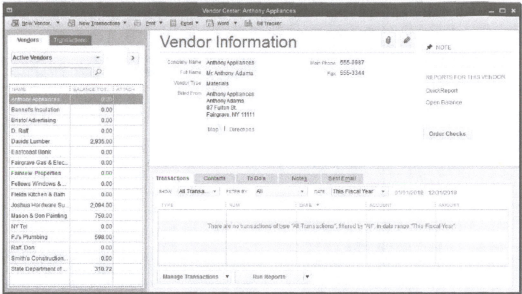

2. Select **PJ's Plumbing** from the list of vendors

All transactions for PJ's Plumbing display on the Transactions tab in the Vendor Information area:

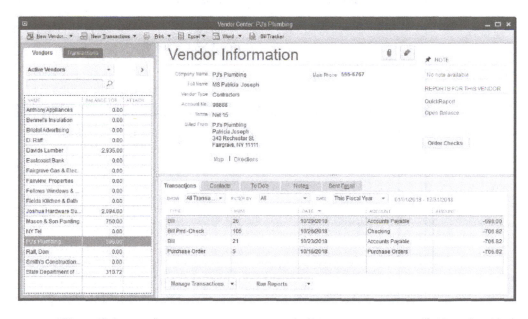

Note: If you did not change your computer's date as recommended in the Before You Get Started lesson, select All from the Date drop-down menu on the Transactions tab in the Vendor Information area.

3. Double-click **Purchase Order** in the Type column on the Transactions tab

The Create Purchase Orders window opens:

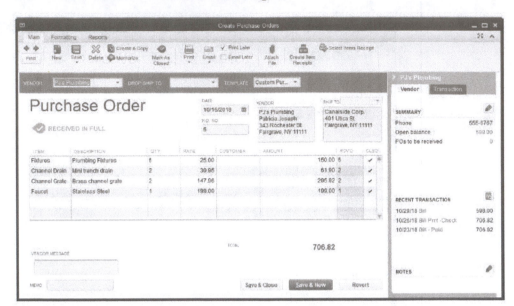

This is the original purchase order used to order the plumbing fixtures from PJ's Plumbing that you have now returned. From the purchase order, you can see that all items were received in full.

4. Close the Create Purchase Orders window to return to the Vendor Center

5. Double-click   Bill (above   in the Type column on the
                   Purchase Order)   Transactions tab

The Enter Bills window opens:

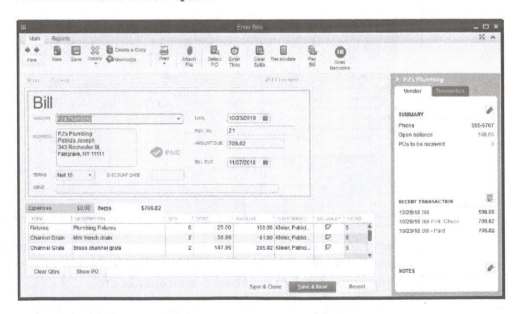

This window displays the bill you entered from PJ's Plumbing for the plumbing fixtures.

6. Close the Enter Bills window to return to the Vendor Center

7. Double-click   Bill Pmt - Check   in the Type column on the
                                               Transactions tab

The Bill Payments (Check) - Checking window opens:

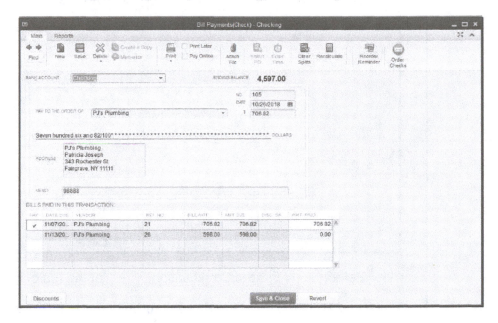

This window shows that the bill to PJ's Plumbing, which included the plumbing
fixtures, was paid.

8. Close the Bill Payments (Check) - Checking window to return to the Vendor
    Center

Now, you will enter the credit for the two plumbing fixtures you returned to PJ's
Plumbing.

9. Click      on the Vendor Center toolbar

A drop-down menu displays:

10. Select   Enter Bills   from the drop-down menu

The Enter Bills window opens with PJ's Plumbing displayed in the Vendor field:

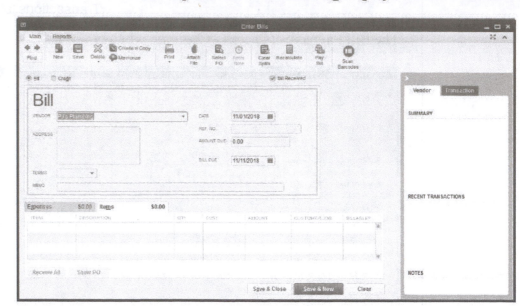

11. Select   the Credit option   at the top of the window

The Enter Bills window is updated with fields for entering credit:

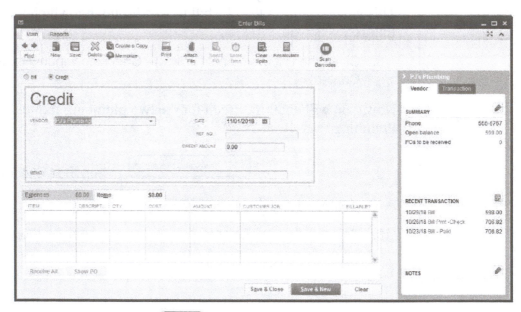

12. Press   Tab   twice to move to the Ref. No. field

13. Type   **21**   in the Ref. No. field

This number identifies the bill you want to associate with this credit.

14. Press   Tab   to move to the Credit Amount field

You returned two plumbing fixtures that were each $25.00.

15. Type   **50.00**   in the Credit Amount field

16. Select   Fixtures   from the Item drop-down menu on the Items tab

QuickBooks fills in the Description, Cost, and Amount fields with information about this item.

17. Press   Tab   twice to move to the Qty field

18. Type   **2**   in the Qty field

19. Press   Tab

QuickBooks updates the Amount field based on the quantity entered.

The plumbing fixtures were returned for Patricia Kleier's bathroom remodel job and you want to pass this credit on to the customer.

20. Select   Kleier, Patricia : Remodel Bathroom   from the Customer:Job drop-down menu

21. Click   Save & Close   to record the credit

The Enter Bills window closes and you return to the Vendor Center.

Applying Vendor Credit to a Bill

After you have saved a credit from a vendor, you can apply it to bills from that vendor.

To apply vendor credit,

1. Click   New Transactions   on the Vendor Center toolbar

A drop-down menu displays:

2. Select   Pay Bills   from the drop-down menu

The Pay Bills window opens:

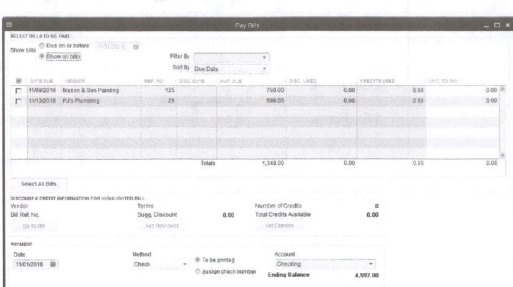

3. Click   the check box   to the left of the PJ's Plumbing bill to select it

QuickBooks displays a check mark next to the bill and decreases the amount in the checking account Ending Balance field to reflect a payment of $598.00.

Notice the Total Credits Available field displays 50.00.

To apply the credit to this bill,

4. Click

The Discount and Credits window opens with the Credits tab displayed:

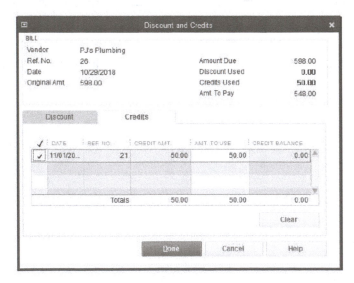

QuickBooks automatically selects the one credit available for PJ's Plumbing.

Quick Tip. *If you only want to use a portion of a credit, change the amount in the Amt. To Use column.*

5. Click to apply the credit to the bill

The Pay Bills window should resemble the figure below:

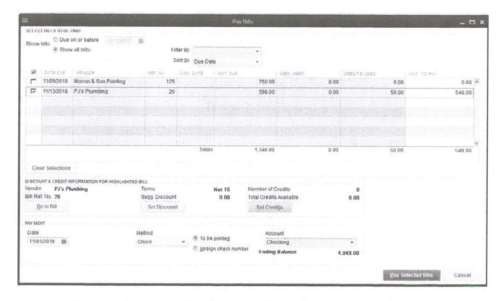

The Credits Used column for the PJ's Plumbing row now displays 50.00, the amount of the credit, and the amount to pay has been reduced by 50.00 to 548.00. The ending balance of the checking account has also increased by 50.00.

6. Click

A Payment Summary window opens displaying the total amount of the payment to PJ's Plumbing:

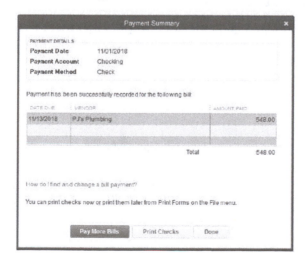

7. Click to return to the Vendor Center

8. Close the Vendor Center to return to the Home page

Review

In this lesson, you have learned how to:

- ☑ Handle expenses
- ☑ Use QuickBooks for accounts payable
- ☑ Use the Bill Tracker
- ☑ Enter bills
- ☑ Pay bills
- ☑ Enter vendor credit

Practice:

1. Enter a bill received from T.J.'s Auto Repair for $437.56 for truck repairs. Enter 525 as the reference number, select payment terms of 2% 10 Net 30, and apply the $437.56 to the Automobile Expense account.

2. Pay the bill for T.J.'s Auto Repair from the Checking account. Apply the 8.75 discount to the bill and charge it to the Automobile Expense account.

3. Using the Chart of Accounts, view the Automobile Expense Account QuickReport. Then, view the bill payment to T.J.'s Auto Repair in the Checking account register and the Accounts Payable register.

4. Enter a vendor credit from Mason & Son Painting for the return of one exterior wood door for 105.00. Use reference number 125 and associate the credit with Patricia Kleier's Family Room job.

5. Pay the bill to Mason & Son Painting using a check and apply the $105.00 credit to the bill.

6. View all paid and unpaid bills in the Bill Tracker.

7. Close the company file.

Using the EasyStep Interview

In this appendix, you will learn how to:

❑ Use the EasyStep Interview

Concept

The QuickBooks EasyStep Interview walks you through the company setup process and helps you tailor QuickBooks to suit your business. The interview also automatically creates some of the QuickBooks accounts and items you will need based on your type of business.

Scenario

In this appendix, you are Sheila Rhodes, the owner of Canalside Corporation, which does new construction and remodeling. You will set up your company using the QuickBooks EasyStep Interview.

Practice Files: Created in this appendix

Using the EasyStep Interview

The EasyStep Interview walks you through the process of setting up your entire business in QuickBooks. We recommend that you complete the EasyStep Interview process in its entirety when setting up your business.

Each screen in the EasyStep Interview asks a different question about your business. QuickBooks uses your answers to these questions to set up your business. The screens that display in the interview process depend on the type of business you are setting up and your answers to the questions asked.

Note: For this lesson, it is recommended that you do not change your computer's date as recommended in the Before You Get Started lesson. Changing your computer's date may prevent certain steps in this lesson from working properly. This lesson works with the QuickBooks Premier version of QuickBooks.

To start the EasyStep Interview,

1. Start QuickBooks

QuickBooks opens displaying the QuickBooks application window with a No Company Open window:

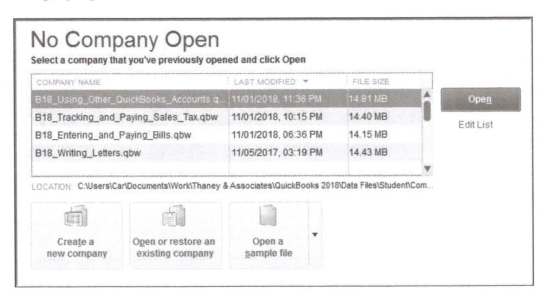

Note: Your No Company Open window will list different company names.

2. Click

QuickBooks opens, displaying the QuickBooks Setup window:

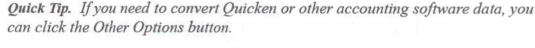

The QuickBooks Setup window allows you to create a new company file using an express or detailed setup process. For this lesson, you will use the detailed setup process, which takes you through the EasyStep Interview.

 Quick Tip. If you need to convert Quicken or other accounting software data, you can click the Other Options button.

3. Click Detailed Start

The first screen in the EasyStep Interview displays:

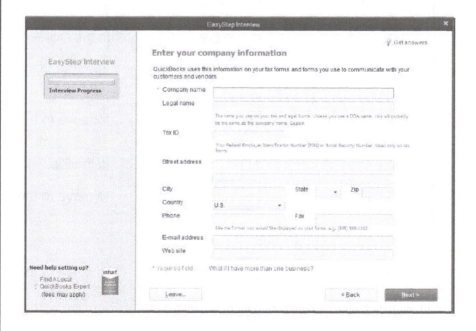

This screen allows you to enter your company name, legal name, tax ID, company address, phone and fax number, E-mail address, and Web site address.

All required fields in the EasyStep Interview will contain an asterisk (*) next to them. You cannot proceed to the next screen unless you enter information in all of the required fields. Notice that the only field that is required on this screen is the Company Name. Although many fields may not be required, it is best to enter as much information as possible when setting up your company.

4.	Type	**Canalside Corporation**	in the Company name field
5.	Press	Tab	to move to the Legal name field

Notice that **Canalside Corporation** automatically displays in the Legal name field. You may change your legal name if you want; however, for this lesson, you will keep the company name and the legal name the same.

6.	Press	Tab	to move to the Tax ID field

The Tax ID field allows you to enter your Federal Employer Identification Number (EIN) or your Social Security Number, which will be used on tax forms. Because Canalside Corporation is a corporation, you will enter your EIN in this field.

7.	Type	**11-2345678**	in the Tax ID field
8.	Press	Tab	to move to the Street address field
9.	Type	**401 Clearview Lane**	in the Street address field
10.	Press	Tab	twice to move to the City field
11.	Type	**Fairgrave**	in the City field
12.	Select	NY	from the State drop-down menu
13.	Press	Tab	to move to the Zip field
14.	Type	**11111**	in the Zip field
15.	Press	Tab	to move to the Country field

You will accept the default country of U.S.

16.	Press	Tab	to move to the Phone field
17.	Type	**555-555-5555**	in the Phone field

18. Press [Tab]   to move to the Fax field

19. Type   **555-555-5556**   in the Fax field

20. Press [Tab]   to move to the E-mail address field

21. Type   **[your e-mail address]**

For this exercise, you will not enter a Web site address.

On some screens, you will be given the option of learning more about a subject by clicking underlined text that represents a link. On this screen, you have the ability to learn more about what to do if you have more than one business.

22. Click   <u>What if I have more than one business?</u>

The Have a Question? dialog box opens along with a separate Help Article dialog box displaying information about having more than one business:

23. Click      to close the dialog box

Quick Tip. *You can also click the Get answers link in the upper-right corner of any EasyStep Interview screen to display QuickBooks Help relevant to that screen.*

To move through the interview process, you click the Next button to proceed to the next screen or click the Back button to go to the previous screen and change the entries on that screen.

24. Click   [Next >]

The next screen in the EasyStep Interview displays:

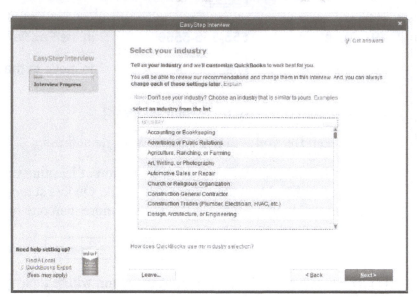

This screen allows you to select your type of industry in order to customize QuickBooks to work best for your business. When you create a new QuickBooks company, you should select an industry type that most closely matches your type of business. QuickBooks will then automatically create a preset Chart of Accounts for your company. If your business does not fall into a specific industry listed, select the one that is closest to get a head start on creating your own Chart of Accounts. After you have created your new company file, you can modify the Chart of Accounts to suit your needs.

25. Select   **Construction General Contractor**   from the Industry list

26. Click   Next >

The next screen in the EasyStep Interview displays:

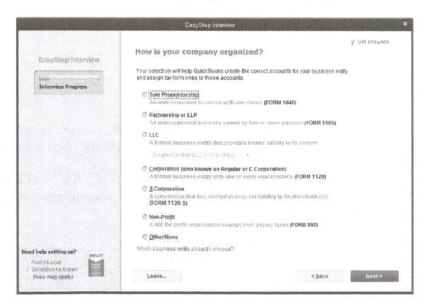

This screen allows you to select how your company is organized so that QuickBooks can create the appropriate accounts for your business and assign tax form lines to those accounts.

27. Select   S Corporation

28. Click   Next >

The next screen in the EasyStep Interview displays:

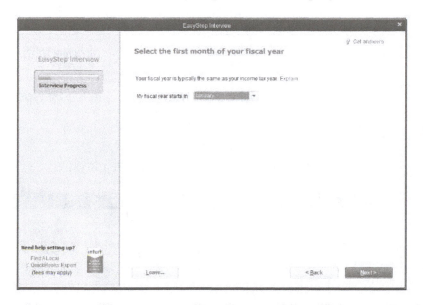

This screen allows you to select the month in which your fiscal year begins. Your fiscal year is typically the same as your income tax year.

Because January already displays in the My fiscal year starts in field,

29. Click   Next >

The next screen in the EasyStep Interview displays:

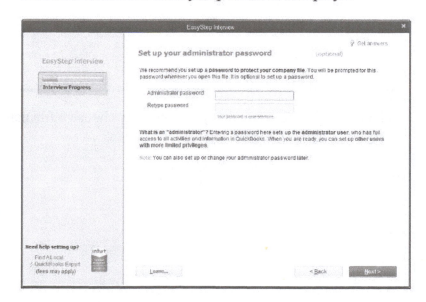

This screen allows you to set up an administrator password. When you are creating a company file, you can password-protect the file in order to prevent unwanted users from accessing your company's information. This will require anyone who opens this file to enter this password.

Note: Although setting up an administrator password is optional, it is recommended that you use this feature to protect your company's data.

30.	Type	**[a password]**	in the Administrator password field

Note: Passwords are case-sensitive.

31.	Press	Tab	to move to the Retype password field

32.	Retype	**[the password]**	in the Retype password field

33.	Click	Next >

The next screen in the EasyStep Interview displays:

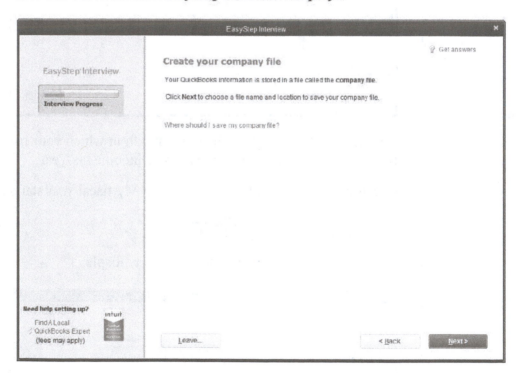

QuickBooks informs you that you must now choose a file name and location to save your company file.

34.	Click	Next >

The Filename for New Company window opens:

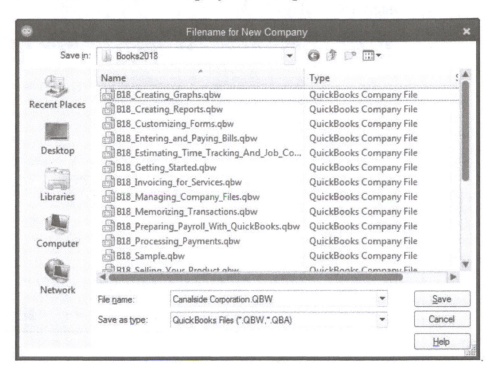

Note: If you did not display file extensions as recommended in the Before You Get Started lesson, the .QBW file extension may not display in your window.

The Filename for New Company window is similar to a Save As window and allows you to specify a name and location for your company file on your computer. By default, QuickBooks names the new file using the company name and places it in the directory where you last saved or opened a file. You will accept the default file name and directory.

Note: If the Books2018 folder does not display, click the drop-down arrow in the Save in field and navigate to the folder.

35. Click | Save |

A Working dialog box displays while the new company file is created.

Quick Tip. After you have saved the company file, you can leave the interview process at any time by clicking the Leave button to close the company file. QuickBooks will remember what screen of the interview you were on, so that the next time you open the company file, you will return to that same screen in the EasyStep Interview.

When the file creation process is complete, the next screen in the EasyStep Interview displays:

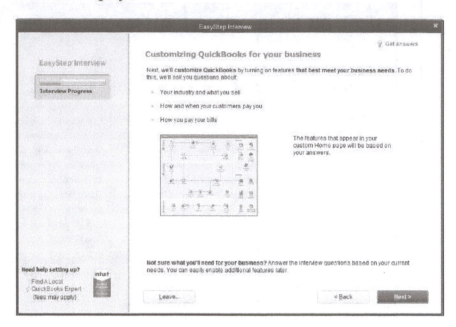

This screen explains how the next steps in the interview process will help you customize your business.

 Quick Tip. *As you proceed through the interview process, your completion status is displayed in the Interview Progress bar.*

36. Click

The next screen in the EasyStep Interview displays:

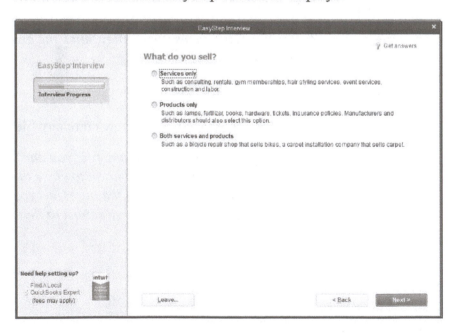

This screen allows you to select whether your business sells services, products, or both services and products. Because your construction business completes new building construction and remodeling (services), as well as sells building materials (products), you will select the Both services and products option.

37. Select   Both services and products

38. Click   Next >

The next screen in the EasyStep Interview displays:

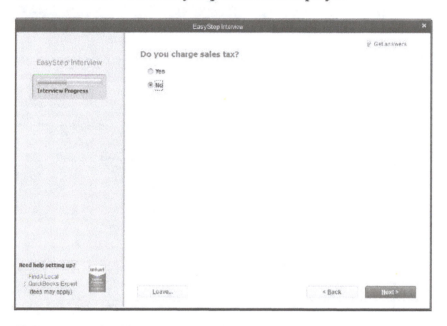

This screen asks if you charge sales tax.

39. Select   Yes

40. Click   Next >

The next screen in the EasyStep Interview displays:

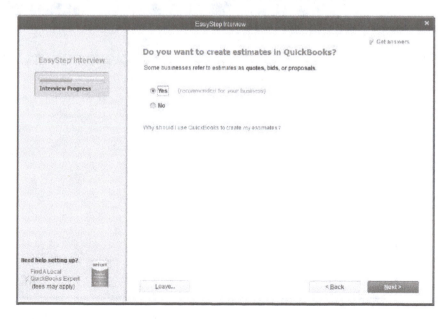

This screen asks if you would like to create estimates in QuickBooks. Because it is very likely that your construction company will need to create estimates for jobs, you will leave the default selection of Yes.

41. Click

The next screen in the EasyStep Interview displays:

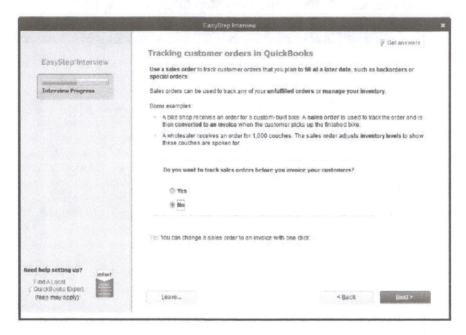

The screen asks if you will use a sales order to track customer orders. You will accept the default selection of No.

42. Click

The next screen in the EasyStep Interview displays:

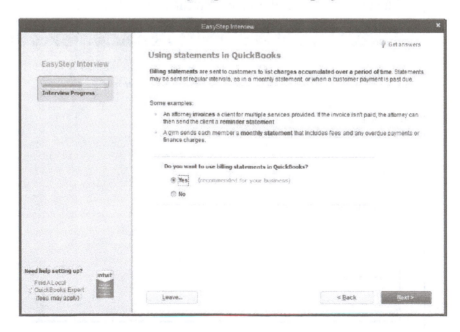

This screen asks if you will be using billing statements in QuickBooks. You will accept the default selection of Yes.

43. Click

The next screen in the EasyStep Interview displays:

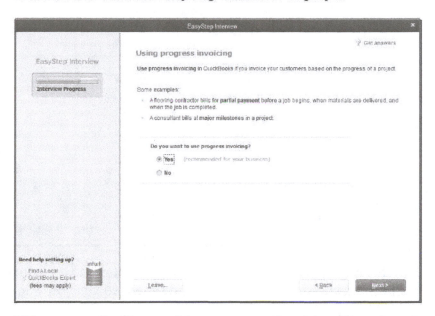

This screen asks if you will use progress invoicing if you invoice your customers based on the progress of a project. You will accept the default selection of Yes.

44. Click

The next screen in the EasyStep Interview displays:

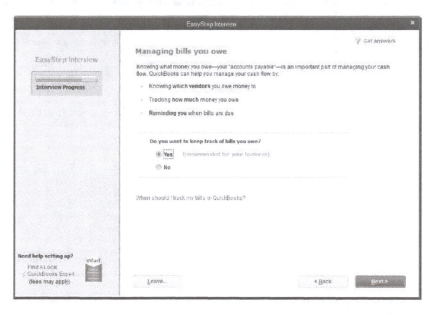

This screen asks if you want QuickBooks to help manage bills that you owe. You will leave the default selection of Yes.

45. Click

The next screen in the EasyStep Interview displays:

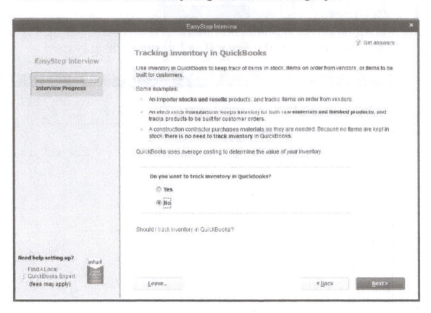

This screen asks if you want to use QuickBooks to track inventory. You will be keeping building materials on hand to sell, so you will want to track inventory.

46. Select   Yes

47. Click

The next screen in the EasyStep Interview displays:

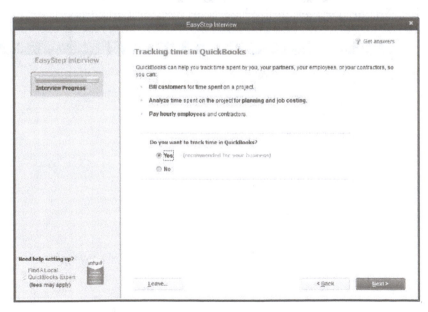

This screen asks if you want to track time in QuickBooks. Your business is largely project-based and you track hours per project, so you will leave the default selection of Yes.

48. Click

The next screen in the EasyStep Interview displays:

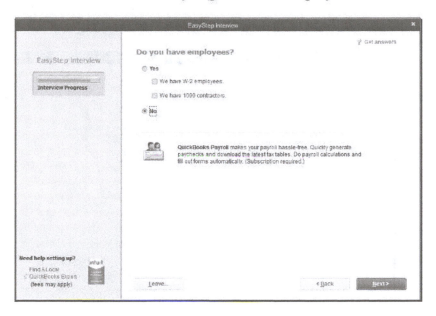

This screen asks if you have employees.

49. Select   Yes

50. Select   We have W-2 employees

Note: QuickBooks also allows you to track 1099 contractors. 1099 contractors are considered vendors in QuickBooks. To enter a contractor, you create a new vendor and specify the vendor is eligible for 1099 status.

51. Click

The next screen in the EasyStep Interview displays:

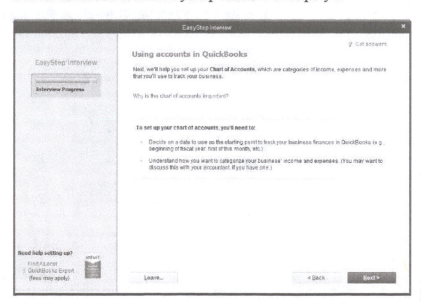

This screen explains what you will need to set up your Chart of Accounts.

52. Click

The next screen in the EasyStep Interview displays:

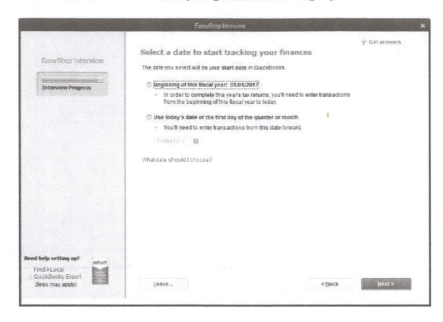

Note: The Beginning of this fiscal year date on your screen will be different.

This screen allows you to select the date you want to begin tracking your finances in QuickBooks.

53. Select   Beginning of this fiscal year

54. Click

The next screen in the EasyStep Interview displays:

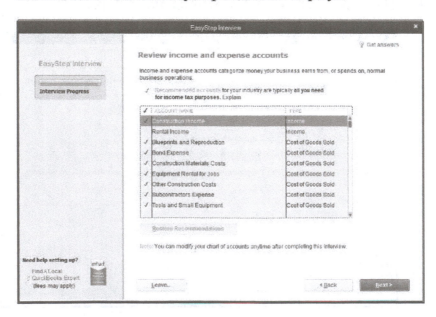

This screen displays the income and expense accounts QuickBooks has chosen for your construction business. All accounts recommended by QuickBooks for your business will display a check mark in the left column. If you would like to use other accounts listed, simply select those accounts.

55.	Select	Advertising and Promotion	in the Account Name column (scroll down)

A check mark displays next to the account to indicate it is selected.

Quick Tip. *You can deselect any account you don't anticipate using.*

56.	Click	Next >

The final screen in the EasyStep Interview displays congratulating you for completing the EasyStep Interview:

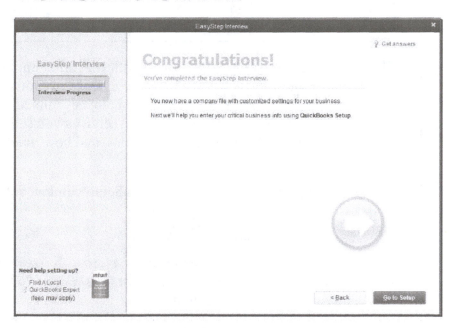

57.	Click	Go to Setup

Note: If a time-saving features window opens, close it.

QuickBooks opens with the QuickBooks Desktop Setup window displayed:

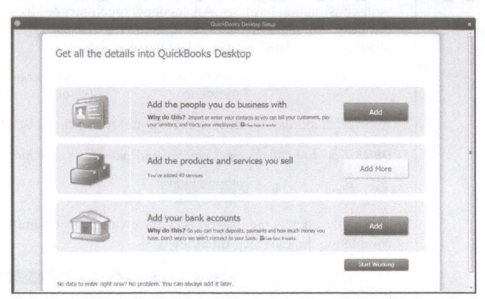

The QuickBooks Desktop Setup window allows you to import business contacts directly into QuickBooks from other address books, so you can start billing customers, paying vendors, and tracking employees immediately. From this window, you can also add the products and services you sell, and add bank accounts so you can track deposits, payments, and how much money your business has.

You will not use the QuickBooks Desktop Setup window at this time.

58. Click

Note: If a New Feature Tour window opens, close it. You can open the New Feature Tour at any time to view the new features in QuickBooks 2018 by selecting Help > New Features > New Feature Tour.

The QuickBooks Home page opens:

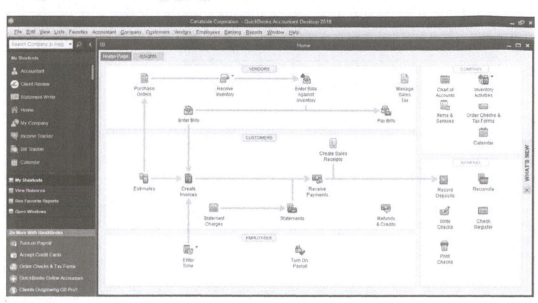

The Home page displays clickable icons and is designed to allow for direct access to common business tasks. Workflow arrows are displayed to help you understand how tasks are related to one another and to help you decide what task to perform next. These workflows are displayed in an easy-to-follow format that helps you work more efficiently. From here, you can start using QuickBooks.

Quick Tip. *The What's New message boxes describe QuickBooks new features and display whenever a new feature is accessed. You can open or close the What's New message boxes by selecting Help > New Features > What's New.*

59. Select   File : Close Company   to close the company file

Review

In this appendix, you have learned how to:

☑ Use the EasyStep Interview

Practice: None

Before Training Skill Evaluation

This training guide is designed to meet the following course objectives. Prior to using the guide, rate your skill level for each objective using the numbered scale on the right. If you have not had prior experience with the objective, indicate as not applicable (n/a). This evaluation helps to determine whether the objectives of the training have been met.

COURSE OBJECTIVES *Get Going With QuickBooks® 2018*	SKILL LEVEL					
	low					high
	n/a	1	2	3	4	5
Get Started	❏	❏	❏	❏	❏	❏
Set up a company	❏	❏	❏	❏	❏	❏
Work with lists	❏	❏	❏	❏	❏	❏
Set up inventory	❏	❏	❏	❏	❏	❏
Sell your product	❏	❏	❏	❏	❏	❏
Invoice for services	❏	❏	❏	❏	❏	❏
Process payments	❏	❏	❏	❏	❏	❏
Work with bank accounts	❏	❏	❏	❏	❏	❏
Enter and pay bills	❏	❏	❏	❏	❏	❏
Use the EasyStep Interview	❏	❏	❏	❏	❏	❏

Company Name:

User/Student Name:　　　　　　　　　　　　　　　**E-mail:**　　　　　　　**Date:**

Instructor's Name:

Comments:

After Training Skill Evaluation

This training guide is designed to meet the following course objectives. After completing the guide, rate your skill level for each objective using the numbered scale on the right. If you did not work on the objective, indicate as not applicable (n/a). This evaluation helps to determine whether the objectives of the training have been met.

COURSE OBJECTIVES	SKILL LEVEL					
Get Going With QuickBooks® 2018	low					high
	n/a	1	2	3	4	5
Get Started	❏	❏	❏	❏	❏	❏
Set up a company	❏	❏	❏	❏	❏	❏
Work with lists	❏	❏	❏	❏	❏	❏
Set up inventory	❏	❏	❏	❏	❏	❏
Sell your product	❏	❏	❏	❏	❏	❏
Invoice for services	❏	❏	❏	❏	❏	❏
Process payments	❏	❏	❏	❏	❏	❏
Work with bank accounts	❏	❏	❏	❏	❏	❏
Enter and pay bills	❏	❏	❏	❏	❏	❏
Use the EasyStep Interview	❏	❏	❏	❏	❏	❏

Company Name:

User/Student Name: **E-mail:**   **Date:**

Instructor's Name:

Comments:

Training Guide Evaluation

RETURN BY MAIL TO: TLR
2024 W. Henrietta Rd
Bldg 4B
Rochester, NY 14623

RETURN BY FAX TO: 585.223.6981

RETURN BY EMAIL TO: sales@tlr-inc.com

Training Guide Title

Company Name

User/Student Name   **E-mail**   **Date**

TRAINING GUIDE OBJECTIVES	SATISFACTION LEVEL				
	low 1	2	3	4	high 5
The guide thoroughly covered all topics and functions.	❑	❑	❑	❑	❑
Information contained in the guide was organized in a logical manner.	❑	❑	❑	❑	❑
Files from the Training CD were accurate and helpful.	❑	❑	❑	❑	❑
Step-by-step instruction was accurate and easy to understand.	❑	❑	❑	❑	❑
Screen captures and illustrations were accurate and helpful.	❑	❑	❑	❑	❑
Practice lessons were helpful in evaluating skills.	❑	❑	❑	❑	❑
Icons denoting special information were accurate and helpful.	❑	❑	❑	❑	❑
Lessons and topics were easy to find in the guide.	❑	❑	❑	❑	❑
The guide is well-designed and visually appealing.	❑	❑	❑	❑	❑

What did you like most about the guide?

What aspects of the guide could be improved?

Comments: